William Scrope

Days and Nights of Salmon Fishing

in the River Tweed

William Scrope

Days and Nights of Salmon Fishing
in the River Tweed

ISBN/EAN: 9783337234478

Printed in Europe, USA, Canada, Australia, Japan

Cover: Foto ©Andreas Hilbeck / pixelio.de

More available books at **www.hansebooks.com**

DAYS AND NIGHTS

OF

SALMON FISHING

In the River Tweed.

BY

WILLIAM SCROPE, ESQ.

Author of "Days of Deer-Stalking."

ILLUSTRATED BY

SIR DAVID WILKIE, SIR EDWIN LANDSEER
CHARLES LANDSEER
WILLIAM SIMSON AND EDWARD COOKE.

LONDON: HAMILTON, ADAMS, & CO.
GLASGOW: THOMAS D. MORISON.
1885.

TO

THE LORD POLWARTH

The following Pages are inscribed

IN REMEMBRANCE OF

THE HAPPY DAYS SPENT IN HIS COMPANIONSHIP ON THE BANKS OF

THE TWEED

AND THE SOCIAL INTERCOURSE ENJOYED FOR SO MANY YEARS

AT MERTOUN

BY HIS SINCERE AND FAITHFUL FRIEND

THE AUTHOR.

PREFACE.

"I will write a sort of a Book on Fishing," said I to my friend Mr. Lobworm; when a fresh breeze from the gentle south swept over the meadows, "stealing and giving odours," and reminded me of the many calm and pleasant hours I had spent by the margin of some crystal stream.

"You really had better do no such thing," replied Lob.—He was a man of few words.

"Your very polite reason, if you please?"

"Why, the subject is utterly exhausted; ninety-nine books have been written upon it already, and no man was ever the wiser for any one of them, although many are clever and entertaining, and moreover abound in excellent instructions."

"Hold! you forget dear old Izaak," said I, "whose dainty and primitive work, the emanation of a beautiful mind, has made many a man both wiser and better; for it is dictated throughout by that wisdom of which it is written, 'Her ways are ways of pleasantness, and all her paths are peace.'"

"Therefore it is," replied Lobworm, "that I would have you by all means to refrain: that book will always stand unrivalled and unapproachable. Excuse me, but 'ex quovis ligno non fit Mercurius.'"

"Nay, nay, you cannot for a moment imagine that I shall attempt such a flight as that. I have read of Icarus, and also of the Ulm Tailor, who on the first trial of his patent wings fell into the Danube, instead of pitching upon the opposite bank; so, as I cannot touch the summits, I must perforce be content to creep on level lands,—'timidus procellæ:'—mine shall be a work quite of another character."

"There is not the least doubt of that, I think," said Mr. Lobworm. "Know likewise," continued he (I never knew him so loquacious or so disagreeable before),—"Know likewise to thy discomfort, nay, to thy utter confusion, that a book has lately appeared yclept 'The Rod and the Gun,' so amusingly written, and so complete in all its parts, that there is not the least occasion for you to burthen Mr. Murray's shelves with stale precepts that no one will attend to."

"Pretty discouraging that, most certainly," I responded. "And then we have 'Salmonia,' which is, or ought to be, a settler too; and also a scientific work by Mr. Colquhoun, who touches deftly on the subject. But I tell you this, Sir Oracle, that although I see a hundred good reasons why I should abandon my design, yet I am resolved to persist: it is my destiny —that is a classical reason. You know that, to the great edification of our youth, the pious Æneas gives no better reason for the hundred rascally and much admired things he was in the habit of executing in his expedition to Latium.

"I only hope the public will be so good as not to be discerning; because if they are, I shall have you, my most tender and amiable friend, eternally dinging in my ears, 'There, did not I tell you so? But you would not be ruled by me, so you must take the consequences.'"

At the end of this colloquy, and when left alone, I began to reflect a little; and although at first I could not help thinking my gentleman somewhat hasty, yet I came to the conclusion that he was partly, if not entirely, in the right. So I began to listen a little to reason, and contracted my plan, resolving to treat on *Salmon Fishing* alone, as it is practised in the *Tweed;* for although various authors have written some pages on the sport, yet I am not aware that any one has as yet gone far into the subject, or given any precepts, or treated of the various methods available to the sportsman of killing these valuable animals in the rod-fisher's part of a river throughout *the whole of the lawful season.* This I have attempted to do in the following pages, having had more than twenty years' practice in that border river alone, above twelve miles of which I rented at different periods.

To the *Tweed* I have confined myself; and I beg my readers to observe, that my remarks and instructions are meant to apply to that river alone; and consequently that I am not accountable for what salmon choose to do in other waters, and for the different means that people may employ for catching them there.

Deer-stalking and salmon-fishing are at the head of field and river sports : having written what has been very generously received upon the first and best of these subjects, I have

been encouraged to take up the other. This
I have done the more readily, as I have been
fortunate enough to bring to my aid the talents
of artists, who are amongst the most eminent
in their various departments that this country
can boast of. I must not, however, impute the
landscape part to them : this it was unfortu-
nately necessary that some one should under-
take who was acquainted with the scenery,
and I must hold myself in a great measure
responsible for such portion of the plates.

It will be seen that in the letter-press I
have attempted little more than to give a
correct and faithful account of the manner and
spirit in which the sport of salmon fishing is
carried on in various ways where the scene is
laid, and to bring before the sportsman the
characters of such people as he is likely to fall
in with in his excursions.

Among those whom I have taken this liberty
with, as the type of his class, will be found the
late Tom Purdie, Sir Walter Scott's faithful
right-hand man, well-known to the readers
of Mr. Lockhart's delightful Biography, and
the genuine parent of the stories here attributed to him.

Since the following pages have been printed,

Mr. Yarrell has put into my hands "The An-
nals and Magazine of Natural History for Feb.
1843," containing an account of Mr. Young's
experiments on the growth of salmon I have
inserted an extract in the Appendix, for the
benefit of those who are interested in the
subject.

I hope I am correct in saying that, judging
from the outline, my statements will agree
with Mr. Young's experiments. This, however, will be more accurately seen when the
Proceedings of the Royal Society of Edinburgh
are published.

CONTENTS.

CHAPTER IV.

CHAPTER V.

CHAPTER VI.

CHAPTER VII.

CHAPTER VIII.

CHAPTER IX.

CHAPTER X.

CHAPTER XI.

APPENDIX.

LITHOGRAPH ILLUSTRATIONS.

For list of Woodcut Illustrations see next leaf.

WOODCUT ILLUSTRATIONS.

DAYS AND NIGHTS

OF

SALMON FISHING.

CHAPTER I.

CITIZEN ANGLERS.

"John Gilpin was a citizen
Of credit and renown.'   Cowper.

SALMON fishers do not fall from the clouds all perfection at once, but generally acquire some skill in
river angling for trout, and such like pigmies, before
they aspire to the nobler spoil;—pretty work, indeed,
would they make of it, if they began at the wrong end :
nemo repentè fuit *fishissimus*. We will venture to say,
that many beginners have been frightened out of their
wits by the sprightliness of a decent-sized trout ; would
they then have the presumption to encounter a salmon
without fortifying their nerves with previous practice
of some sort or another ?   I would advise each, one and
all, to try their hands at something less powerful, before
they throw their gauntlet at Entellus.   In short, we
ourselves, experienced as we are, stand in perfect awe of
a salmon to this day ; and think it meet to approach

2

him by degrees, by mentioning, in the first instance, the pursuits of less aspiring anglers, and their various grades of ambition. Thus, we shall show the strength of the passion for fishing, even of the most humble description, and by comparison set off the followers of *Salmo Salar* to the highest possible advantage.

We omit giving any particulars of such holiday folk as disturb the puddles in the commons about London, and beg to introduce our worthy friend Mr. Pooley, who being counter-bound nearly all the year, takes his pastime occasionally on the river Lea. A pedestrian he, and a man of pretty considerable pretensions. Behold ! he casts aside his domestic garb disdainful, and packs himself up in a shooting jacket, which distinguishes him from the common herd of travellers, and becomes him admirably. Indeed he shows much address in the skilful use of its buttons ; and it is really surprising to see what an effect he produces by fastening the two last in the waist, thereby making the rereward of his person stick out in bold relief ; for Mr. Pooley is a man of a commendable rotundity. The short rod which he trails merrily in his hand, and the basket that irritates the vertebrae of his back, proclaim his high resolve. At early morn he quits the dusky city, with a temporary distaste for the sound of Bow bells, and with pity for such as are doomed to business whilst it is his pleasure to angle.

At length, behold him arrived at thy lazy waters, O Lea ! With joyous voice he evokes the miller ; orders a dinner, as he is pleased to suppose, of three dishes, the principal one consisting of the fish he is about to catch, with Izaak Walton's instructions for cooking them. The miller generally puts on a somewhat distressing smile on this occasion, as the said dish of fish is rather addressed to the imagination than otherwise—food for the mind alone. Behold him now, seated on a spot which has long borne his name *(Mr. Pooley's Seat)*. The story runs, that he once caught a pike there of five pounds; but the truth is, that the said pike was actually only two pounds, but he added a pound to its weight every passing year, because he said that the fish would have gained as much had he lived up to the present day of reckoning. This was a mode of calculation that some even of his most intimate friends could not assent to, but he was always peremptory on the subject. His person now being fairly disposed on the bank, with his short and comely legs dangling over the weir, he becomes deeply intent upon his neatly painted float. On this his longing eyes are bent. He sees but askance the swallows that flit by him, and the willow that droops over the pool—he sees only his float. By Jupiter, it bobs!— now is the decisive moment. Prompt and energetic, he gives a scientific jerk, and up comes the light line obedient. Is there the semblance of a fish at the end of it? O no, certainly not. What then made the float move? Who can say? Perhaps it was only a delusion of the optics brought on by a sanguine temperament, or a slight ruffle occasioned by the zephyrs that kissed thy Cockney waters, O gently slumbering Lea! You were excited, Mr. Pooley, you must own, dreadfully excited,—and it well became you to be so, for the moment was awful; but we will leave you to resume your tranquillity.   We grant you our sympathy, but deny you our company.

Pass we on to the more ambitious angler, even to our adventurous acquaintance, Mr. John Poplin. He cannot submit to the worm, paste, or float—not he. His skilful arm is practised to wave his rod gracefully, with nothing less at the end of the line than the green granam fly. Reclining on his sofa, and tinted with a slight effusion of bile, he has seen on one auspicious morn a seductive advertisement, headed "*Trout Fishing.*" With eager pen he responds to A.B.; pays a guinea for a ticket to enable him to angle for trout during a whole season, in a part of the river Wandle that is strictly preserved. How very cheap! After pulling about monstrous fish in his dreams all night, he pays his guinea, and drives off to the Elysian fields: there he beholds the whole extent of the fishery lying before him,—a mill-pond full seventy yards long, one side only belonging to the advertiser in right of a small water meadow. The spot seems a favourite one; for a goodly company of citizens are extended along the bank in line at three feet asunder—a similar number on the opposite bank. Now three feet is a liberal allowance, for only two are granted for a soldier standing in close order. With graceful obeisance and skilful tact he apologises, and wedges himself into line; hooks his neighbour's tackle on the right the very first throw, whilst he on his left hooks his. They remonstrate, and extricate with proper courtesy. Not particularly admiring his position, which he deems crowded, he backs out, quits the ranks, and in evil hour trespasses on the water below. Then was thy wrath awakened, O jolly miller! White in apparel, but rubicund in complexion, you sally forth, portly and irascent: lofty is your language.

"Who gave you toleration to fish in my mill tail?" In return, Mr. Miller, you are called an uncivil brute, and you well deserve it; for, in civility, you should first of all have remonstrated, and, in prudence, should afterwards have endeavoured to exact a handsome fine for the trespass. But you did neither of these; on the contrary, I am sorry to say, you were personal and unpleasant, and forcibly deprived our amiable friend Mr. John Poplin of his rod; so that he returned to London with an accumulation of bile, and scolded his wife, maid, and footboy. Hard was the fate of the caster of the green granam!

Mount we now one step higher, nay, a goodly stride or two; and let us celebrate the real scientific fly-fisher, to whom fortune has been more propitious. Possessed of ample means, he roves from river to lake, rich in rods of various dimensions, and the joyful possessor of all the flies that have been named or engraved in all the ninety-nine books that have been published on the art of angling, not forgetting that distinguished fly called the *professor*. We have a boundless respect for this young gentleman. We like his custom of roving about. He does not scruple to mount his tilbury, and to flourish his rod over the rivers and lakes of Wales, and to lash also with zeal all the waters of Westmoreland and Cumberland. He is not a mere angler, but somewhat of an artist also; at least he thinks so himself. So when the sun rides high, and the lake lies hot and motionless, "and the flies make strange streaks, albeit skilfully thrown, on the mirror-like surface of the water," as that most capital penman, " the organist," has described it, he plants his sketching stool in some shady nook, and, armed at all points with the necessary implements, imagines that he transmits to his canvas a vivid impression of what he sees before him.

Well skilled to select his subjects, he does not take a general view of the broad expanse, but gets a glimpse of the lake between the bolls of the trees opposed to it in shadow. Proud of his ultra marine, he touches in the distant mountain, and the rugged brae nearer the fore-ground he paints rich and sunny; nor does he forget those accessories that give interest and character to the scene,—the smoke issuing from the cottage lying in some shady nook, the boat hauled up on the gravelly beach, or the cattle that stand listless on some point of land that juts into the lake. Perhaps, too, some shepherd lies sleeping with his flock around him in a sequestered glade. Thus he paints the images of rural life; and who happier than himself, when he retires to the clean little inn, and selects the trout for his dinner, giving a cut behind the dorsal fin to descry those of the reddest tint? Self-complacent are his regards when he eyes his ample capture,—beaming are his looks when he contemplates his coloured canvas. It is with pain we take leave of the happy man: we would willingly write his memoirs, but we have a higher duty to perform. We are about to sing of Harry Otter, even of ourselves, doing battle with the lusty Salmon as we ride on the waves of the Tweed in our little

bark, or wade amongst its rapid cataracts.   It becomes
us first, however, to preface our pages with a short
description of the Salmon itself, as well as of Harry
Otter; and we will begin with the fish, as being the
most interesting animal of the two.

CHAP. II.

" So dainty salmons, chevins thunder-scarred
Feast-famous sturgeons, lampreys speckle-starr'd,
In the spring season the rough seas forsake,
And in the rivers thousand pleasures take."

Du Bartas.

THE three species of the genus *Salmo* which are to be found in the Tweed, and which afford most sport to the angler, are the common Salmon, or *Salmo Salar ;* the Grey, or Bull Trout, *Salmo Eriox ;* and the Salmon Trout, *Salmo Trutta.* The *Salmo Fario* also, or common Trout, is, or rather used to be, in great abundance there; but of this latter species I do not mean to treat.

Although the salmon fisheries are of considerable national importance, affording a great supply of food and employment to thousands ; yet, surprising as it may appear, the natural history and habits of the fish itself have almost up to this time been very imperfectly known. Indeed naturalists have been altogether mistaken as to the appearance of the fry, which at a certain growth they have supposed to be a distinct species of fish ; and had it not been for the skill and diligence of Mr. Shaw, who has demonstrated this their mistake by a series of scientific and interesting experiments, they would still have continued in error.

But not naturalists alone, who are apt to copy their predecessors with somewhat too liberal a faith, but even practical men, who have made their observations from nature, have arrived also at false conclusions.

Mr. Yarrell, in the second edition of his beautiful work on British Fishes, has given so ample and so scientific an account of the Salmon, deduced from the late recent and important discoveries, that little remains to be said on its natural history.

I shall therefore be as brief on this subject as possible; adding, however, such remarks on the habits of the three most valuable species of the *Salmonidæ* as my practical acquaintance with the subject may enable me to supply.

And, first, for the

COMMON SALMON.

Salmo Salar.

Generic Characters.—"Head smooth, body covered with scales; two dorsal fins, the first supported by rays, the second fleshy and without rays; teeth on the vomer, both palatine bones, and all the maxillary bones; branchiostegous rays, varying in number, generally from ten to twelve, but sometimes unequal on two sides of the head of the same fish."—*Yarrell.*

This splendid fish leaves the sea, and comes up the Tweed at every period of the year in greater or lesser quantities, becoming more abundant in the river as the summer advances; that is, provided sufficient rain falls to swell the water to such an extent as will discolour it, and enable the fish to pass the shallows with ease and security. It travels rapidly; so that those Salmon which leave the sea, and go up the Tweed on the Saturday night at twelve o'clock, after which time no nets are worked till the Sabbath is past, are found and taken on the following Monday near St. Boswell's—a distance, as the river winds, of about forty miles.

This I have frequently ascertained by experience. When the strength of the current in a spate is considered, and also the sinuous course a Salmon must take in order to avoid the strong rapids, this power of swimming must be considered as extraordinary.

As Salmon are supposed to enter a river merely for the purposes of spawning, and as that process does not take place till September, one cannot well account for their appearing in the Tweed and elsewhere so early as February and March, seeing that they lose in weight and condition during their continuance in fresh water. Some think it is to get rid of the sea-louse; but this supposition must be set aside, when it is known that this insect adheres only to a portion of the newly run fish, which are the best in condition. I think it more probable that they are driven from the coasts near the river by the numerous enemies they encounter there, such as porpoises and seals, which devour them in great quantities. However this may be, they remain in the fresh water till the spawning months commence.

On the first arrival of the spring Salmon from the sea, they are apt to take up their seats in the rear of a scull of kelts; at this early period they are brown in the back in the Tweed, fat, and in high condition. In the cold months they lie in the deep and easy water; and as the season advances they draw into the principal rough streams, always lying in places where they can be least easily discovered. They are very fond of a stream above a deep pool, into which they can fall back in case of disturbance. They prefer lying upon even rock, or behind large blocks of stone, particularly such as are of a colour similar to themselves. They are not to be found all over the river like Trout, but only in such rough or deep places as I have mentioned; it is therefore very necessary for a stranger to take out some one with him who is acquainted with the water he means to fish, for there are large continuous portions of almost all salmon rivers where no fish ever take up their seats. It is true that a very practised eye, which is well acquainted with water, needs little assistance; but there are not many such nice observers.

At every swell of the river, unless a very trifling one, the fish move upwards nearer the spawning places: so that no one can reckon upon preserving his particular part of the river, which is the chief reason of the universal destruction of these valuable animals. Previous to a flood, the fish frequently leap out of the water, either for the purpose of filling their air-bladder to make them more buoyant for travelling, or from excitement, or, perhaps, to exercise their powers of ascending heights and cataracts in the course of their journey upwards. Of the nature of these spates, or floods, I will speak hereafter.

That Salmon will leap a great height I have read, and heard asserted continually; but even the subdued account which Mr. Yarrell has mentioned, placing their powers of leaping ten or twelve feet perpendicularly, I hold to be beyond the mark. I have frequently watched their endeavours to surmount falls, and I do not think I ever saw a Salmon spring out of the water above five feet perpendicularly. There is a cauld at the mouth of the Leader-water, where it falls into the Tweed, which Salmon never could spring over; this cauld I have lately had measured most carefully by a mason, and its height varies from five feet and a half to six feet from the level above to the level below it, according as the Tweed, into which the Leader falls, is more or less affected by the rains. Hundreds of Salmon formerly attempted to spring over this low cauld, but none could ever achieve the leap; so that a Salmon in the Leader-water was formerly a thing unheard of. The proprietors of the upper water have made an opening in this cauld of late years, giving the owner of the mill some recompense, so that Salmon now ascend freely. Large fish can spring much higher than small ones; but their powers are limited or augmented according to the depth of water they spring from : in shallow water, they have little power of ascension; in deep, they have the most considerable. They rise rapidly from the very bottom to the surface of the water by means of rowing and sculling, as it were, with their fins and tail; and this powerful impetus bears them upwards in the air, on the same principle that a few tugs of the oar make a boat shoot onwards after one has ceased to row. It is probably owing to a want of sufficient depth in the pool below the Leader-water cauld, that prevented the fish from clearing it; because I know an instance where Salmon have cleared a cauld of six feet belonging to Lord Sudely, who lately caused it to be measured for my satisfaction, though there were but few out of the numerous fish that attempted it that were able to do so. I conceive, however, that very large fish could leap much higher.

Although I think the powers of Salmon to leap perpendicularly have been much overrated, yet I know that they will ascend steep cataracts in a wonderful manner. Mr. Smith of Deanston, in the Carse of Stirling, has invented a sort of stair, by means of which Salmon are enabled to ascend streams in full waters in spite of natural or artificial obstructions. One side of the river under a weir or cauld is separated from the main stream, and intersected by transverse pieces of wood or stone, each of which reaches about two thirds of the width of the gap. There are two ranges of these steps, one on each side, and the steps on one side face the centre of the interval between the steps on the other; so that the fish ascend from side to side in a zigzag direction, and can rest in their ascent, should they find it necessary. This is a very ingenious contrivance, and it has been constructed on the Teith, near Doune, with complete success. But I conclude it can only come into operation in such floods as raise the water to a higher level than is required for the mill-dam; and therefore if rude steps of rolling stones were constructed at a portion of the back of the cauld, the end would be answered in a better manner, since the ascent might be made more gradual.

The fish pass every practicable obstruction till they arrive at their spawning ground, some early, and some late in the season. The spawning in the river Tweed continues throughout the autumn, winter, and beginning of spring. It commences about September, and I have caught full roeners as late as May; but the principal months are December, January, and February. Mr. John Crerar, who was fisherman to the Duke of Atholl for sixty years, and who left behind him some pages in manuscript on the habits of the Salmon, has recorded in them that fish full of mature roe may be caught in the Tay in every month of the year.

The fish become weak and wasted before the spawning time, and change in colour. The male loses its silvery hue, and is deeply tinged in the cheeks and body with orange, and is also dappled with red spots, when, in the upper parts of the Tweed, it is sometimes called a "Soldier." The under jaw also becomes longer, and a cartilaginous substance grows from the point of it, and extends upwards till it buries itself in the nose above. In this state the fish is very thin in the back, and altogether much wasted; but its flesh is sometimes eatable, and at any rate infinitely superior to that of a fish which has newly spawned. The female, when ready to spawn, is dark in colour, and her flesh is soft and worthless.

Salmon are led by instinct to select such places for depositing their spawn as are the least likely to be affected by the floods. These are the broad parts of the river, where the water runs swift and shallow, and has a free passage over an even bed. Here they either select an old spawning place, a sort of trough left in the channel, or form a fresh one. They are not fond of working in new loose channels, which would be liable to be removed by a slight flood, to the destruction of their spawn. The spawning bed is made by the female. Some have fancied that the elongation of the lower jaw in the male, which is somewhat in the form of a crook, is designed by nature to enable him to excavate the spawning trough. Certainly it is difficult to divine what may be the use of this very ugly excrescence; but observation has proved that this idea is a fallacy, and that the male never assists in making the spawning place; and indeed, if he did so, he could not possibly make use of the elongation in question for that purpose, which springs from the lower jaw, and bends inwards towards the throat.

When the female first commences making her spawning bed, she generally comes after sunset, and goes off in the morning: she works up the gravel with her snout, her head pointing against the stream, as my fisherman has clearly and unequivocally witnessed, and she arranges the position of the loose gravel with her tail. When this is done, the male makes his appearance in the evenings, according to the usage of the female; he then remains close by her, on the side on which the water is deepest. When the female is in the act of emitting her ova, she turns upon her side, with her face to the male, who never moves. The female runs her snout into the gravel, and forces herself under it as much as she possibly can, when an attentive observer may see the red spawn coming from her. The male in his turn lets his milt go over the spawn ; and this process goes on for some days, more or less, according to the size of the fish and consequent quantity of the eggs.

During this time, Trout will collect below to devour the spawn that floats down the river ; and numerous *Parrs,* so called, are always seen about and in the spawning beds,—an explanation of which will be found in the sequel. If a strange male interferes, the original one makes at him, and chases him with great fury, and in these combats they often inflict great injury on each other. John Crerar once had his attention attracted by a great noise of dashing and plunging, at King's Ford in the Tay, and upon looking round he found it was occasioned by the fighting of two Salmon. After a short contest one of them set off ; and the water being shallow, Crerar fired at and killed him ; he was a male of course, and weighed thirty-two pounds. This occurred in June, 1799.

When the female has done spawning, she sets off, and leaves the place. The male remains waiting for another female ; and if none comes in twenty-four hours, he goes away in search of another spawning place. In the spawning beds on the Tweed, great injury is done with the leister and rake hooks ; and the fishermen, who know how to profit by their cruel slaughter, are in the habit of spearing the male which first comes to the female, leaving the latter as a decoy fish, and killing the other males in succession as they arrive to consort with her. By this barbarous and poaching practice all the largest spawning fish are destroyed, to the great destruction of the river. These foul Salmon are bad and unwholesome food, and used to be sold by the fishermen for about half a crown the stone, Dutch weight: they were afterwards salted. Trifling as this price is, the fishermen in the upper parts of the Tweed formerly made up the chief part of their rent in this manner; for there is no law against killing foul fish, except in close time.

I have now given a brief account of the Salmon, from his first entry into fresh water till he has spawned. It remains only to trace him back to the sea.

When the spawning is finished, the fish become very lank and weak, and fall into deep easy water, where they have not to contend with the current: here, after a time, their strength is recruited, when, as the spring advances, the strongest fish leave the depths and draw into the streams. At this time they become clear in colour, and are comparatively well-made; but their flesh is soft, and without flavour. They now move down the river by degrees, in their passage to the sea. When they arrive in the deep pools where the water runs evenly, they lie in sculls, and take a rest for some days; here they are caught in great quantities by anglers, as they take the fly and other baits freely. March is usually the best month for this sport,—if, indeed, it can be called sport to kill an animal that is worth a mere trifle, and resists but little. If there are freshes, the *Kelts* (for so the females that have spawned are called) quit the Tweed before the month of May, and the *Kippers*, or male fish, at the same time. Very many do so in March and April, according to the time that they have spawned and regained their powers. In going downwards they are taken about Kelso, or at least

3

they used to be so in my time, with the long net, in pools where they rest, such as that below Kelso bridge; but they cannot be caught by the cairn nets, which are so destructive to them in ascending.

Having now despatched the Salmon to the sea, it remains to me to explain what becomes of the spawn, and how and when the young fry arrive at maturity; and as there have been various doubts and contradictions on this subject, I think it more prudent to lead the reader to a consideration of the following pages, than to make a positive assertion on my own unsupported authority.

Mr. Shaw's ingenious experiments have lately had a very wide circulation; but still I have thought it proper to make a very short abstract of them, as they are of too great importance to be omitted in any publication relating to Salmon.

Up to a late period it was universally thought that the spawn deposited as above mentioned was matured in a brief time, and that the young fry of the winter grew to six or seven inches long, were silver in colour, and went down to the sea in this state with the first floods early in the May of the coming spring. They were then called *Smolts*. In the summer months there are always multitudes of little fry in every salmon river, which in the Tweed are called *Parrs*, and have been thought to be a different species from the Salmon. I have formerly held several tiresome arguments, both with practical men and also with naturalists, with an intent to convince them that they were one and the same species.

The late Mr. James Hogg, the Ettrick Shepherd, was particularly stiff and bristly in opinion against me. But

WORKING THE NET

he recanted afterwards, and caused to be published in the famed "Maga" an account of experiments made by himself, all tending to confirm my theory. I suppose it would have been better for my credit had I abstained from any colloquy with the said James, which appears not to have been particularly entertaining; for lately, upon asking my friend Sir Adam Ferguson if he recollected the circumstance, " Perfectly well," said he, " and it was at your own table ; but I cannot say who had the best of the argument, as I fell asleep soon after it began."

But indeed I had not resided long on the banks of the Tweed, before I came to the conclusion that the Parr was not a distinct species, but, as I have said, was actually the young of the Salmon : and very many years ago, long before Mr. Shaw's experiments, Mr. Kennedy having brought in a bill for the better preservation of the salmon fisheries, I wrote to him the following letter, which I transcribe from the first draught, which I preserved :—

" Pavilion, Melrose.

" Sir,

" Your Salmon Bill being in progress, permit me to have the honour of addressing you on a point that is at present overlooked, and that you will at once perceive is of vital importance to its successful operation.

" It is a fact, that whilst the legislature has imposed penalties for the destruction of Smolts or Salmon fry, not only those whose duty it is to put the law in force, but the public, and even fishermen themselves, cannot ascertain what these are at all seasons of the year.   On the contrary, for most part of the year they go by the name of Parrs, and are destroyed daily with impunity, and in incredible quantities. Hitherto the Parr and the Smolt have been considered as different species; but that they are precisely the same, I think may be demonstrated.

"The received opinion, and that which the present law of Scotland acts upon, is, that the Salmon fry of the winter and spring congregate and go down to the sea in the May of the same season, and that they are of a pure silver colour, as indeed more or less they are. Now in all salmon rivers Parrs are to be found in abundance throughout the summer, and early in the spring; and in the summer they are not of a silver colour, but marked with red spots, and are shaded with vertical bars on their sides at intervals. From the appearance of these bars, they are very generally supposed to be of a distinct species from the Smolt. Permit me to give my reasons for entertaining a contrary opinion.

"After May the large Parrs totally disappear, and such few as may be found afterwards are very small; but as the summer advances they become larger, and in the spring following, the bars and red spots above mentioned gradually die away, and a stronger armour or scale supervenes; and as that is more or less advanced in growth, the bars and spots are more or less visible.

"When they are in this silvery state, that is, when the new scales are perfected, they become what are called Smolts or Salmon fry; but by removing such new scales, you will find the bars and spots of the Parr underneath as clear and vivid as ever. I have therefore a positive conviction that the Salmon fry, instead of falling down to the sea the same year they are produced, remain in the river, under the name of Parrs, till the year following.* That they increase little in size we cannot be surprised at, as it is universally known that the Salmon himself wastes from the moment he comes into fresh water.

"If the Committee make themselves perfectly acquainted with the natural history of the Salmon, they will be aware of the peculiar construction of the eye of that fish. Dr. Brewster† has been so obliging as to examine for me the eyes of some Parrs, which I sent him for that purpose; and replies, 'I have examined very carefully the crystalline lenses of the Parr, which I find to be the same with those of the Salmon, which is a strong confirmation of your opinion.'

"I must add, that these Parrs, as they are called, are never found but in salmon rivers, or in such as have an uninterrupted communication with them; and that they cannot be the young of the Bull Trout, as the formation of the tail in that fish is wholly different.

"When it is considered that trout fishing is enjoyed by every class of people in Scotland, and that, speaking with reference to the river Tweed only and its different tributary streams, hundreds and hundreds of people are trouting daily, and that each person catches several dozen Parrs in a morning, except in that interval between the disappearance of the old fry and the appearance of the new in a forward state, it will be found

---

* Mr. Shaw has since proved that they remain in fresh water still longer.

† Now Sir David Brewster.

that the young Salmon (for such I contest they are) so destroyed will amount to considerably more than the whole marketable produce of the river.

"By your present bill I know not how far the local Scotch Acts may be repealed; but I take the liberty of suggesting that it would be for the public benefit if the usage of a pout net in close time were made punishable by a fine. The inhabitants of almost every cottage have these nets, which are taken out under pretence of catching Trout, which no one but a proprietor has a right to do in such a way. I have heard that above a thousand Salmon have been taken in a small space of the Tweed by these nets during close time. They are most destructive below the backs of caulds, where the fish collect in order to ascend.

" I should have mentioned before, that what we call the Parr in the Tweed goes by various other names in the different rivers of Great Britain, which is a material circumstance to note.

" If you are desirous of any further information on this subject, I shall most readily give you such as may be in my power. What I have already said is of a nature that cannot make me be suspected of having any private or party view to answer.

" I have the honour to be," &c., &c.

The above being the first draught, I omitted to put a date to it; but it was written many years before Mr. Shaw's experiments. For Mr. Kennedy's bill, to which my letter alludes, was brought in on the 15th of April, 1825, and thrown out on the second reading.

I received a very obliging answer from that gentleman, the purport of which was to say, that as his bill had failed, it was not necessary to trouble me any farther on the subject.

This letter contains evidence that Sir David Brewster's experiments were made previously to its being written; and when I had thought of publishing, being desirous to know the exact time when they were made, I wrote to Sir David to call his attention to the subject. His answer, dated 16th of April, 1840, was as follows:

" I am pretty sure that my experiments on the structure of the crystalline lens of the *Parr*, which is identical with that of the Salmon, were made previous to 1828.*   I remember well your stating to me that when the silver scales of the young Salmon (which in Roxburghshire we call Smouts) were carefully rubbed off, the colours of a darker hue which characterise the Parr were invariably and distinctly seen. I think you showed me the experiments, but I am not sure of this. With the view of confirming this your theory, or of overturning it, I mentioned to you that the fibres of the lens of the salmon," etc.

Then follows the account of his experiments, as detailed a little farther on.

Besides the reasons mentioned in the above letter, there were other causes which influenced me in the opinion I had formed; the two principal of which were—

* The date of Mr. Kennedy's Bill, *which I have but just ascertained*, proves that they were made in or before the year 1825; whereas Mr. Shaw's first account of his interesting experiments appeared in the "New Edinburgh and Philosophical Journal" for 1836, vol. xxi. p. 99—eleven years after.

Firstly, That no one ever saw a clear silver-looking fry below the usual dimensions of those which are ready to go down to the sea; that is, till the new dress comes over them, and obliterates the distinguishing marks of what is called the Parr.

Secondly, That Parrs are found above falls which Salmon can, but they cannot possibly, surmount.

A high spate might certainly bring some of these falls more to a level; but it would be as impossible for a Parr to swim up them in a raging flood, as it would be for the sere leaf that falls into the waves to find its passage upwards. Mr. Shaw, who has carefully watched shoals of *Parr* (correctly speaking, *Smolts*) in their descent to the sea, affirms that they pass down the current with the greatest caution, keeping their heads up the stream, and rowing gently with their fins against it, so as to steady themselves and prevent a too rapid descent; and thus they drop down by degrees, tail foremost, precisely in the same manner that we manage a boat in the Tweed when descending the rapids.

When the fry were congregating in May I caught these little fish in various stages of the growth of the new scale. In some it had supervened so as to obliterate the bars and spots entirely, when their sides became silver; in others they were partially obliterated, so as to leave only a mere stain of colour; whilst some retained them almost entire. As I caught these fry I sent them up to Sir David Brewster, who was then residing at his beautiful place on the banks of the Tweed. After a careful examination he could find no distinction in the structure of the organs between any of these little creatures, however differing in colour.

The Salmon has a peculiar formation of the eye, the crystalline lens having the fibres of which it is composed arranged as in the annexed sketch A, the

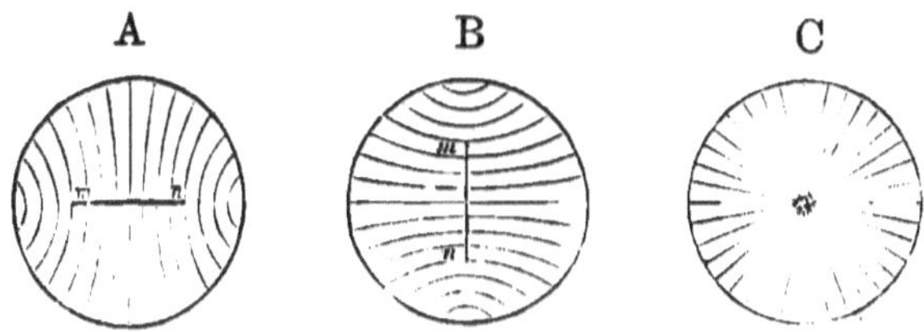

line *m n* being horizontal on one side, and vertical on the other; whereas in many of the Trout species the fibres are arranged as at C, crossing one another, or rather meeting at two opposite poles, like the meridians of a globe, the line joining the two poles being the axis of vision of the eye.

"After examining the lenses of the *Parr* you sent me," says Sir David Brewster in a letter now before me, "I found the structure to be exactly the same as that of the *Salmon.* I have frequently had occasion to mention the proofs that you gave me of the identity of the *Parr* with the *Salmon,* and to mention my own experiments on the lenses as confirmatory of your opinion that the Parr and the Salmon are one and the same species."

Salmon begin spawning as early as September, and continue to do so throughout the winter months; December, January, and February being the principal ones for that operation. They continue on the spawning ground, or Rade, as it is termed in Scotland, also during the spring months, though in diminished quantities. I myself have caught full roeners, as they are called, in the month of May in the Tweed. Now we know from the proofs of experiments that have been made by various persons, that the spawn of the Salmon continues imbedded in the gravel from ninety to one hundred and fifteen days, according to the temperature of the water, before it vivifies; and indeed remains there some weeks after its exclusion from the egg. Mr. Shaw has stated the exact time of this latter period to be fifteen days; at the end of which time, says he, the egg which was attached to its abdomen, from which it derived its nourishment, "contracted and disappeared; the fin or tadpole-like fringe also divided itself into the dorsal, adipose, and anal fins, all of which then became perfectly developed; the little transverse bars, which for a period of two years characterise it as a Parr, also made their appearance; so that a period of at least 140 days is required to perfect this little fish, which even then measured little more than one inch in length."

The above not being matter of conjecture, but having been demonstrated by experiment, how by any possibility can the old doctrine be true, that the fry which go to sea about the first or second week in May, six or seven inches long, can be the spawn of the winter immediately preceding it? And what and where are the young of the Salmon all the summer, if they are not indeed Parr; for no silver-coloured fry are at that time to be seen in the river? I must add also, that it is incumbent upon those naturalists who assert that the Parr is a distinct species, to prove that it is so from comparative anatomy. But they have not been able to do this; on the contrary, as far as I can learn, they confess they have discovered no variation of organic structure.

I have heard it objected that the growth of the Salmon being very rapid, it seems out of the order of nature to suppose that a creature should remain so long in fresh water with so little increase of size. But Salmon never grow in fresh water; on the contrary, they begin to waste from the moment they enter a river, whether they are clean at that period, or forward in spawning. Besides, as the full latitude of the spawning season endures for six months, some of the fry, acknowledged by all to be Smolts, must be six months older than others, and yet when they congregate to go to sea they will all be found to be nearly of the same size. Now if the fry, confessed by all to be Smolts, or the young of the Salmon, do not increase during so many months, why should it be objected that the Parr is not the young of the Salmon on the same account?

These and other arguments have occurred to me from time to time. All reasoning, however, on this subject is now become superfluous; Mr. John Shaw of Drumlanrig having demonstrated, by a number of careful and scientific experiments, that the Parr is actually the young of the Salmon. His first paper announcing this important fact, was published in the " Edinburgh New Philosophical Journal" for July, 1836, vol. xxi. page 99. His second was read before the Royal Society of Edinburgh on the 18th December, 1837, and was published in the "Edinburgh New Philosophical Journal" for January, 1838, vol. xxiv. page 165. His third and concluding communication, by far the most interesting, and which has been lately received by the Royal Society of Edinburgh, contains a continuance and confirmation of the results of the experiments mentioned in the two first papers above alluded to, together with the very extraordinary fact, that the milt of a Parr eighteen months old, and only weighing an ounce and a half, is capable of impregnating the ova of a full-grown Salmon.

Before proceeding to make the experiments related in his last communication, he made three ponds, the banks so raised, and constructed otherwise in such a manner, that it was impossible for the young fish to escape, or for any other fish to have access to them. Accurate drawings and descriptions of these ponds are given in his printed pages, now before me, which he was so obliging as to present me with. " Being thus prepared," says Mr. Shaw (alluding to the construction of his ponds), " with every means of carrying my experiments into practice, I proceeded to the river Nith on the 4th of January, 1837, and readily discovered a pair of adult Salmon engaged in depositing their spawn. They were in a situation easily accessible, the water being of such a depth as to admit of my net being employed with certain success." The fish were accordingly captured by means of a hoop net. The ova were then pressed with the hand from the body of the female, and impregnated in the same manner by the milt of the male, and the spawn in this state was transferred to a private pond previously prepared for its reception. That there might be no doubt as to the species, the skins of the parent Salmon were kept, and may be seen at any time.

On the 28th of April, 114 days after impregnation, the young Salmon were excluded from the egg, which was not the case when they were visited the preceding day. On the 24th of May, twenty-seven days after being hatched, the young fish had consumed the yolk which remains attached to the lower part of the body, and which serves him for nourishment, and the *characteristic bars of the Parr had become distinctly visible.* From a deposition of mud, as Mr. Shaw apprehends, all these fry, except one individual, were found dead at the bottom of the ponds, so that there was no opportunity of watching their future progress ; but an ingenious experiment was made, which proved that an increased temperature hastened the development of the infant fish.

But we shall see that Mr. Shaw was too indefatigable to be daunted by such an untoward accident, and that he persevered in his experiments, till his efforts were rewarded by complete success.

On the 27th of January, 1837, he captured a male fish of sixteen pounds, and a female of eight, and expressed the ova of the female, and impregnated it with the milt of the male in the manner above related, and deposited the spawn in this state in a private pond as before, and to which no fish could by possibility have access.

"On the 21st of March," says Mr. Shaw (that is, fifty-four days after impregnation), " the embryo fish were visible to the naked eye. On the 7th of May (101 days after impregnation), they had burst the envelope, and were to be found amongst the shingle of the stream. The temperature of the water was at this time 43°, and of the atmosphere 45° ; and it is this brood which I have now had an opportunity of watching continuously for a length of time, that is, for more than the entire period which was required to elapse from their exclusion from the egg, until their assumption of those characters which distinguish the undoubted Salmon fry."

Mr. Shaw then proceeds to describe the size and appearance of the Salmon fry at different periods of their age, accompanied with several very accurate and well-executed engravings illustrating the text. "One of these is a specimen *two years* old, when it has assumed its migratory dress, and measures about six inches and a half, being about the average size of the brood." *Two years,*—mark this,—and only six inches and a half long! It then goes to the sea the first floods in May, and returns in two or three months, as it may happen, when it is called a Gilse, and is increased to the size of from four to seven pounds, and indeed very considerably more, being larger or smaller in proportion to the time it has remained in the sea. A second visit to the sea gives it another increase, when it returns to the river as a Salmon. This appears so wonderful and extraordinary a departure from the general laws of nature, that it is no wonder that the most scientific men have been misled.

But if the Salmon fry attain but to such pigmy growth in fresh water, still less is that element favourable to adult Salmon, which, as I have elsewhere observed, fall off in size and condition from the moment they enter a river for the purpose of spawning. When they have spawned, however, they certainly do mend greatly in condition, or, more correctly speaking, recover from their state of weakness.

But to return to Mr. Shaw.—" The circumstance," says he, "of male Parrs with the milt matured, and flowing in profusion from their bodies, being at all times found in company with the adult female Salmon while depositing her spawn in the river, and the female Parrs being in every instance absent, suggested the idea that the males were probably present with the female Salmon at such seasons for sexual purposes.

"To demonstrate the fact," he continues, "in January, 1837, I took a female Salmon weighing fourteen pounds from the spawning bed, from whence I also took a male Parr weighing one ounce and a half, with the milt of which I impregnated a quantity of her ova, and placed the whole in a private pond; where, to my great astonishment, the process succeeded in every respect, as it had done with the ova which had been impregnated by the adult male Salmon, and exhibited, from the first, visible appearance of the embryo fish up to their assuming their migratory dress, the utmost health and vigour.

" The result from this experiment was of so startling a nature, that it was not thought prudent to give it publicity till the trial was repeated. It was so early in the following January, 1838, when two lots of eggs of a Salmon, weighing eighteen pounds, were impregnated with the milt of two male Parrs, and there ensued precisely the same result as before. Again, in December, 1838, four lots of ova from an adult Salmon were impregnated with the milt of four Parrs with similar success; and the same Parrs, being afterwards placed in a private pond, assumed the migratory dress in the following May, not in the most minute degree differing from what in the Tweed are universally called Smolts, and are acknowledged by all to be the young of the Salmon."

All these experiments appear to me to be quite conclusive, and of a nature to satisfy any one who has not pledged himself to an opposite theory. But if any thing were still wanting, it has been completely supplied by an additional experiment, which clenches the proof.

On the 4th of January, 1837, a male Parr, *itself the produce of a male Parr and female adult Salmon,* was made by expression of the milt to impregnate the eggs of a Salmon weighing twelve pounds; and for the better security of the lot, the whole was placed in a wooden trough, over which a sheet of fine copper wire-gauze was fixed. The trough was then placed in a stream of water previously prepared for its reception, and the results were precisely of a corresponding nature to those already detailed.

Now, if the Parr and the Salmon were distinct species, their produce would be hybrids, and would not, therefore, breed again, according to the rules of nature established to prevent the confusion of different species by a conservative law; but this last and most important experiment has proved that the produce from the male Parr and female adult Salmon will breed again with the old Salmon, and therefore that such produce are not mules, but of the same species with their parents.

In a letter to Mr. Shaw, written in the spring (1840), I suggested to him to impregnate the ova of the Salmon with the milt of the common river Trout, imagining that the produce, if any, might be what is called in the Tweed the Bull Trout, which exactly resembles in outward appearance and general size what one would conceive such a process would create.

I learn from Mr. Shaw's last paper that he has succeeded in breeding the Sea Trout by artificial impregnation with their own species; so that the produce of this cross, that is, of the River Trout and Salmon, cannot be the Sea Trout of the Spey and other rivers, but may possibly prove what I suggested. It is at least a very curious coincidence, that the Tweed, which abounds in common Trout, abounds also in Bull Trout; whereas in the Annan and the Tay, where Trout are very scarce, the Grey or Bull Trout is very scarce also. But though crosses may be produced by mechanical impregnation, it is a matter of grave consideration whether such take place naturally. Trout, however, are always seen near the spawning beds of the other *Salmonidæ*.

"The young of these Sea Trout," says Mr. Shaw, "at the age of six months bear no very marked resemblance to the young of the real Salmon, either in the parr or fry state; and as they advance in age and size the resemblance becomes still slighter. But upon comparing them with the common Trout, the resemblance is very striking, the general outline of the fish being much less elegant than that of the young Salmon or Parr; the external markings being also more pecu-

4

liarly those of the Trout species; so that in the absence of the parent skins, which I carefully preserved, it would be a matter of difficulty to determine to which kind of Trout they actually belong."

Mr. Shaw afterwards impregnated the ova of the Salmon with the milt of the common River Trout, according to my suggestion; and in a letter with which he favoured me, dated 26th of April, 1841, he says :— " I am happy to inform you that my experiments with the ova of the common Trout and Salmon have been quite successful, and the young hybrids are now hatched, and in good health."   Mr. Shaw will, of course, publish the details of his late experiments, and thus add to the obligations which those who are interested in this subject already owe him.

I will only add, that his papers are written with such candour, and all his experiments conducted with such care and ability, and so often repeated with similar results, without any effort or intention to make them bend to a favourite theory, that every one, I think, who reads his pages, must consider that the Parr and the Salmon are of the same species, and that the question is so far set at rest for ever.

To sum up,—it appears that the young fry had burst the egg 101 days after impregnation, the temperature of the water being at that time 43°, and the temperature of the atmosphere 45°: a former brood, which died and were excluded in a colder temperature, did not come into life till 114 days after impregnation.

It further appears from a part of Mr. Shaw's publication, which I have not hitherto quoted, but which I have now before me, that the fry, at two months old are only one inch and a quarter long; at four months, two inches and a half; and at six months, three inches and a quarter: that makes nine months and eight days after the impregnation of the spawn. At eighteen months old the fry measure six inches in length, and the milt of the male is matured, and can be made to flow from the body freely by the slightest pressure; but the females of a similar age do not exhibit a corresponding appearance as to the maturity of the roe. The male is at this time in the autumn of his second year, and lies about and in the spawning beds of the large Salmon, where he impregnates the ova. The following spring he is about seven inches and a half long, when beautiful silver scales grow over the spots and bars which have characterised him up to this period; and the majority of the breed then congregate, and go to sea with the first floods in May.

In the latter end of April, 1842, Mr. Shaw obligingly sent me two parcels of the Salmon fry, which arrived in good condition; and although not so glossy as when first captured, were made brighter in appearance by the application of water. I carried them immediately to Barnes, the residence of Mr. Edward Cooke; and having selected the most silvery amongst them, I begged him to paint it as faithfully as possible; and after he had so done I desired that, *during my absence*, he would remove the scales from the upper half of the *same fish*, and paint it again as it should appear after such removal. The result will be seen in the accompanying lithograph, with the execution of which I did not at all interfere. It proves what has been asserted as to change of outward appearance.

All the fry, however, which go to sea at this period, have not their silver scales perfected; but many have the bars and spots faintly indicated, as represented in the lithograph (No. 3.) introduced a few pages forward, —another fish selected from the same lot; and although the majority of these little emigrants go to the sea in large masses about the first swells of the river in May, yet I have no doubt but that some are continually going down to the salt water in every month of the year,—not with their silver scales on, but in the parr state. I say not with their silver scales, because no clear Smolt is ever seen in the Tweed during the summer and autumnal months. As the spawning season in the Tweed extends over a period of six months, some of the fry must be necessarily some months older than others,—a circumstance which favours my supposition, that they are constantly descending to the sea; and it is only a supposition, as I have no proof of the fact, and have never heard it suggested by any one. But if I should be right, it will clear up some things that cannot well be accounted for in any other mode. For instance, in the month of *March*, 1841, Mr. Yarrell informs me that he found a young Salmon in the London market, and which he has preserved in spirits, measuring only fifteen inches long, and weighing only fifteen ounces. And again, another the following *April*, sixteen and a half inches long, weighing twenty-four ounces. Now, one of these appeared two months and the other a month before the usual time when the

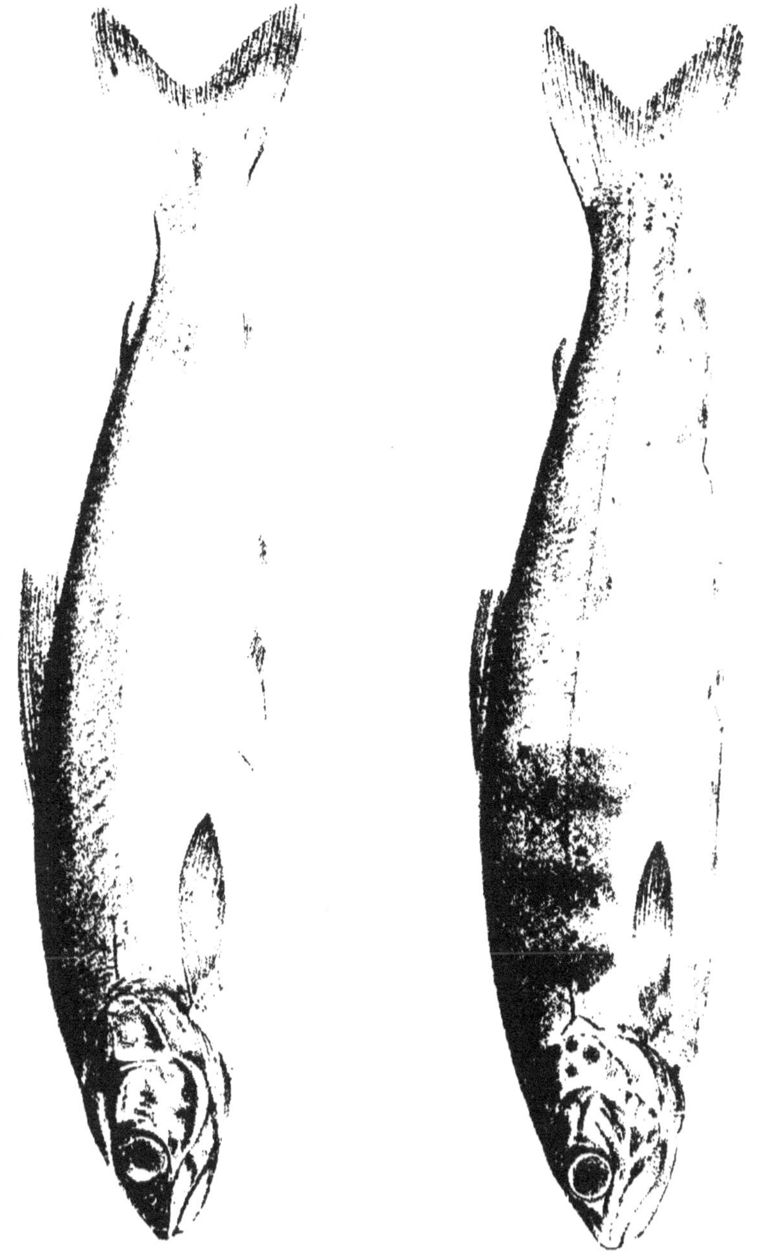

fry congregate. According to the received doctrine, therefore, these animals were two of the migration of the preceding year; and thus it must necessarily follow that they remained in salt water, one ten and the other eleven months, with an increase of growth so small as to be irreconcilable with the proof we have of the growth of the Gilse and Salmon during their residence in salt water.

Having now sent these tiresome little creatures to sea, it remains to me to trace their progress till they become Salmon.

A few, but a very few of these Smolts, return from the sea to the Tweed as early as the month of May; that is, during the same month in which the *general* emigration takes place: they then weigh from a pound to two pounds each, and are long and thin, and very forked in the tail. They keep on ascending the river during the summer months, the new-comers increasing afterwards about a pound and a half a month on an average, but much less in their very young state. The most plentiful season in the Tweed, if there is a flood, is about St. Boswell's Fair, namely, the 18th of July, at which period they weigh from four to six pounds; and those which leave the salt for the fresh water at the end of September, and during the month of October, sometimes come up the river of the weight of ten and eleven pounds, and even more. All these fish are known in the North by the name of *Gilses*, but by the London fishmongers are generally, I believe, called *Salmon Peel.* Some of them are much larger than small Salmon; but by the term Gilse I mean young Salmon that have only been once to sea. They are easily distinguished from Salmon by their countenance and less plump appearance, and particularly by the diminished size of the part of the body next to the tail, which also is more forked than that of the Salmon. They remain in fresh water all the autumn and winter, and spawn at the same time with the Salmon, and in the manner which I have already described. They return also to sea in the spring with the Salmon. It seems worthy of remark, that Salmon are oftentimes smaller than moderate-sized Gilse; but although such Gilse have only been once to sea, yet the period they have remained there must have exceeded the two short visits made by the *small* Salmon, and hence their superiority of size.

When these fish return to the river from their *second* visit to the sea, they are called *Salmon*, and are greatly altered in their shape and appearance; the body is more full, and the tail less forked, and their countenance assumes a different aspect.

It has formerly been suggested that the Gilse was a separate species from the Salmon; but they have been proved to be one and the same by very conclusive testimony. Many years ago, when I was on the Tweed, two were put in a salt pond by Mr. Berry: one of them was found dead, and supposed to have killed himself by rushing against a stake; the other was taken out some time afterwards a complete Salmon. But I shall mention a recent experiment, made by a tacksman on the Duke of Sutherland's salmon fishings on the river Shin.

In the course of February and March, 1841, he took

a considerable number of Gilses, and marked them with wire in various places sufliciently efficacious to be again recognised.   Of these, ten were retaken in the course of the months of June and July following, by which time they had assumed the size and all the distinctive marks of the genuine Salmon.   The following table shows when each was taken, and its weight at that time, and its increased weight when recaptured.   In addition to the fact which it establishes of the identity of the Gilse with the Salmon, it shows also how rapid the growth of the Gilse is in his process of becoming a Salmon :—

When marked.	When retaken.	Weight of Gilse.	Weight of Salmon.
		lbs.	lbs.
February 18	June 23	4	9
18	25	4	11
18	25	4	9
18	25	4	10
18	27	4	13
18	28	4	10
March 4	July 1	4	12
4	1	4	14
4	10	12	18
4	27	4	12

The above disparity of growth is easily accounted for, since it is not probable that these fish, which were caught and returned to the river in February, went down to the sea before March, if, indeed, so early : of course they would not increase in growth in fresh water, though they would mend somewhat in weight after their weak spawning state.   Setting these, therefore, aside, it appears that the growth of the last four fish averaged two pounds each per month when they were at sea; and if they remained in the river after the 4th of March, as it is reasonable to suppose they did, then their growth must have been proportionally greater.

For the scientific and successful experiments of Mr. Shaw, the Keith medal was awarded to him for the biennial period of 1838 and 1839: it is of gold, and of the intrinsic value of sixty guineas.

The importance of his proof is immense; for the Parrs not having been before considered to be young Salmon, have not been hitherto protected by the law beyond the short period in which they assume their silver dress, and thus have been killed by hundreds of thousands, by the multitude of boys and men who angle in the various tributary burns and rivers that pour their waters into the Tweed.

Mr. John Wilson says, in his evidence before the Select Committee, taken in 1824—" I have seen from my own window upwards of seventy or eighty people angling within the distance of half a mile on the Tweed." Then there is the Teviot; the Adder, comprising the White Adder and Black Adder; the Till, the Eden, the Kale, the Oxnam, the Jed, the Ale, the Rule, the Slitrig, the Gala, the Carter, the Borthwick, the Leader, the Ettrick, the Yarrow, the Lyne, the Eddlestone, the Manor, the Quhair, with many smaller burns and mountain streams. In floods Salmon enter and spawn in most of these rivers, if not in all of them; at the subsiding of the waters some of them fall back, and some are left nearly dry, and easily captured. It is ordained by nature that the Parr should in these cases impregnate such ova as have been deposited, perhaps because he is not so easily discovered, or such an object of attraction as a Salmon. What an ample space the above streams present for the destruction of the fry! And not only are they killed by the rod, each urchin, perhaps, taking eight or ten dozen a day, but by various other means in a wholesale manner.

Mr. William Laidlaw,* a gentleman mentioned with so much merited praise in the best biographical work extant, perhaps, who formerly lay under the general misapprehension regarding the Parr, writes to me as follows :—

" So great was the number of Parrs in the rivulet of *Douglas Burn*, that I have seen five dozen taken out of one small pool with aid of a pair of old blankets; and I and my playfellows, when boys, have committed great havoc by damming up one of the streams, where the rivulet happened to divide into two, and laying the other as dry as we could. The Parrs were so numerous, that we used to make the water white with the milt of those we killed. When the water was lowering, the poor creatures, instead of swimming downwards, where they would have had a chance of safety, all kept *swattering* upwards, and we actually killed them by hundreds. But a fact, which I could not account for, was this,—namely, that they appeared to come up the rivulet during the early part of the summer only ; but after the month of September there were very few to be seen, and not any in October; and when this discovery relative to the Parr was first made, and *I think*

* I am greatly indebted to this gentleman for his communications respecting T. Purdie.

it was from yourself I had it twenty years ago, I used to notice that there were scarcely any Parrs in the Tweed during the winter months."

So far Mr. Laidlaw. The disappearance of the Parrs from the burns is easily accounted for. They would naturally avoid the cold shallow rivulets, and fall into the deep and warmer water of the Tweed during the winter months, where they could not be well discovered, or be so subject to the action of torrents.

Besides the destruction of the fry in this and similar modes, we must add the thousands that are illegally taken at mill-dams, and the injury which the long net occasions in sweeping over the spawning beds. In the evidence taken before a Committee of the House of Commons in 1824 or 1825, there was an attempt to prove that no harm could be done in this latter manner, as there was no weight, but only a rope attached at the bottom of the net. This is very true; but the rope itself is sufficiently heavy to sink to the bottom, and disturb the gravel of the spawning beds, which, being newly raked up, and put together by the Salmon, must be easily displaced. It is fair, however, to observe, that the long net is not used in the generality of such places as fish commonly spawn in.

To these sweeping modes of destruction we must add the great havoc committed by the eels and trout, which devour the spawn; and when we consider the peculiar powers and habits of the eel, a fish most abundant in the Tweed, we must at once see that a ruinous devastation is occasioned by these creatures which bore through the gravel.

Strongly, however, as all these causes operate, there is one more destructive than all of them put together; namely, the effects of the furious spates which are continually taking place in the Tweed, and which put the channel in motion, and often sweep away the spawning beds altogether.

Before the hills were so well drained as at present, this was not so much the case; as the mosses gave out the water gradually, and the river continued full for a long time, to the great solace of the rod fisher. But now every hill is scored with little rills which fall into the burns, which suddenly become rapid torrents and swell the main river, which dashes down to the ocean with tremendous violence. Amidst the great din, you may hear the rattling of the channel stones, as they are borne downwards. Banks are torn away; new deeps are hollowed out, and old ones filled up; so that great changes continually take place in the bed of the river either for the better or the worse.

When we contemplate these things, we must at once acknowledge the vast importance of Mr. Shaw's experiments; for if ponds were constructed up the Tweed at the general expense, after the model of those made by him, all these evils would be avoided. The fry might be produced in any quantities by artificial impregnation; be preserved, and turned into the great river at the proper period of migration. There might at first be some difficulty in procuring food for them; but this would easily be got over. At a very small expense, and with a few adult Salmon, more fry may be sent to sea annually than the whole produce of the river at present amounts to, after having encountered the sweeping perils I have mentioned.

Proprietors should call meetings for this purpose; and Parrs, hitherto so called, should be protected by law. Let all who have an interest in the river consider the wisdom of mutual accommodation. The proprietors of the lower part of the river are dependent on the upper ones for the protection of the spawning fish and the fry; and they on their part depend upon the lower ones for the strict adherence to the weekly close time.

I think this method of artificial impregnation would prove somewhat more successful than the method said to be adopted by the Chinese, which, for the better enlightening of barbaric nations, I will transmit to posterity, from the authority of "The English Chronicle" of the 25th July, 1839:—

"The Chinese have taken a fancy to hatch fish under fowls. For this purpose they collect from rivers and ponds the gelatinous matter which contains the eggs of fish, put it into vessels, and sell it to the proprietors of ponds. When the hatching season arrives, a fowl's egg is emptied of its usual contents, and this gelatinous matter is put in. The entrance is hermetically sealed, and the egg is then put under a hen. After some days it is opened, and placed in a vessel of water heated by the sun; it is kept in the rays until the little fish become strong enough to bear the external temperature."

Not to derogate from the ingenuity of the celestial nation, I have no doubt but that fowls may be dispensed

with, and that a river may be stocked with any sort of
common fish by transmitting the ova and milt amalga-
mated, embedded in gravel, and placed in a vessel filled
up with water. One of our best fish, namely Trout, cannot
be sent alive even to a moderate distance. It is worth
while, therefore, to try the experiment. According to a
letter published by the late Sir Anthony Carlisle, something nearly approaching to this was done by him in
the river Wandle about thirty years ago. He then imbedded the ova of the Salmon in the gravel without the
milt of the male, leaving the River Trout to impregnate
them: he asserts that they did so, and that the river
was afterwards full of the fry so produced. It would
be interesting to put the Salmon eggs properly impregnated with the milt of the same species in one of our best
streams,—in the upper parts of the Test, for instance,
—and to investigate the result from year to year.

Salmon keep on increasing in size until they attain a
prodigious weight, even up to eighty-three pounds;
which, says Mr. Yarrell, is the largest fish on record,
and was exhibited at Mr. Grove's, fishmonger, in Bond
Street, about the season of 1821. This was a female
fish; and, from the observation of the same eminent
authority, those fish which attain a very unusual size
have always proved to be females.

But the devices and intelligence of fishermen have
increased as Salmon have become more marketable, so
that few escape all the perils that beset them long
enough to gain any considerable size; and we no more
hear, as in days of yore, of a fish being exchanged,
weight for weight, for a Highland wedder, and the

butcher having to pay. The Salmon in the Tweed are no longer large ; far from it. During my experience of twenty years I never caught one there above thirty pounds, and very few above twenty. I have remarked that the largest fish are found in the most considerable rivers, which I attribute to the superior chance of longevity where fish have a greater scope for escape.

It appears, from the above facts and observations, that Salmon are not uniform in their habits. Some come into the river many months before they are in a spawning condition, and remain in it till the time comes for depositing their spawn ; getting worse in condition every day they are in fresh water, and thus, as it should seem, doing unnecessary penance all that time. Others, again, remain in the sea, thriving all the while, and do not enter the rivers till their spawn is nearly matured. I have said above that I believe the Smolts singly, or in small quantities, are continually falling down to the sea in nearly if not quite every month of the year, according to their age ; but that they congregate, and go there in vast shoals in the beginning of the month of May. There seems to be a corresponding habit as to the time of their return; for they come back at first in small quantities, and periodically in the spring and summer months, and in July they arrive in vast quantities ; and this sudden abundance consists, I think, of the fry that have assembled and gone to sea the preceding May, whilst the others that ascend at different periods are the Smolts that go down in the same manner.

The accompanying lithograph represents a fry in the state when the silver scales just begin to appear, and

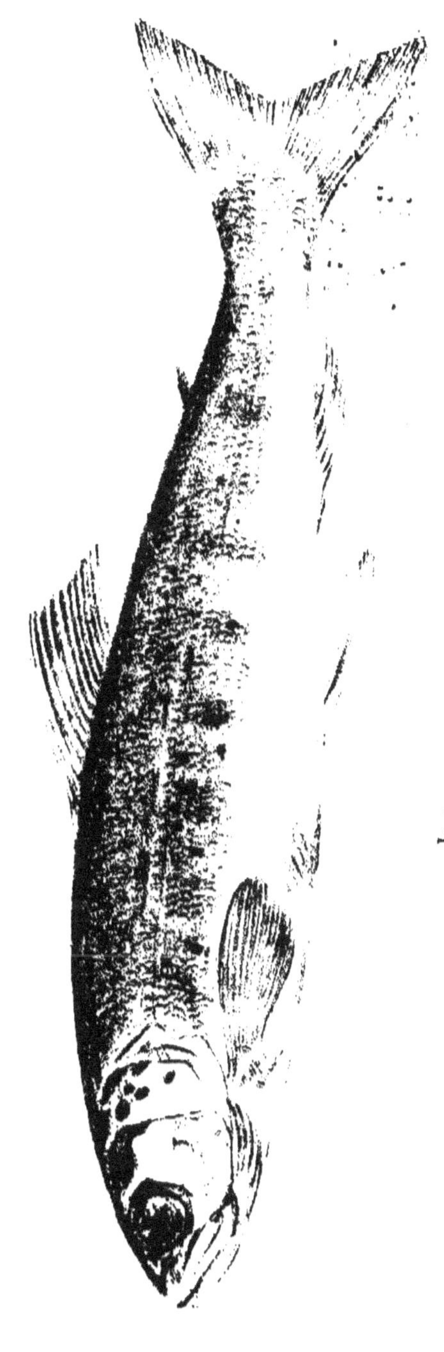

Intervening State.

soften the bars and spots,—the intermediate state
between the summer Parr and Smolt.

As to the belief that Salmon return to the same river
in which they are bred, I hold it to be a well-founded
one. But I think it is not invariably the case; and that
should their native river be too low for their ascent,
owing to an extraordinary drought, and continue so
when the period of spawning approaches, most of the
Salmon will seek and ascend some other river that may
be contiguous to it, whose volume of water is more
abundant. Thus many Tweed Salmon have been
caught in the Forth, and a very successful fishing there
is generally followed by a scarce one in the Tweed.

It appears that Salmon will live, and even breed, in
fresh water, without ever making a visit to the sea.
Mr. Lloyd, in his interesting and entertaining work on
the Field Sports of the North of Europe, says, " Near
Katrinebergh there is a valuable fishery for Salmon,
ten or twelve thousand of these fish being taken
annually. These Salmon are bred in a lake, and in
consequence of cataracts cannot have access to the sea.
They are small in size, and inferior in flavour. The
year 1820 furnished 21,817."

Mr. George Dormer of Stone Mills, in the parish of
Bridport, put a female of the Salmon tribe, which
measured twenty inches in length, and was caught by
him at his mill-dam, into a small well, where it remained
twelve years, and at length died in the year 1842.
The well measured only 5 feet by 2 feet 4 inches, and
there was only 15 inches depth of water. In this confined spot she remained up to Saturday the 12th of last

month, when death put a period to her existence. This fish has been the means of great attraction since the time she was mentioned in the newspapers, which was about five years ago, many persons having come a great distance to see her; and those who have witnessed her actions (of whom there are many in the city of Exeter) can bear testimony to the truth of the following statement:—

" She would come to the top of the water and take meat off a plate, and would devour a quarter of a pound of lean meat in less time than a man could eat it; she would also allow Mr. Dormer to take her out of the water, and, when put into it again, she would immediately take meat from his hands, or would even bite the finger if presented to her. Some time since a little girl teased her, by presenting the finger and then withdrawing it, till at last she leaped a considerable height above the water, and caught her by the said finger, which made it bleed profusely : by this leap she threw herself completely out of the water into the court. At one time a young duckling got into the well to solace himself in his favourite element, when she immediately seized him by the leg, and took him under water; but the timely interference of Mr. Dormer prevented any further mischief than making a cripple of the young duck. At another time a full-grown drake approached the well, and put in his head to take a draught of the water, when Mrs. Fish, seeing a trespasser on her premises, immediately seized the intruder by the bill, and a desperate struggle ensued, which at last ended in the release of Mr. Drake from the grasp of Mrs. Fish, and no sooner freed than Mr. Drake flew off in the greatest consternation and affright; since which time to this day he has not been seen to approach the well, and it is with great difficulty he can be brought within sight of it. This fish lay in a dormant state for five months in the year, during which time she would eat nothing, and was likewise very shy." *

That Salmon and some other fish assume in some degree the colour of the channel they lie upon, from whatever cause, is a circumstance pretty generally admitted by those who have paid any attention to the subject; and this, perhaps, is the reason why fishermen tell you that they can distinguish the Salmon of one river from those of another contiguous to it. Indeed, I myself could easily distinguish the Isla from the Tay Salmon by their colours, when I rented fisheries on both those rivers. This fact I thought so curious, that I had some correspondence with my eminent friend Sir David Brewster on the subject; and at the Literary and Philosophical Society of St. Andrews, Dr. Gillespie read the following paper, entitled " Recollections of the Habits, Colours, and Sufferings of Fishes."

"' My chief experience is with trouts,—such as are found in our mountain lakes and streams; and it is mainly to these that my few recollections refer. Trouts seem to have a generic type, comprehending several apparently different species; which difference, however, in many cases, disappears when the circumstances under

---

* This account seems to have been sent to a Devonshire newspaper by Mr. Dormer himself, or some of his family.

5

which they are viewed are the same. I know a locality in Dumfries-shire, amidst the hills of Queensberry, where three mountain streams, all of different character, meet—the one proceeding from a moss; the other running over a clear channelly bed; and the third, from its clayey banks and bottoms, exhibiting a milk-and-water aspect, like the 'flavus Tiberis' (or Albula) of Italy. Now the trouts in all these streams were of the same generic type; but differed, notwithstanding, in external appearance or colour. The moss race were of the Roderick Dhu tint—aspect grim and swarthy: the clear channel produced those of a brightly spotted appearance; and the clay bottom exhibited a correspondingly bluish race. Now, you might convert the blue fish into bright, and the bright again into black, by merely transferring them into the corresponding streams. This often took place, more or less, after what is called a thunder plump, which falls partially, and is quite local. I have seen one of these streams overflowing its banks, and carrying all before it, whilst its two mountain sisters remained calm and unmoved. Upon the ebbing of this partial flood, the trouts in the two conjoining streams immediately rush in quest of food (particularly after a long drought) into the other; and, in less time than any one who has not marked the fact could believe, they all become of the same appearance. Upon returning again into their native waters, they reassume their former colour. Fill your basket with fish from all the three streams, and in a little while that part of the bodies which presses against the others will exhibit the same appearance, whilst the other parts will remain as before ; and hence the clouded aspect they exhibit. I once threw a trout by accident, from a clear channel stream over my head into a peat-moss pool behind me, which had no communication with the running water ; and after a few months I caught him as black and portly as possible. Such facts certainly prove, to my own satisfaction at least, that trouts do not vary in original and indelible type so much as is generally imagined. In regard to what follows upon the changing colours of fish when in the act of dying, I cannot speak with the same certainty ; but either my eyes deceived me very much (and at the period of life to which I refer they were pretty good), or I observed the following phenomena :—I usually killed my fish, not by breaking their necks, as is now generally the method adopted, but by slapping their heads against a stone, the edge of my shoe, or the butt of my fishing-rod ; and even when a boy I was sensible of some change which took place in the colour of the dying victim. A kind of streamer, or phosphorus light, seemed to shoot along the quivering flesh and only ceased with the life of the trout. In salmon I should think the fact is still more manifest. The salmon fishery at the Eden afforded me an accidental proof of this. Some summers ago I was in the habit of bathing near the stakes at ebb tide, when the salmon were removed from the nets. I had a pleasure in walking into the inside of the nets, and seeing the finely-shaped living salmon plunging about, and still in their native element. Upon securing the fish, the men were in the habit of giving them the *coup de grace* on the forehead with a wooden mallet,—analogous to my fishing-rod butt; and at each successive stroke on the brain, the colours undulated away in the most delicate and beautiful radiance. All this is, indeed, exceedingly revolting to humanity, and presents a tempting theme for the reprobation of the poet and sentimentalist; and yet I confess that I cannot enter completely into this feeling, not only from my enjoyment of, and relish for, the sport of rod-fishing, but even from considerations of a more legitimate bearing. I do not think that cold-blooded animals suffer equally with warm-blooded; and my grounds for forming this opinion I shall shortly state. I have often lost a trout which had gorged my bait, and yet recaptured him in a short time with the former hook deep fastened in his stomach, and the broken line pending from his jaws. I, for one, certainly should have had little appetite to dine so soon after swallowing a fork. I have seen a large trout enjoying the amplitude of a clear pond with a couple of my fly-hooks appended to his nose. Nay I have even witnessed him rising to a natural fly in this situation, whilst, fisher-like, he caught a smaller companion by the depending hook. Nature is wonderfully benevolent to her children. The absence of all kind of medical aid in the waters seems to be fully compensated by the *vis medicatrix naturæ*— an old experienced practitioner, by whose management the most severe wounds made by the pike upon the trout, and the grampus upon the salmon, are safely and rapidly cured. I have caught trouts, particularly in the neighbourhoood where pike harbour, in various states of mutilation, yet seemingly in good health and spirits; from all which I infer that their physical sufferings are less than we suppose, and that the quiverings which they exhibit when dying are rather of a galvanic (which the change of colour seems to countenance) than of a convulsive or very painful character. It is, at least, comfortable for those who have been accessory in early life to much apparent suffering, to find out afterwards that the suffering was more apparent than real.'

"Sir David Brewster stated to the Society that he had been led to consider this subject in consequence of a correspondence with W. Scrope, Esq., who had paid much attention to the change of colour in fishes. Mr. Scrope was of opinion that a real change of colour took place, if not voluntarily, at least very quickly; and he supported his views by the following opinions of Mr. Yarrell and Mr. Shaw:—

"'An interesting account (says Mr. Yarrell) of some experiments made by Dr. Stark, was published in Jamieson's Edinburgh Journal for 1830, page 327. It shows that the colour of sticklebacks, and some other small fishes, is influenced not only by the colour of the earthenware or other vessel in which they are kept, but also modified by the quantity of light to which they are exposed; becoming pale when placed in a white vessel in darkness, even for a comparatively short time, and regaining their natural colour when placed in the sun. From these circumstances, observed also in some species of other genera, Dr. Stark is led to infer that fishes possess, to a certain extent, the power of accommodating their colour to the ground or bottom of the waters in which they are found. The final reason for this may be traced to the protection such a power affords to secure them from the attacks of their enemies, and exhibits another beautiful instance of the care displayed by Nature in the preservation of all her species. Dr. Stark often observed that on a flat, sandy coast, the flounders were coloured so very much like the sand, that, unless they moved, it was impossible to distinguish them from the bottom on which they lay.'

" Mr. Shaw, who has the charge of the salmon cruive at Drumlanrig, has observed that the Salmon taken in it change their colour in consonance with the turbid or refined state of the water. In the experiments he has made with Parr in different-coloured earthenware vessels, the change of colour is perfected in the space of four minutes. If Parr is taken from the dark-coloured vessel, and put immediately to the Parr in the light-coloured one, the difference of colour between the two fish will be found strikingly observable.

" Mr. Scrope himself had observed that the Trout at Castle Combe are white in a chalky spate, resuming their colour when the water clears ; and that in all the rivers in which he had fished, the fish are clear in a gravelly bottom, and dark in that overhung with trees. All this he considered as resulting from the same principle of preservation by which the ptarmigan and alpine hares have their colours changed with the approach of snow.

" Notwithstanding these distinct statements by so many observers in whom confidence might be placed,

Sir David thought that the experiments required to be repeated by persons acquainted with those branches of physical optics with which the phenomena were intimately allied. It is very easy to explain why a fish may appear dark in a dark vessel, and light in a coloured one; and why it should have a still different appearance when taken out of both vessels and exposed to the light of the sun. All bodies assume the colour of the light which they reflect, and a brilliant light will develop colours which are invisible in light of ordinary intensity. As the peculiar colours of fishes depend on the thickness or size of certain minute transparent particles, it is not easy to understand how the fish could voluntarily alter the size or thickness of those particles, or how exposure to another colour could permanently produce the same mechanical effect. If a fish is kept in mossy or muddy water, it will doubtless absorb the colouring matter which the water may contain; but this is rather a process of dyeing than one of physiological action. The changes said to take place in the colour of fishes when dying might arise from the drying of their scales, which produces a change in all colours, but particularly in those of thin films, which are quite different when they are dry from what they are when immersed in a fluid.

"A conversational discussion then took place, in which Professor Connell supported Dr. Gillespie's views, and Dr. Reid those of Sir D. Brewster."

This subject is in such good hands, that I shall not intrude any speculative observations of my own. We have lately seen such wonderful effects produced by the agency of light, that these things are become less startling.

It is very certain that Trouts and Salmon are less vivid in colour, and in fact more grey, when they have been some time out of their element; fishmongers throw water from time to time over their fish, as well to preserve their colour as to keep them fresh. I would recommend any one who wishes to show his day's sport in the pink of perfection, to keep his Trouts in a wet cloth, so that on his return home he may exhibit them to his admiring friends, and extract from them the most approved of epithets and exclamations, taking the praise bestowed upon the fish as a particular compliment to himself.

Since our writing the above remarks, I have paid more attention to the subject, and am enabled to state that in one particular part of the river Chess, I have been in the habit of taking Trouts of a darker and greyer colour than those which I captured in the other parts of this little stream; and, observing this to be invariably the case, I desired my fisherman to scoop up some of the channel with his landing net, which proved upon inspection to be part of a stratum of black flint.

I can state farther,—what appears to me to be altogether a curious circumstance. I had often observed that the largest of those Trout which almost continually lay under the *hides*, which were constructed in the stream and covered with boards,—being, in fact, large troughs open at the lower end so as to admit the fish, and staked within so as to preserve them from being poached out,—were of a very black colour : this arose, no doubt, from the privation of light. Sometimes I have seen them lying on the shallows within a few yards of the hide, where they still retained their black hue. I caught with a minnow one of these dirty-looking animals in the month of June last. He was not only black in the back, so that he could be seen at a considerable distance in the water, but was also of a granulated inky cast on his sides and underneath : his resort was under a hide in comparative darkness. He was not wasted, but of the same proportions with his brighter companions. I concluded, however, that from his African appearance he would cut but a sorry figure at the table ; but being about three quarters of a pound, with no promise of amendment, I bagged him notwithstanding. As this was the first trout I took that morning, he lay at the bottom of my basket. After catching a few more lower down in the river, I thought I would have another look at my swarthy captive. I found him more praiseworthy than at first ; for the upper side, which came in contact with the other fish, became also bright, and of a colour exactly similar to them, whilst the lower side that touched the dry basket retained its original dark hue ; but by turning that part of the fish also towards the others, the whole Trout after a time became of a uniform bright colour, and was not in that respect dissimilar to the rest. I do not mean to hint that the blackamoor was dyed by his dead companions, because I think that a wet cloth would have produced the same effect ; but it seems extraordinary that the water, which had no effect upon his colour when living in the river, should have so decided a one after he was dead,—not bringing back the original dye, but removing the dark tint entirely.

But to return to my subject.

It is an undoubted fact that Salmon ascend some rivers much earlier than others. I have rented fisheries both in Tweed and Tay, and to my own knowledge the latter river is a month earlier than the former. The Esk and the Eden both fall into the Solway Firth, and are only separated at their mouths by a sharp point of land; yet, according to the statement of Mr. Howard,* a proprietor and renter of the river Eden, new fish go up that river three months before they ascend the Esk, and the month of February is one of the greatest produce there. The Irthing falls into the Eden, and may be a fourth of its water; but no Salmon run up it, except in spawning time. Now the waters of the Eden may be presumed to be of a warmer temperature than those of the Esk, which latter is a brawling shallow stream, wider also than the Eden, which is of a deeper and more tranquil nature.

Snow water is offensive to fish, and they will not ascend a river whilst it is impregnated with it. Setting aside this impediment, and *cœteris paribus*, I believe the season of all rivers depends upon the temperature of their waters during the winter and spring months Thus the Ness is the forwardest river in Scotland which the following table of monthly captures produced by Mr. Alexander Fraser† will prove.

* Evidence before Select Committee in 1825, p. 140.
† Ibid. p. 42.

Statement of the Number of Salmon Killed in the Ness in Twelve Years.

1811.	1811-12. Sal.	Gr.	1812-13. Sal.	Gr.	1813-14. Sal.	Gr.	1814-15. Sal.	Gr.	1815-16. Sal.	Gr.	1816-17. Sal.	Gr.	1817-18. Sal.	Gr.	1818-19. Sal.	Gr.	Total Salmon monthly in Eight Years.
Dec.	226	-	454	-	301	-	240	-	324	-	422	-	128	-	220	-	2405
1812.																	
Jan.	427	-	565	-	354	-	204	-	370	-	1052	-	388	-	194	-	3554
Feb.	194	-	874	-	289	-	206	-	208	-	696	-	326	-	266	-	3230
Mar.	103	-	591	-	522	-	164	-	645	-	490	-	270	-	244	-	3029
April	157	-	461	-	227	-	195	-	283	-	370	-	248	-	206	-	2147
May	29	-	157	-	359	-	152	-	102	-	246	-	34	-	48	-	1127
June	6	39	18	27	69	180	7	20	16	11	40	-	10	-	4	-	170
July	25	211	38	208	21	263	51	97	40	164	57	184	12	147	9	84	253
Aug.	236	1361	318	700	221	710	202	186	187	406	604	340	260	286	74	240	2192
Sept.	77	482	74	169	15	97	21	142	18	126	178	187	19	170	28	120	430
	1480	2093	3550	1104	2408	1250	1022	435	2283	707	4155	711	1005	603	1293	444	18,546

						Sal.
1819-1820	-	·	·	·	·	1215
1820-1821	-	·	·	·	·	1806
1821-1822	-	·	·	·	·	710
1822-1823	-	·	·	·	·	344

Now it must be observed that the Ness never freezes even with the most intense frost. In the year 1807, when the thermometer at Inverness was from 23 to 30 and even 40 degrees below the freezing point, it made no impression upon the river or the lake. " The Ness (says Mr. Fraser) was always privileged earlier than any river in Scotland from this cause; and it will be evident that the Salmon taken in December and January are the most valuable produce : for though they appear to be only one third of the total number, yet from their size they constitute more than half the weight."

The most forward rivers in Ireland, I am informed by the London fishmongers, and from other sources, are those on the western coast. In England, perhaps the Severn produces the finest Salmon during the winter months ; and the Lord Viscount Clive, proprietor of a salmon fishery in the Severn, near Poole Quay, says[*] the best fish are commonly taken there in November, December, and January, though they are not numerous, and that in the Dovey and Tivey, two rivers with which he is well acquainted, the Salmon are always in the best season at the period when the Severn Salmon are in the worst condition.

But if Salmon prefer the warmest rivers in the winter, they spawn earliest in those that are most cold. Thus in the shallow mountain streams which pour into the Tay nearer its sources (I do not mean such as may issue from lochs), the fish spawn much earlier than those in the main bed of the river. The late John Crerar, head fisherman and forester to the Duke of Atholl, wrote thus in his manuscript:—

"There are two kinds of creatures that I am well acquainted with,—the one a land animal, the other a water one : the red deer, and the salmon. In October the deer ruts, and the salmon spawns. The deer begins soonest, high up amongst the hills, particularly in frosty weather; so does the salmon begin to spawn earlier in frosty weather than in soft. The master hart would keep all the other harts from the hind, if he could; and the male salmon would keep all the other males from the female, if he was able."

The gross rental of the salmon fishings in Tweed is very considerable; but has varied very much in amount from time to time, according to the plenty or scarcity of fish. Mr. John Wilson[†] states, that during the seven

<hr>

[*] Minutes of Evidence taken in 1825, &c., p. 14.
[†] Minutes of Evidence, &c. in 1824, p. 9.

years previous to 1824 it averaged £12,000 a year but in that year only about £10,000. With the present rental I am unacquainted.

"The fishings, as regards their relative value, may be divided into the following classes :—The first comprehends the short distance from the mouth of the river to Berwick Bridge, where alone there are probably a greater number of salmon captured than in all the remainder of the river. From Berwick Bridge to Norham, to which place the tide reaches, may be considered the second class: as far as this place the net and coble only are in use. From Norham to Coldstream Bridge the fishings are of still less value ; and here, besides the net and coble, the various modes of fishing practised in the upper parts of the river are also in use—*rod fishing, setting, leistering;* cairn, hanging, and straik nets. From Coldstream to the Bridge of Kelso the net and coble are used only partially in floods ; and on Mondays, says Mr. Houy, when, by the cessation of the lower fishings on Sunday, the salmon get further up, I have seen from 100 to 500 salmon and gilses caught at Kelso in the morning by the net and coble. From Kelso to the higher districts of the river the principal modes of fishing are by the rod, leister, cairn and straik net."

When fish are ascending the river the cairn net is very destructive. In the parts of the river most favourable for placing it a cairn is built, *as in the vignette.* This projection into the current makes the water comparatively still and easy below ; and Salmon in travelling naturally take to it, as finding there some relief to the labour of ascending. They pass between the net and the shore; and endeavouring to get forward, at the point of the cairn become entangled in the net, and are taken in great quantities.

THE SALMON TROUT.

SALMO TRUTTA, *Linn.*

THIS fish is called by different names in various localities,—*White Trout, Phinock, Sea Trout, Whitling, Hirling.* It is little inferior to the Salmon in flavour; and being less rich, is I presume more wholesome. It is distinguished, says Mr. Yarrell, by the gill-cover being intermediate in its form between that of the Salmon, and Grey or Bull Trout. The teeth likewise are more slender, as well as more numerous than in those fish. The tail is less forked than in Salmon of the same age, and smaller in proportion, but becomes ultimately square at the end.

It is found in most, if not in all salmon rivers; but it is now very scarce in the Tweed, which I attribute to the spates that are become more sudden and violent in that river than formerly, owing to a more complete drainage of the mountains and adjoining lands; for these fish always prefer the smaller and less turbulent streams. Like the Salmon, it remains in the river two years before it puts on the migratory dress, and the males also shed their milt at 18 months old, similar to the Parr (so called) of a corresponding age. The Orange Fin, for so the fry of the Sea Trout is called, so much resembles the common River Trout, that it is with very great difficulty it can be distinguished from it. Like the Gilse, it returns to the river the summer of its spring migration, weighing about a pound and a half upon an average. It afterwards increases about a pound and a half a year; but is seldom seen above six or seven pounds, though it probably attains to a much greater weight.

By the aid of the cruive, Mr. Shaw traced this fish from the Orange Fin of three ounces to the Hirling or Whitling, up to the Sea Trout of seven pounds; and he has now a specimen in his possession exhibiting the four several marks he had put on it in the course of its annual migrations. At the size of six pounds the central rays of the tail were considerably increased in length, so much so in the males that their tails became actually rounded: the fish altogether at this time loses a great deal of its former elegance. The tails of the females of a corresponding age are more square, and their general shape is more slim.

These fish may be crossed with Salmon; I mean that by artificial impregnation hybrids may be thus produced. Mr. Shaw says in a letter to me, dated November 25th, 1840:—"I put some of your suggestions regarding the ova of the Salmon, and the common Trout, Sea Trout, and Salmon, into practice about a month ago, and shall let you know the result." The following year I had the pleasure of a letter from him, dated October 14th, 1841, saying that "The hybrids which I produced by artificial impregnation last autumn are all in a very healthy state, the cross not having in the slightest degree affected their constitution. Those produced between the Salmon and the Salmon Trout (*Salmo Trutta*) appear to partake more of the external markings, silvery coating, and elegance of form of the Parr (young Salmon) than any of the others. Those produced between the Salmon and common Trout (*Salmo Fario*), and between the common Trout and Salmon Trout, have in every respect more the appearance of the common Trout than the former."

Some have imagined that the Whitling or Hirling are the young of the Bull Trout. But this is a mistake, as the Hirling abounds in the Annan, where the Bull Trout is very rarely seen; and also in the Nith, where Mr. Shaw has never been able to discover one of the other species. Lord Home likewise, whom I consider the very best practical authority, says, " The Whitling

of the Tweed is the Salmon Trout, and not the young
Bull Trout, which now goes by the name of Trout
simply."

THE GREY, BULL TROUT, OR ROUND TAIL.

SALMO ERIOX, *Linn.*

"THE Grey Trout," says Mr. Yarrell, "is distinguished
from the Salmon and Salmon Trout by several specific
peculiarities. The gill-cover differs from them decidedly
in form, and the teeth are longer and stronger." The
tail grows square at an earlier period than in the
Salmon; and the central caudal rays continuing to
elongate with age, the whole tail, originally concave,
eventually becomes convex, and from thence it has
been called the *Round Tail.* The elongation of the
under jaw is peculiar to the males only, and is less
than in the Salmon. The scales also are less, the
shoulders thicker, and the tail more muscular. In
short, it is altogether a more thick and powerful fish
than the Salmon, and consequently gives the angler
more sport; but to the epicure it gives less, as it is
inferior in flavour and colour, and if not very fresh
from the sea its flesh is short and woolly. It is very
much the colour of the Salmon, but tinted with grey
or brown spots.

These fish are found in many salmon rivers, but not
in all. It is very abundant in the Tweed, which it
visits principally at two seasons; in the spring about
the month of May, and again in the month of October,

G

when the males are very plentiful; but the females are scarce till about the beginning or middle of November. With salmon it is the reverse, as their females leave the sea before the males. The Bull Trout is also more regular in his habits than the Salmon, for the fishermen can calculate almost to a day when the large black male Trouts will leave the sea. The foul fish rise eagerly at the fly, but the clean ones by no means so. They weigh from two to twenty-four pounds, and occasionally, I presume, but very rarely indeed, more. The largest I ever heard of was taken in the Hallow-stell fishing water at the mouth of the Tweed, in April, 1840, and weighed twenty-three pounds and a half.

The heaviest Bull Trout I ever encountered myself weighed sixteen pounds, and I had a long and severe contest with his majesty. He was a clean fish, and I hooked him in a cast in Mertoun Water called the *Willow Bush*, not in the mouth, but in the dorsal fin. Brethren of the craft, guess what sore work I had with him! He went here and there with apparent comfort and ease to his own person, but not to mine. I really did not know what to make of him. There never was such a hector. I cannot say exactly how long I had him on the hook; it seemed a week at least. At length John Haliburton, who was then my fisherman, waded into the river up to his middle, and cleiked him whilst he was hanging in the stream, and before he was half beat.

Besides the three species I have mentioned, I have sometimes, though very rarely, caught a fish very

ASCERTAINING THE WEIGHT.

similar in shape to the Grey or Bull Trout, but much cleaner, which the fishermen call a North-country Salmon. It is clearly not a Bull Trout, for that fish is as well known in the Tweed as the Salmon itself. I have no doubt but that it is rightly named, and a wanderer from the northern coasts.

I have also occasionally caught in the Tweed a small silver fish, between a quarter and half a pound, which seems of the Salmon tribe; its flesh is of a pale pink, and good eating. In the river Isla I have taken many of them with a net.

I have now given a brief account of all the fish of the Salmon Tribe in the Tweed, except the *Salmo Fario*, or common Trout, which I do not profess to treat of. Much more has been said by naturalists as to distinctive character and organisation. Whoever wishes for minute information on these points cannot do better than consult the new edition of Mr. Yarrell's unrivalled work on British Fishers—a gentleman to whom I feel much indebted for some very liberal and scientific communications; nor must they omit to look into the pages of a most highly entertaining and clever work lately published, called "The Rod and the Gun."

I shall only add, that in allusion to the consequence attributed to these beautiful fish in the Tweed, and in consideration of the favourable places for spawning in the upper parts of the river, the Royal Burgh of Peebles wears for arms—vert, three salmon counter naiant in pale argent, with the motto, "Contra nando Incrementum."

In the arms of the city of Glasgow, and in those of the ancient see, a salmon with a ring in its mouth is said to record a miracle of St. Kentigern, the founder of the see, and the first Bishop of Glasgow.

"They report," says Spotswood, "of St. Kentigern, that a lady of good place in the country, having lost her ring as she crossed the river Clyde, and her husband waxing jealous, as if she had bestowed the same on one of her lovers, she did mean herself unto Kentigern, entreating his help for the safety of her honour; and that he going to the river after he had used his devotion, willed one who was making to fish to bring the first fish he caught, which was done. In the mouth of this fish he found the ring, and, sending it to the lady, she was thereby freed of her husband's suspicion."

The classical tale of Polycrates, says the very clever author of "The Heraldry of Fish," related by Herodotus a thousand years before the time of St. Kentigern, is, perhaps, the earliest version of the fish and the ring, which has been often repeated with variations. The ring, says Herodotus, was an emerald set in gold, and beautifully engraved, the work of Theodorus the Samian; and this very ring, Pliny relates, was preserved in the Temple of Concord in Rome, to which it was given by the Emperor Augustus.

In the Koran of Mahomet the legend of the ring, and its recovery by means of a fish, is introduced. "Solomon entrusted his signet with one of his concubines, which the Devil obtained from her, and sat on the throne in Solomon's shape. After forty days the Devil departed, and threw the ring into the sea. The signet was swallowed by a fish, which being caught and given to Solomon, the ring was found in his belly, and thus he recovered his kingdom."*

* Sale's Translation of the Koran.

CHAP. III.

" *Hostess.*   Say what beast, thou knave thou.
Falstaff.   What beast ? Why, an otter.
Hostess.   An otter, Sir John ! why an otter ?
Falstaff.   Why she's neither fish nor flesh. A man knows not
where to have her. '

BEFORE I enter upon the practical part of Salmon Fishing, I will just say a few words about my natural tendency to the sport, to the end that it may be evident that my maxims are not drawn from books, but originate in my own experience.

I declare, then, that I, Harry Otter, am by nature a person of considerable aquatic propensities, having been born under the sign of Aquarius, or Pisces—it matters not which. My delight in water, however, has its limits, and extends only to external applications: the placid amusement of wading in a Salmon river is very much to my taste—quite captivating. Showers, and even storms, if not of too long a continuance, are exceedingly refreshing to my person; but I must in candour admit that the decisive action of a water-spout may not possibly be so gratifying—*ne quid nimis.* Macintosh's invention I consider as wholly uncalled for, accounting it, as I do, an unpardonable intrusion to place a solution of india-rubber between the human body and a refreshing element. It is like taking a shower-bath under shelter of an umbrella.

Thus far I can extend; but desire me to drink water by itself, and I am your very humble servant. Had I been at a symposium of brandy and the said vapid element with that worthy Magnus Troil, he should not have drunk all the brandy himself, and put me off with the water, as he is recorded to have done to his very simple friend. I beg to say that I am not one of those two thousand patients who have been relieved by a *water cure,* administered by James Wilson, Esq., physician to his Serene Highness the Prince of Nassau, as advertised. Internally, in its pure state, I totally discard it. But I like the society of fish; and as they cannot with any convenience to themselves visit me on dry land, it becomes me in point of courtesy to pay my respects to them in their own element.

Next to wading in water, comes, I think, the pastime of trudging over bogs and fens—ground intimately allied to it, and which Colonel Hawker has made quite classical. This is a sort of debateable land, and the natural inhabitants of it reject you with most unequivocal signs of disapprobation. The red shank, the pewet, the curlew, and all their allies, scream and dart around you, inhospitable as they are, and tell you, as plainly as bills can speak, to sheer off, and not invade their premises. But we are a sort of Paul Pry, and love to persist responding now and then with our double barrel, which we more especially direct towards the ruff, snipe, wild duck, and teal—birds whose merit we particularly appreciate. Thus we are, as may be seen, of an amphibious nature, and respond to the fat knight's description, when he compared Hostess Quickly to our namesake. That this predilection for humidity is with me an instinct, may be seen from the following brief notice of my infant propensities.

When I was an urchin I stole off, and wandered up the stream that came winding through the verdant meadows of my native valley, till I arrived at the foot of the Castle Hill; following the little path that dived into a thicket, and wound round its base near the margin of the river; thence, amongst irregular clumps of thorn bushes, holly trees, and other wild wood, stopping a while to gather the cowslips and white violets that dappled the sunny slopes, I pursued my way through a tangled thicket, whose branches overhung the stream. I remember even now that the sunbeam glittered on the leaves, struck through the masses here and there

and pierced to the surface of the water, which shone in
spots through the gloom like the fragments of a broken
mirror : these lucid touches caught my childish fancy ;
but my favourite spot was not yet attained.   Not until
I had rounded the rib of the promontory on which
stood the grey castle, and came to another face of it,
did I obtain the object of my ramble.   At this turn of
the stream I found myself in a small lonely meadow
sprinkled with cowslips, upon which opened two
wooded valleys, each watered by a small stream, which
at their junction washed out a deep hole ; and at the
foot of the hole a small gravel heap was thrown up,
upon which grew the yellow iris, and some other
vegetation.   In Lilliput it would have been termed an
island : so in truth it was. I know not how it happened,—
unless, indeed, that I was strictly enjoined not to go near
the water,—but I had a decided propensity to establish
my little person on this insular spot.   For some time I
was either very good, or very much afraid—it matters
not which,—and the achievement was dubious.   At
length the demon of temptation appeared in the form
of a dragon-fly, which, glancing from some branches
that extended across the stream a little above, danced
up and down in the air in all its gaudy trim, and at
length settled on an iris in this enchanted island.   I
stood enraptured on the bank with my arms out-
stretched, and my longing eyes fixed upon the beauty.
It was irresistible—I could hold out no longer.   So
mustering up my naughty courage, and letting myself
gently down the bank, I paddled through a little
shallow water, till I actually set foot safely on the

desired spot.   Here I found that my love for the *libella* was not mutual; or, if it was, I may say,

> " Love, free as air, at sight of human ties
> Spreads its light wings, and in a moment flies."

Even so did the dragon-fly: he and my hopes vanished at once.   Nevertheless I showed a decided taste for an insular life, and sat down watching the trout rise on all sides, as happy as a king; and I might have remained there to this day, had not that kill-joy Martha, who was blest with the care of me, and from whom I had escaped in the morning, come upon my trail.   Infuriated she was (for the whole Xantippe possessed her).   She sallied forth like another Ceres in quest of her lost child.   Half frightened, half pleased, I could see her toiling up the hill.   " Master Harry! Master Harry!" resounded shrilly through the woods and valleys: even now methinks her voice rings in my ears.   In vain—

> " Nor at the lawn, nor at the wood, was he."

But when at length she returned, " alla solinga valle," I stood confessed within the range of her animated optics.   She declared her sentiments without reserve in very fluent language.   I was an *obstropolous* brat; a perfect *dæmon* (demon), as fond of dabbling in water as a *sallymander*.   I should *catch it* when she got hold of me, that I should.   This being intelligibly explained, I thought I would delay that period as long as possible. To all this eloquence, therefore, answer made I none; but I believe I looked and felt rather oddly. At length, seeing her amble to and fro upon the banks, and perceiving that she had the hydrophobia strong upon her,

I told her if she wanted me she must come and fetch
me, as I was forbidden to go into the water. "Hang
your imperance, I says, Master Harry, but I'll find one
as shall fetch you in a twinkling!" So saying, the
eloquent Martha suited the action to the word, and ran
round the turn of the river, where it seems she knew
the keeper was fishing, who, I believe, in village phrase,
" kept company with her." Down comes John, a good-
natured fellow; tickles me with the point of his fishing
rod in gamesome mood ; makes two or three casts with
his fly at me ; and at length wades to me, and places
me on the mainland at the gentle Martha's side. Peace
was made, but without promise for the future.

Henceforth, when I could escape control, I divided
my time between the water and the meadows : in warm
weather the water, in cold the land possessed me.
Then I began to tamper with the minnows ; and,
growing more ambitious, after a sleepless night full of
high contrivance, I betook me at early dawn to a wood
near the house, where I selected some of the straightest
hazel sticks I could find, which I tied together and
christened a fishing-rod : a rude and uncouth weapon
it was. I next sought out *Phyllis*, a favourite cow so
called, in order to have a pluck at her tail to make a
line with. But Phyllis was coy, and withheld her
consent to spoliation ; for when I got hold of her
posterior honours, she galloped off, dragging me along,
tail in hand, till she left me deposited in a water-course
amongst the frogs. The dairy-maid, I think, would
have overcome this difficulty for me, had I not discovered that horse-hair, and not cow's tail, was the

proper material for fishing lines; so the coachman, who was much my friend, plucked *Champion* and *Dumplin*, at my request, and gave me as much hair (black enough to be sure) as would make a dozen lines. For three whole days did I twist and weave like the Fates, and for three whole nights did I dream of my work. Some rusty hooks I had originally in my possession, which I found in an old fishing-book belonging to my ancestors. In fact, I did not put the hook to the rod and line, but my rod and line to the hook. I next proceeded to the pigeon-house, and picking some coarse feathers, made what I alone in the wide world would have thought it becoming to have called a fly; but call it so I did, in spite of contradictory evidence. Thus equipped, I proceeded to try my skill; but exert myself as I would, the line had domestic qualities, and was resolved to stay at home. I never could get it fairly away from the hazel sticks; therefore it was that I hooked no fish. But I hooked myself three times: once in the knee-strings of my shorts, once in the nostril, and again in the lobe of the ear. At length, after sundry days of fruitless effort, like an infant Belial, I attempted that by guile which I could not do by force; and dropping the fly with my hand under a steep bank of the stream, I walked up and down trailing it along: after about a week's perseverance, I actually caught a trout. Shade of Izaak Walton, what a triumph was there! That day I could not eat,— that night I slept not. Even now I recollect the spot where that generous fish devoted himself.

As I grew up I became gradually more expert, and

at length saved money sufficient to buy a real fishing rod, line, reel and all, quite complete. Down it came from London resplendent with varnish, and many cunning feats did I perform with it. About this time I learned to shoot; not that I was strong enough to hold a gun, but that the keeper put the said implement to his shoulder, when I took aim at larks and sparrows, and those sort of things, and pulled the trigger. So I waxed in years and wisdom. All the time I could steal from my lessons (for I was not quite a Pawnee) I spent in this edifying manner; at length I was fully initiated in all the mysteries of sporting by a relation, himself the prince of sportsmen, who took a fancy to me. The reason was as follows :—

In the depth of winter, the ground being smothered with snow, and the blast bitter, I followed him out a wild-fowl shooting. I was devoid of hat, an article that I looked upon as superfluous, and that I always lost or mislaid as soon as it was given me. Equipped I was in white cotton stockings ; and my shoes, which were of the thinnest, I had tied to my feet with a string which passed over the instep. I could not put them up at heel with any comfort, because I had large chilblains there, which were broke. At length, after creeping a space on my gloveless hands and knees in the snow, and under cover of some sedge and willow bushes, up flew some wild ducks before my patron. "Quack, quack !" —down came one to his shot, and fell with a splash into the river. In I plunged after him like a Newfoundland dog: you might have heard the flounce in a still day at Chippenham, about six miles off. The duck not being dead, made a swim and a dive of it. Long and dubious was the chase; but in the end I descried his bill amongst the sedges, where he had poked it up to take a little breath. Making a dexterous snatch, I seized him underneath by the legs,—Chinese fashion, with the exception of the pumpkin,—and drew him loud quacking to the bank. When landed, I squeezed my clothes a little, according to order; but I do not believe that benefitted my chilblains.

At a rather more advanced period of my life I used to make long fishing excursions, generally with prosperous, but occasionally with disastrous results. I remember well, when a pair of bait-hooks was to me a valuable concern, I hooked two large black-looking trouts in a deep pool at the same time. As I had to pull them several feet upwards against the pressure of the stream, my line gave way, and left me proprietor of a small fragment only. For some time I looked alternately at my widowed rod and my departed fish; which last were coursing it round and round the pool, pulling in opposite directions. like coupled dogs of dissenting opinions : Durum—sed levius fit patientiâ. So I sat down with somewhat of a rueful countenance, and began to spin with my fingers some horse-hair which I had pulled that morning, at the risk of my life, from the grey colt's tail. This being done in my own peculiar manner, and my only remaining hook being tied on with one of the aforesaid hairs, I continued to follow my sport down the stream for about half a mile. After the lapse of a considerable time, I had occasion to cross bare-legged from one bank to the other. In my transit through the current, I found something

like a sharp instrument cutting the calves of my legs.
I scampered ashore, under the impression that I was
trailing after me some sharp-toothed monster, perhaps
a lamper eel; when, upon passing down my hand to ascertain the fact, I found to my great astonishment and
delight that I was once more in possession of my lost
line, hooks, fish, and all. The fish had fairly drowned
each other, and, by a curious coincidence, were passively
passing in the current at the time my legs stemmed it.

Originally I had what in Scotland is called a *poke* or
bag to carry my trouts in. This being rather of a
coarse appearance, I panted after a basket. One of my
school-fellows had exactly the thing; and I bargained for
it by giving in return all my personal right in perpetuity
to two young hawks. Proud of my acquisition, I set
out with no small share of vanity, carrying my basket
through the whole length of a neighbouring village,
which was considerably out of the way. When I arrived
at the happy spot where my sport lay, I was successful
as usual. At length the declining sun admonished me
of some ten miles betwixt me and home; so I resolved
only to take a few casts in a dark and deep pool which
was close at hand, and then to bend my course home-
ward. There I hooked a fine fish, which I was obliged to
play for some time, and then, after he was fairly tired,
to lift out with my hands, not having yet arrived at
the dignity of a landing net. In stooping low to perform
this process, the lid of my new pet basket, which from
want of experience I had omitted to fasten, flew open,
and two or three of my last-killed fish dropped into the
deep water immediately before me. In suddenly reach-

ing forward to secure these, round came my basket, fish, and all, over my head, and fairly capsized me. With some difficulty, and even risk of drowning, I got my head above water, and my hand on the crown of a sharp rock. There I stood, screaming and disconsolate, casting a wistful look at the late bright inmates of my basket, which were tilting down the weeds through the gullet into a tremendous pool, vulgarly called Hell's Cauldron. Into that same pool with the ominous name had I myself very nearly passed, and thus had followed my hat, which was coursing about in the eddy or wheel of this fearful depth. Thus vanished before my eyes my whole day's sport, for dead fish immediately sink ; and it was not without some skilful fishing up that my hat and I renewed our acquaintance. I have before observed that when I was quite an urchin I never wore a hat, or any covering over my hair; but as I grew older, I thought it decorous to follow the fashion.

At another time, whilst still a *puer*, and only possessed of one single bait-hook, to my utter confusion I found that solitary hook had been swallowed by a duck, which a mass of sedges under the bank had concealed from my view. There we were, Mrs. Duck and I, dashing, swashing, and swattering down the stream ; the duck all the time declaring her sentiments by the utterance of a fearful noise, and I endeavouring by every means in my power to prevent my only hook from being ravished from me by my feathered opponent. In the meantime a group of lasses, who were washing clothes at the river side, and were friendly to the bird, set upon me, first with their tongues, of the use of which they seemed to be in full possession, and latterly with their pails and watering pans, in consequence of which I was compelled to snap my line, and turn upon my fair tormentors. But let no boy of fourteen ever try to face a batch of lasses. In fine, I was terribly mauled, and did not feel my ears at all comfortable in their externals for a considerable time afterwards.

But enough of these idle anecdotes. The reader will now understand that I, Harry Otter, was an idle scamp. If he chooses to keep company with me in my rambles, he will, nevertheless, find no very particular harm in me, and I on my part shall be delighted to hold good fellowship with an indulgent brother of the craft.

"I saw young Harry with his beaver off."

CHAP. IV.

" I in these flowery meads would be ;
These crystal streams shall solace me."

MUCH has been said by various humane persons about the cruelty of fishing ; but setting aside that, according to the authority of the eminent author of *Salmonia*, and of Dr. Gillespie also, who, by-the-by, is professor of humanity at St. Andrews, fish seldom feel any pain from the hook. Let us see how the case stands. I take a little wool and feather, and, tying it in a particular manner upon a hook, make an imitation of a fly; then I throw it across the river, and let it sweep round the stream with a lively motion. This I have an undoubted right to do, for the river belongs to me or my friend ; but mark what follows. Up starts a monster fish with his murderous jaws, and makes a dash at my little Andromeda. Thus he is the aggressor, not I ; his intention is evidently to commit murder. He is caught in the act of putting that intention into execution. Having wantonly intruded himself on my hook, which I contend he had no right to do, he darts about in various directions, evidently surprised to find that the fly, which he hoped to make an easy conquest of, is much stronger than himself. I naturally attempt to regain this fly, unjustly withheld from me. The fish gets tired and weak in his lawless endeavours to deprive me of it. I take advantage of his weakness, I own, and drag him, somewhat loth, to the shore, where one rap at the back of the head ends him in an instant. If he is a trout I find his stomach distended with flies. That beautiful one called the May-fly, who is by nature almost ephemeral—who rises up from the bottom of the shallows, spreads its light wings, and flits in the sunbeam in enjoyment of its new existence,—no sooner descends to the surface of the water to deposit its eggs, than the unfeeling fish at one fell spring numbers him prematurely with the dead. You see, then, what a wretch a fish is; no ogre is more blood-thirsty, for he will devour his nephews, nieces, and even his own children, when he can catch them; and I take some credit for having shown him up. Talk of a wolf, indeed, a lion, or a tiger! Why these are all mild and saintly in comparison with a fish. When did any one hear of Messrs. Wolf, Lion, and Co. eating up their grandchildren? What a bitter fright must the smaller fry live in! They crowd to the shallows, lie hid among the weeds, and dare not say the river is their own. I relieve them of their apprehensions, and thus become popular with the small shoals.

When we see a fish quivering upon dry land, he looks so helpless without arms or legs, and so demure in expression, adding hypocrisy to his other sins, that we naturally pity him; then kill and eat him with Hervey sauce, perhaps. Our pity is misplaced—the fish is not. There is an immense trout in Loch Awe in Scotland, which is so voracious, and swallows his own species with such avidity, that he has obtained the name of *Salmo ferox.* I pull about this unnatural monster till he is tired, land him, and give him the *coup de grace.* Is this cruel? Cruelty "should be made of sterner stuff." There is a certain spurious sort of humanity going about that I cannot understand. Thus I know a lady who will not eat game, because, she says, shooting is a cruel amusement; but she is very much addicted to fowls, and all domestic poultry, feeding them one day, and eating them up the next, with treacherous alacrity and amiable perseverance. It would be more candid in her, therefore, to say to us sportsmen, like the fox in the fable,—

> " Go, but be moderate in your food;
> A pheasant too might do me good."

" I once saw," says the learned and accomplished Dr. Gillespie, " one of those all-devouring fish in a curious predicament. In fishing, or rather strolling, within these few years, with a rod in one hand and a book in the other, so as to alternate reading and fishing, as the clouds came and went, I observed a great many June-flies, at which the fish were occasionally rising, and which at the same time were picked up by the swallows, as they skimmed over the surface of the still water. It so happened that a trout from beneath and a swallow from above had fixed their affections upon the same yellow-winged and tempting fly. Down came the swallow, and up came the open mouth of the fish, into which, in pursuit of his prey, the swallow pitched his head. The struggle was not long, but pretty severe; and the swallow was once or twice nearly immersed, wings and all, in the water, before he got himself disentangled from the sharp teeth of the fish." It is true that the trout had no intention of encountering the bird; but every one knows that pike will pull young ducks under the water, and devour them.

"The Tay trout," says John Crerar (I quote from his MS.), "lives in that river all the year round. It is a large and yellow fish, with a great mouth, and feeds chiefly on salmon spawn, moles, mice, frogs, &c. A curious circumstance once happened to me at Pulney Loch. One of my sons threw a live mouse into it, when a large trout took the mouse down immediately. The boy told me what had happened; so I took my fishing-rod, which was leaning against my house close to the loch, and put a fly on. At the very first throw I hooked a large trout, landed it, and laid it on the walk: in two seconds the mouse ran out of its mouth, and got into a hole in the wall before I could catch it." Thus far John Crerar.

> " The mouse that is content with one poor hole
> Can never be a mouse of any soul."

I believe every author on the subject, from the time of dear Isaak Walton to the present day, has taken some pains to vindicate the amusement of angling. For this purpose they have quoted men eminent for humanity, illustrious for science, and famed for high achievement—philosophers, warriors, divines,—who have been dear lovers of the sport.* But does it require this vindication? For myself, far from being surprised that distinguished men have delighted in fishing, I only wonder that any man can be illustrious

---

* When Sir Humphrey Davy was at Gisburn, the late Lord Ribblesdale took him to see the celebrated Gorsdale Rocks, expecting they would astonish and interest him, and call forth some very learned remarks; but the great philosopher noticed only the stream beneath them, which he scrutinised minutely, saying he was sure there were no fish in it, or he should have discovered them.

who does not practise either angling or field sports of some sort or another. They all demand skill and enterprise. If you ask me to reconcile angling to reason, you may possibly distress me. It is an instinct, a passion, and a powerful one, originally given to man for the preservation of his existence. The waters as well as the land yield forth their increase. In the joyless regions of the north, when the bear famishes on the iceberg, and the gaunt wolf howls amongst the snow-drifts, the miserable tenant of the land stalks along the desolate shores, and with his javelin, or hooks of bone, acquires by his rude skill a precarious subsistence for his family. Everlasting winter has stamped her iron foot upon the soil : the snow whitens all interminably, except where the blasts drive it from the face of the bleak rocks ; and without this resource he must perish,—he and his sad family together. Even it is ordained from above.

Thrice happy are we, who live in a more genial climate, and who inherit the instinct given to our less fortunate fellow-creatures, and exercise it not from hard necessity, but as a means of recreation. Man being thus evidently destined to fish, let us consider the style of thing that is likely to give him the most gratification.

When I read of the whale fishery, and of that animal running out a mile of rope, for an instant my thoughts were bent on the seas of Greenland ; but I was taken aback by the frontispiece of Captain Scoresby's entertaining narrative, which represents his boat thrown aloft in the air by a playful jerk of a whale's tail, and all the crew tumbling seaward in very sprawling and unstudied attitudes. Now this is a sort of adventure which I do not covet myself, or recommend others to seek. In such case, perhaps, the heroes of the harpoon might be caught at their descent by some ravenous shark; and unless people have a curiosity about the construction of that animal's intestines for the sake of scientific purposes, a visit to his interior would be useless, and I think imprudent. Besides, whale fishery is a sort of unsavory butchery, which does not suit all tastes. We will take leave, therefore, to discard it at once.

The truth is, that I like no sea fishing whatever, being of opinion that it requires little skill; neither do I enjoy sailing in the salt element, for very particular reasons relating to health. But my mind is full of solemn thoughts as I stand on the sounding shore, and see the gallant vessel pass away into the great desert of waters, till her misty hull rests lonely in the horizon. Then, as shades of night set in, and as she fades in the general gloom, I meditate on the perils of storm and battle, and all the adventurous scenes her crew may encounter, for good or for evil,—far, far away from the land of their affections.

> " Nos patriam fugimus, nos dulcia linquimus arva :
> Nos patriam fugimus."

No; the wild main I trust not. Rather let me wander beside the banks of the tranquil streams of the warm South, " in yellow meads of asphodel," when the young spring comes forth, and all nature is glad; or if a wilder mood comes over me, let me clamber among the steeps of the North, beneath the shaggy mountains, where the river comes raging and foaming everlastingly, wedging its way through the secret glen, whilst the eagle, but dimly seen, cleaves the winds and the clouds, and the dun deer gaze from the mosses above. There, amongst gigantic rocks, and the din of mountain torrents, let me do battle with the lusty salmon, till I drag him into day, rejoicing in his bulk, voluminous and vast.

But, alas! we run riot. Let me now set forth by what chance I became a fisher for salmon. Dining one auspicious day with a friend in London, after a sultry morning gratifying to nothing but a lizard or a serpent, —the town hot, still, and deserted, as the ruins of Pompeii,—we turned from the base thraldom to which we had subjected ourselves, and resolved to wander over the blue hills of Scotland; "for we had heard of *grouse-shooting*, and we longed to follow in the field some lusty *heath-cock*." It was Wednesday. On Friday we would depart, that was certain; for we were young and ardent. Our travelling means were not very rich : they consisted of a curricle with one horse (his companion having died lately), and a tilbury without any. But the next day there was to be a sale at Tattersall's, which all juveniles delight in ; so away we went to the hammer, rejoicing in our *soi disant* judgment, and purchased two animals most indubitably of the horse species. My friend accommodated himself with a chestnut, I with a mottled grey; and it would be difficult to say which of the two had the best bargain.

Now it chanced that these two nags never had harness on their backs from the time of their foalhood; but this

did not interest us in the least: they had it on soon at
all events, all at the door of Thomas's Hotel, Berkeley
Square. The chestnut shone as off-horse in the curricle,
the grey was resplendent in the tilbury. As for the start,
I cannot boast much of that,—kicks, plunges, rearings
to match. There was evidently some misunderstand-
ing. My fellow-traveller, wheeling round in spite of
"curb or rein," passed me in an opposite direction. My
thoughts were intent on Davies Street; the *grey* differed
with me widely in opinion, and was ambitious of the
Square; round which (if I may use the expression) he
galloped with unnecessary haste, till he met my fellow-
traveller at the bottom, and we passed each other in
grand style, our nags being considerably animated by
the "lumbering of the wheels." Not once alone did this
happen; and before our coursers could be gained over to
our opinion, Charing Cross possessed the curricle, and
Hanover Square could boast of the tilbury. Our skill
might reasonably be questioned, our perseverance could
not; for before midnight we rallied, and urged our re-
luctant beasts to the dulness of Stilton. From henceforth everything went on smoothly with them; except
that the chestnut died of the distemper, and the grey
fell out of a crazy boat into Loch Lomond, ran away
some time afterwards, overturned the vehicle, broke my
unfortunate servant's leg, and lamed himself for life.

We journeyed on to Selkirk in juvenile mood. From
hence my friends went to Edinburgh, where I agreed to
join them. And now comes the point—what made me,
Harry Otter, a fisher for salmon? Why thus it was—I
went forth, after my arrival at the aforesaid town, at

the hour of prime. I asked no questions, for I cannot endure to hear beforehand what sort of sport I am likely to have. Sober truth is sometimes exceedingly distressing, and brings one's mind to a lull; it puts an end to the sublimity of extravagant speculation, which I hold to be the chief duty of a sportsman. So, as I said, I asked no questions; but I saw the river Ettrick before me taking her free course beneath the misty hills, and brushing away the dew-drops with my steps, I rushed impatiently through the broom and gorse with torn hose and smarting legs, till I arrived at the margin of that wild river, where the birch hung its ringlets over the waters.

Out came my trusty rod from a case of "filthy dow-lass." Top-varnished it was, and the work of the famous Higginbotham: not he the hero of a hundred engines, "who was *afeard* of nothing, and whose fireman's soul was all on fire;" but Higginbotham of the Strand, who was such an artist in the rod line as never appeared before, or has ever been seen since. "He never joyed since the price of *hiccory wood* rose," and was soon after gathered to the tomb of his fathers. I look upon him and old Kirby, the quondam maker of hooks, to be two of the greatest men the world ever saw, not even excepting Eustace Ude, or Michael Angelo Bonarotti.

But to business. The rod was hastily put together; a beautiful new azure line passed through the rings; a casting line, made like the waist of Prior's Emma, appended, with two trout flies attached to it of the manufacture even of me, Harry Otter. An eager throw to begin with: round came the flies intact. Three, four, five,

six throws—a dozen : no better result.   The fish were
stern and contemptuous.   At length some favourable
change took place in the clouds, or atmosphere, and I
caught sundry small trout; and finally, in the cheek of
a boiler, I fairly hauled out a two-pounder.   A jewel of
a fish he was—quite a treasure all over.   After I had
performed the satisfactory office of bagging him, I
came to a part of the river which, being contracted,
rushed forward in a heap, rolling with great impetuosity.   Here, after a little flogging, I hooked a lusty
fellow, strong as an elephant, and swift as a thunderbolt.   How I was agitated say ye who best can tell,
ye fellow-tyros !   Every moment did I expect my trout
tackle, for such it was, to part company.   At length,
after various runs of dubious result, the caitiff began
to yield ; and at the expiration of about half-an-hour,
I wooed him to the shore.   What a sight then struck
my optics !   A fair five-pounder at the least; not fisherman's weight, mark me, but such as would pass muster
with the most conscientious Lord Mayor of London
during the high price of bread.   Long did I gaze on
him, not without self-applause.   All too large he was
for my basket; I therefore laid the darling at full
length on the ground, under a birch tree, and covered
over the precious deposit with some wet bracken, that
it might not suffer from the sunbeam.

I had not long completed this immortal achievement
ere I saw a native approaching, armed with a prodigious fishing-rod of simple construction, guiltless of
colour or varnish.   He had a belt round his waist, to
which was fastened a large wooden reel or pirn, and the
line passed from it through the rings of his rod ; a sort

of Wat Tinlinn he was to look at. The whole affair seemed so primitive,—there was such an absolute indigence of ornament, and poverty of conception, that I felt somewhat fastidious about it. I could not, however let a brother of the craft pass unnoticed, albeit somewhat rude in his attire; so, "What sport," said I, "my good friend?"

"I canna say that I ha'e had muckle deversion; for she has quite fallen in, and there wull be no good fishing till there comes a spate."

Now, after this remark, I waxed more proud of my success; but I did not come down upon him at once with it, but said somewhat slily, and with mock modesty—

"Then you think there is not much chance for any one, and least of all for a stranger like myself."

"I dinna think the like o' ye can do muckle; though I will no say but ye may light on a wee bit trout, or maybe on a happening fish. That's a bonnie little wand you've got; and she shimmers so with varnish, that I'm thinking that when she's in the eye o' the sun, the fish will come aneath her, as they do to the blaze in the water."

Sandy was evidently lampooning my Higginbotham. I therefore replied, that she certainly had more shining qualities than were often met with on the northern side of the Tweed. At this personality, my pleasant friend took out a large mull from his pocket, and applying a copious quantity of its contents to his nose, very politely responded—

"Ye needna fash yoursel' to observe aboot the like o' her; she is no worth this pinch o' snuff."

He then very courteously handed his mull to me.

" Well," said I, still modestly, " she will do well enough for a bungler like me." I was trolling for a compliment.

" Ay, that will she," said he.

Though a little mortified, I was not sorry to get him to this point; for I knew I could overwhelm him with facts, and the more diffidently I conducted myself the more complete would be my triumph. So laying down my pet rod on the channel, I very deliberately took out my two-pounder as a feeler. He looked particularly well; for I had tied up his mouth, that he might keep his shape, and moistened him, as I before said, with soaked fern to preserve his colour. I fear I looked a little elate on the occasion : assuredly I felt so.

" There's a fine fish now,—a perfect beauty !"

" Hoot-toot ! that's no a fish ava."

" No fish, man ! What the deuce is it, then ? Is it a rabbit, or a wild duck, or a water-rat ?"

" Ye are joost gin daft. Do ye no ken a troot when ye see it ?"

I could make nothing of this answer, for I thought that a trout was a fish*; but it seems I was mistaken. However, I saw the envy of the man; so I determined to inflict him with a settler at once. For this purpose I inveigled him to where my five-pounder was deposited; then kneeling down and proudly removing the bracken I had placed over him, there lay the monster most manifest, extended in all his glory. The light,—the eye of the landscape,—before whose

---

* Salmon, salmon trout, and bull trout alone, are called *fish* in the Tweed. If a Scotchman means to try for trout, he does not say " I am going a *fishing*," but " I am going a *trouting*."

brilliant sides Runjeet Singh's diamond, called "the mountain of light," would sink into the deep obscure ; —dazzled with the magnificent sight, I chuckled in the plenitude of victory. This was unbecoming in me, I own, for I should have borne my faculties meekly ; but I was young and sanguine ; so (*horresco referens*) I gave a smart turn of my body, and, placing an arm akimbo, said, in an exulting tone, and with a scrutinising look, " There, what do you think of that ? " I did not see the astonishment in Sawny's face that I had anticipated, neither did he seem to regard me with the least degree of veneration but giving my pet a shove with his nasty iron-shod shoes, he simply said,

" Hoot ! that's a wee bit gilse."

This was laconic. I could hold no longer, for I hate a detractor ; so I roundly told him that I did not think he had ever caught so large a fish in all his life.

" Did you now ?—own."

" I suppose I have."

" Suppose ! But don't you know ?"

" I suppose I have."

Speak decidedly, yes or no. That is no answer."

" Well, then, I suppose* I have."

And this was the sum total of what I could extract from this *nil admirari* fellow.

A third person now joined us, whom I afterwards discovered to be the renter of that part of the river. He had a rod and tackle of the selfsame fashion with

----

* *Suppose*, in Scotch, does not imply a doubt, but denotes a cer-tainty.

THERE'S A FINE FISH NOW

the apathetic man. He touched his bonnet to me: and if he did not eye me with approval, at least he did not look envious or sarcastic.

" Well, Sandy," said he to his piscatorial friend, my new acquaintance, " what luck the morn ?"

" I canna specify that I hae had muckle; for they hae bin at the sheep-washing up bye, and she is foul, ye ken. But I hae ta'en twa saumon—ane wi' Nancy*, and the other wi' a Toppy†,—baith in Faldon-side Burn fut."

And twisting round a coarse linen bag which was slung at his back, and which I had supposed to contain some common lumber, he drew forth by the tail a never-ending monster of a salmon, dazzling and lusty to the view; and then a second, fit consort to the first. Could you believe it? One proved to be fifteen pounds, and the other twelve! At the sudden appearance of these whales I was shivered to atoms: dumb-foundered I was, like the Laird of Cockpen when Mrs. Jean refused the honour of his hand. I felt as small as Flimnap the treasurer in the presence of Gulliver. Little did I say; but that little, I hope, was becoming a youth in my situation.

I was now fairly vaccinated. By dint of snuff and whisky, I made an alliance with the tenant of the water; and being engaged for that year to join my friends at Edinburgh, and go on a shooting excursion to the Hebrides and the north of Scotland, I resolved to revisit the Tweed the summer following.

---

* A fly so called from Nancy Dawson, who was born on the Tweed near Little Dean Tower.

† The Toppy will be described hereafter.

It was the above incident that regulated my residence, in a great measure, for above twenty years of my life.

A year had rolled on since this my first excursion to the North, and I, Harry Otter, was again seated in an open vehicle, enriched with fishing rods, both of small and of ample dimensions; I must say exceedingly ample. The stanch *Arno* lay at my feet; nor was I deficient in a gun, such as Manton used to turn out in that age of flint. My attendant, or groom, was of the freshest fashion,—a youth newly hired. John, who was whilom in my service, understood the arts of travelling better than this man. But, alas! John was a backslider; for when I asked him if he had any objection to go to Scotland, "Pray, sir," said he, "is that the country as is infested with eagles?" I candidly confessed that there certainly were birds of that description there. "Then, I am sorry, sir, but I must beg leave to decline going," was his valorous reply.

Tedious it were to recount the dawdling of a long journey performed by the same man and the same horses. I will not therefore utter such an infliction. It is quite enough to say, that in the end I ensconced myself in an hostel in the little town of Melrose: inn, properly so called, there was none, for Melrose was then unsung. It was late, and I looked forth on the tranquil scene from my window. The moonbeams played upon the distant hill-tops, but the lower masses slept as yet in shadow; again the pale light catched the waters of the Tweed, the lapse of whose streams fell faintly on the ear, like the murmuring of a sea-shell. In front rose up the mouldering abbey, deep in shadow; its pinnacles, and buttresses, and light tracery, but dimly seen in the solemn mass. A faint light twinkled for a space among the tombstones; soon it was extinct, and two figures passed off in the shadow, who had been digging a grave even at that late hour.

As the night advanced, a change began to take place. Clouds heaved up over the horizon; the wind was heard in murmurs; the rack hurried athwart the moon; and utter darkness fell upon river, mountain, and haugh. Then the gust swelled louder, and the storm struck fierce and sudden against the casement. But as the morrow dawned, though the rain-drops still hung upon the leaf, the clouds sailed away, the sun broke forth, and all was fair and tranquil.

The fisherman was sent for express. His apparel may be taken as a general sample of the garb of the piscator on that river, where "Flora discloses her beauties" *par excellence*. A hat with salmon flies round the crown, the loop of each gut being passed over the head of a pin stuck into the said hat, and the barb of the hook fastened into the felt. The bonnet on such occasions is laid aside. A short coat or jacket; waistcoat according to fancy; blue pantaloons; and a pair of colossal shoes, studded with splatter-headed nails.

"Well, Wattie, I am glad you are come; for you shall see me catch a dozen salmon to-day."

"You mun be a warlock then; for the deil a man atween Bolside and Kelso, beside yoursel, wull tak ae saumon the day. If ye were even to throw the *Lady of

---

* The Flower of Yarrow, married to Scott of Harden.

8

Mertoun into the water, they wudna look at her; for the storm cam from the wast last nicht ye ken, and she* wull be waxing the morn; but we can gang doon to her and see." Down we accordingly went, and she was decidedly waxing, he said.

All this was a mystery to me at that time; but I learned from him that when the river is about to flood, the rain that has fallen near its sources comes pouring down from the gullies and drains, and propels the clear water before it, which then climbs the dry stones of the channel, exhibiting a convex surface, like wine in a glass filled to the brim. This effect cannot be perceived where the river is in quick motion; but in the little bays and pools that are here and there in the channel, it is very visible: the water will rise to some height before it is in the slightest degree discoloured, and this in proportion to the quantity of rain that has fallen near the sources; so that a stranger would not notice the change. In strong spates it is afterwards of a reddish cast, and fines by degrees into a porter colour, which gets clearer and clearer till it resumes its wonted transparency. It must be noted that I speak with reference to the Tweed only; for it is obvious that every river is coloured somewhat differently, according to the nature of the soil from which, and through which, it flows. Thus the Tay partakes much of the dark moss and peat colour; and on part of the Inverness coast, where some of the rivers come from a hard stony soil, they are never much discoloured, or, if dis-

---

* The Tweed, like a ship, is always called *she*, the feminine gender giving it its due consequence.

coloured, in a different manner. Thus the fisherman is kept two or three days from his sport. And he may as well go home when the waxing begins, though the water is clear, and the rise is imperceptible, except in the way I have mentioned; for it is a singular truth that the salmon will not take the fly into his mouth when this change takes place, though he will often rise to it, and leap over it. This fact is so well known, that no experienced person on the Tweed thinks of fishing during such an occurrence. This waxing commences sooner or later, according to the violence or quantity of the rain that has fallen, and the situation where the storm breaks. In a moderate spate, with a westerly wind, it is seen at Melrose about ten or twelve hours after the rain, more or less. If the wind is very violent, also, the water which is blown out of the lakes will make the river rise slightly; but in that case no change of colour will afterwards take place.

"Ye canna fish the day; so I wud hae ye advised to gang after the patrigs."

So indeed I did, *auspice* Wattie, who, to my surprise, seemed somewhat loth to attend me. We found birds —Arno stood—we shot to the top of our bent; and Wattie would have marked well, but for one failing, which, lover as he was of the sport, he could not overcome. This failing, to call it by the mildest name, was an apprehension of evil, which possessed him to that absurd degree that he sculked astern, and lay upon the ground the moment he expected a shot to be fired; and I verily believe that he stopped his ears also. Once, when a covey spread beautifully amongst some gorse, for a space he eluded my vision, and when the firing ceased, I detected him in his form couched between two blocks of granite; "for he kent," he said, "that it was no canny to dander aboot, and disturb the patrigs." And I think this was judicious; but it did not seem to account for the paleness of his complexion.

My bag was now sufficiently full; and in returning to the hotel I noticed the form of the Eildon Hills, which, we have since been credibly informed, were cloven in three by the art of gramarye. It was then that I discovered that my companion's mind was completely subdued by superstition.

"Thae hills are pleasant to the view," said he; "and it is the custom on the seventh day for people to ascend the middle one, and enjoy the prospect. On the last Sabbath I gaed up; and instead of the hill being throng as usual, I fund mysel alone, and when I was near the tap a sudden mirkness cam owre me, and I sat doon on the sod in a cauld sweet. Then I cast my een up; and I saw, as plain as I see ye the noo, twa men houking a grave by the licht of a torch; and ither men joined them, walking twa by twa, wi' pale lichts. And when they cam to the grave, they gaed to the far side of it; and an auld wife cam in front wi' a lang white stick in her hand, and a licht like a star a tap o' it: she had an awfu' beard, and beckoned me to the grave. Ou it was dreadfu'! I believe I swooned away, as it was richt I should; and when I cam to mysel, all was vanishit, and it was as mirk as pick. And a' this day I thocht that your gun was the instrument that was to pit me intill that grave."

CHAP. V.

My first visit to the Tweed was before the Minstrel of
the North had sung those strains which enchanted the
world, and attracted people of all ranks to this land of
romance.   The scenery therefore at that time, un-
assisted by story, lost its chief interest; yet was it all

lovely in its native charms. What stranger just emerging from the angular enclosures of the South, scored and subdued by tillage, would not feel his heart expand at the first sight of the heathery mountains, swelling out into vast proportions, over which man has had no dominion? At the dawn of day he sees, perhaps, the mist ascending slowly up the dusky river, taking its departure to some distant undefined region; below the mountain range his sight rests upon a deep and narrow glen, gloomy with woods, shelving down to its centre. What lies hid in that mysterious mass the eye may not visit; but a sound comes down from afar, as of the rushing and din of waters. It is the voice of the Tweed, as it bursts from the melancholy hills, and comes rejoicing down the sunny vale, taking its free course through the haugh, and glittering amongst sylvan bowers,—swelling out at times fair and ample, and again contracted into gorges and sounding cataracts,— lost for a space in its mazes behind a jutting brae, and reappearing in dashes of light through bolls of trees opposed to it in shadow.

Thus it holds its fitful course. The stranger might wander in the quiet vale, and, far below the blue summits, he might see the shaggy flock grouped upon some sunny knoll, or straggling among the scattered birch trees; and, lower down on the haugh, his eye perchance might rest awhile on some cattle standing on a tongue of land by the margin of the river, with their dark and rich brown forms opposed to the brightness of the waters. All these outward pictures he might see and feel; but he could see no farther: the lore had not spread its witchery over the scene,—the legends slept in oblivion. The stark moss-trooper, and the clanking stride of the warrior, had not again started into life; nor had the light blazed gloriously in the sepulchre of the wizard with the mighty book. The slogan swelled not anew upon the gale, resounding through the glens, and over the misty mountains; nor had the minstrel's harp made music in the stately halls of Newark*, or beside the lonely braes of Yarrow.

Since that time I have seen the cottage of Abbotsford with its rustic porch, lying peacefully on the haugh between the lone hills; and have listened to the wild rush of the Tweed as it hurried beneath it. As time progressed, and as hopes arose, I have seen that cottage converted into a picturesque mansion, with every luxury and comfort attached to it, and have partaken of its hospitality: the unproductive hills I have viewed covered with thriving plantations, and the whole aspect of the country civilised without losing its romantic character. But, amidst all these revolutions, I have never perceived any change in the mind of him who made them, "the choice and master-spirit of the age." There he dwelt in the hearts of the people, diffusing life and happiness around him: he made a home beside the border river, in a country and a nation that have derived benefit from his presence, and consequence from his genius. From his chambers he looked out upon the grey ruins of the abbey, and the sun which set in splendour beneath the Eildon Hills. Like that sun, his

---

* The tower of Newark stands near Bowhill.

course has been run; and though disastrous clouds came across him in his career, he went down in unfading glory.

These golden hours, alas! have long passed; but often have I visions of the sylvan valley, and its glittering waters, with dreams of social intercourse. Abbotsford, Mertoun, Chiefswood, Huntley Burn, Allerley,—when shall I forget ye!

But, to our humble business. The swell of the river had been trifling, and it would be fit to fish on the morrow. The later in the day, said Walter the Bold, the better; so I fidgetted away the early part of the morning, and hauled over my London tackle, which proved unseemly to the sight of the Scotchman. The flies, he said, were dressed like dancing dogs; but my rod, he owned, was fine.

At last we started. We had about two or three miles to go to the upper cast called the "Carry-wheel." As I neared it, and saw the sweep of the gallant river, I stepped out in eagerness till I came to the top of a steep covered with wood, gorse, and broom; then I dashed down the rocks, and found myself on the channel, with the rush of a glorious salmon cast before me. Think of this, ye gudgeon fishers! The rod was put together in haste,—out came the London book; and whilst I selected that misnomer a metropolitan salmon fly, a huge fish sprang out of the water before me, bright and lusty. What a challenge! In my agitation the flies got entangled;—confusion worse confounded beset me. The hooks stuck into my quivering fingers, and then a puff of wind scattered them abroad in various

directions. To crown all, Walter kept me in a
perspiration by making as if he would throw for the
fish, which, by anticipation, I considered as my property.
At length I collected my senses, and my flies also; and
it is a wonder that I did so, as the said fish continued
his gambols, and repeatedly claimed my attention.

Now then for it. The cast being narrow at the
throat, I began with a short line, which I kept length-
ening as it got wider; for so it became me. I came
now, step by step, to the spot where I expected to do
for the fish. Excited as I was, I flung with spirit;
but the fly alighted not upon the wave; far from it;
it attached itself most perfectly to a birch-tree in my
rear, and crack went my top-varnished Higginbotham.
Thus I was at once discomfited almost in the arms of
victory. Being totally driven from my propriety, I
cannot be answerable for what I said or did: something
very sublime it was, no doubt; but let that pass. Certain it was that each particular hair of my head stood
on end with horror. As I had spare tops to my rod, I
soon set all to rights again. But throw, and throw as I
would, the salmon would not "come and be killed;" so I
gave up the unreasonable brute at last as unattainable.
Nor could the Scotchman make any hand of him afterwards. In fishermen's language, *I had set him down.*

The tail of the cast now grew broader, and it was
necessary to wade; so in I went, "accoutred as I was;"
that is to say, in light, flimsy walking shoes, without
nails. I soon perceived that the wet stones were slippery and treacherous beyond endurance, and that my
shoes had no adhesive qualities. My untutored feet

took no hold, and I floundered about in the superlative degree, quite innocent of a due balance. At length, joyous to relate, I saw a break in the water, and the switch of a fish's tail : I struck, and found I had him fast. As for playing him, I did no such thing; on the contrary, I honestly confess that he played me, and had all along the best of it too,—for I could not keep my footing. I swayed like a pendulum, only more unevenly, till down I went from a treacherous stone, which joggled under my step, and tilted me in about middle deep. Being thus sufficiently humid, I beat a retreat as soon as I was able, and backed out on the channel : arrived there, I felt the beauty of my new situation, and made certain of a capture. The monster was still strong, and sprung out of water, as if to show me what a prize I was about to obtain, and I acknowledged his value secretly. He next judged it prudent to give a sudden turn, a sort of ill-natured twist,—an obstinate obliquity of motion that I shall never forget, or forgive : at once my muscles ceased to quiver,—the line lost its strain and sprang aloft in thin air, and the rod was as straight as when it came from the maker's hands. Here was an exposition !—here was a horror ! To crown all, Walter stood by and took snuff most provokingly philosophical, and I thought I detected a half-suppressed smile on his visage. Raving as I was internally, I still conducted myself with outward decency, particularly when I found that the fish was lost owing to the bad temper of a London hook, which broke in the animal's jaw ; so that I, Harry Otter, was not to blame after all. I gave one solemn sigh for the death of old Kirby, whose hooks would not have broken in the mouth of a shark.

My Scotch friend now fitted me out with one of his own flies, but desired me not to throw any more in the Carry-wheel; "for," said he, "as sure as deid, the spirit is against ye: he hampered yer heucks, he broke yer goad and yer flee, and he pulled ye doon in the waters; and ye never would hae been seen again in this life, gin I hadna cotched ye by the oxter.* Thae that the Kelpie grips seldom rise again; but nae ither spirit, ye ken, has power in the rinnin' water." Whether I partook of this superstition matters not; but I left the cast because it was unlucky, which is much the same thing.

I was now under the influence of some better spirit of the flood; for I absolutely landed two gilse of six pounds each in a cast called "The Noirs." Wattie, seeing my rod bent, came up: he said but little; but that little was the most unqualified abuse of my mismanagement. The fact is, I treated the gilse just as I would have treated a trout; a very base mistake. I bagged them, however, notwithstanding,—thanks to the excellence of the channel.

The next cast I came to was called "The Brig-end;" and here I hooked a fine salmon: he was brave and strenuous, and so ponderous, that it seemed as if my hook had caught hold of a floating Norwegian pine, "fit for the mast of some high ammiral." After various eccentric courses, Master Fish made a sudden and desperate rush down the river;—out went my line with a whirring rattle, and cut one of my fingers sharply. I

* The arm.

followed as best I might, prancing in the water like a war-horse, with the spray about my ears. Wattie hallooed out, and said I know not what; but the tone of his voice was far from being complimentary. Nearly all my line of a hundred yards was now run out; when the fish made a sudden turn, crossed to the opposite bank, and coasted up it amongst the rocks. Here again Wattie was perfectly wild.

"Gang back, I tell ye,—haud up yer gaud,—shorten yer line,—keep aboon him, ye gomeril! Ou, ye are drounit as sure as deeth! Pirn in, pirn in!—pirn out, pirn out! Gang forrat, gang forrat!—gang ahint, gang ahint!" These contradictory exclamations I could have excused, as I believe they were warranted by the sudden turns of the fish; but the fellow had absolutely the temerity to attempt to take my rod from me, whereat I lashed out behind, and gave him sundry kicks, as strong and hearty as could be managed with my degenerate shoes.

I did shorten my line a little, however; but the water pressed against it so heavily, that I could not extricate it as I wished. I had now receded to the shore, and gained, as I thought, the victory. Being resolved to be canny, I fixed my eyes intently upon the point where the line dipped into the water, under which I conceived the fish to be; but, to my surprise, I caught a glimpse of my playfellow with the tail of my eye, springing out of the water, and towing my tackle after him about twenty yards above the spot where I conceived him to be. I was in a perfect tremor—ye gods, how I did shake! But that did not last long, as the line all of a

DROWNED ALREADY AND ABOUT TO BE CUT
TH BILLON HILL

sudden vaulted into the air, and streamed abroad like
the lithe pennon on a ship-mast, being, at a rude guess,
about twenty yards minus of its pristine proportions.
This was all magic to me at the time,—magic of the most
distressing sort; but in after days I saw what my error
was. I knew that it consisted in giving out too much
line at first, which would have been unnecessary, had I
stepped back at once on the channel, kept my rod aloft,
and ran down the river-side with my fish, still keeping
above him. This, as has been seen, I did not do; but
kept deep in the water, where I could make but little
way. With a shorter line, and good footing, I might have
kept above my fish when he crossed over and made up
the stream, and thus have held the line tight; but as it
was, it hung back in a huge sweep, that would have
gone round the foundations of another Carthage,—
which sweep, coming in contact with a concealed rock,
gave the fish a dead pull, and he broke it incontinently: abiit, evasit, erupit. It was very distressing—very.

Now having your line in this untoward position is
called *being drowned*, and the breaking of the tackle in
the manner described *being cut*,—soul-harrowing,
suicidal miseries, that no one can properly describe
except Mr. Richard Penn.

Here ended my fishing, and in summing up the
events of the day I had not much to congratulate myself upon. I had been guilty of almost every error possible: I broke my hook and my rod; I was moreover
cut and *drowned*, technically speaking. I learned, however, four things: firstly, never to fish in a cast where
the Kelpie has his strong-hold; secondly, to look occa-

sionally behind me before my throw, where the banks are steep and near ; thirdly, to try the strength of my hook *before* I use it, not *after;* and, fourthly, to get into shoes of a proper consistency, and well studded with nails of Brobdignag dimensions. Take warning, gentle readers, from these disasters, which are recounted for your benefit and instruction.

The day following I was more successful ; for I shot twelve brace of partridges, and killed seven salmon in the evening. This I thought good sport, as partridges are scarce by the river side.

I rented various houses and large fisheries on Tweed side for about twenty years after this, remaining there not only during the summer months, but sometimes all the year round except close time; so that my experience reaches to all the methods of catching salmon during the legal time of the year. I shall now proceed to give as good an idea as I can of the sort of thing to be expected by those who are inclined to follow the same amusement, together with such instructions as I would fain hope may increase their success. And, first, for wading.

Wading in the water is not only an agreeable thing in itself, but absolutely necessary in some rivers in the North that are destitute of boats ; and that you may do this in the best possible style, procure half a dozen pair of shoes, with large knob-nails at some distance asunder: if they are too close, they will bring your foot to an even surface, and it will glide off a stone or rock, which in deep water may be inconvenient. Cut some holes in the upper-leathers of your shoes, to give the water a free passage out of them when you are on dry land; not because the fluid is annoying, for we should wrong you to say so, but to prevent the pumping noise you would otherwise make at every step. If you are not much of a triton, you may use fishermen's boots, and keep yourself dry: it is all a matter of taste. When you are wading through the rapids, step on quickly and boldly, and do not gaze down on the stream after the fashion of Narcissus; for running waves will not reflect your beauty, but only make your head giddy. If you stop for a moment, place your legs abreast of each other: should you fancy a straddle, with one of them in advance, the action of the water will operate upon both trip you up, and carry you out to sea. Observe, I am talking of a heavy stream. The body of a man, who probably lost his life in this manner, was found low down the river when I was fishing. I asked John Haliburton, who was then my fisherman, where it came from. "I suppose," said he, "it travelled all the way from Peebles."*

Avoid standing upon rocking stones, for obvious reasons; and never go into the water deeper than the fifth button of your waistcoat: even this does not always agree with tender constitutions in frosty weather. As you are likely not to take a just estimate of the cold in the excitement of the sport, should you be of a delicate temperament, and be wading in the month of February, when it may chance to freeze very hard, pull down your stockings, and examine your legs. Should they be black, or even purple, it might, perhaps, be as well to get on dry land; but if they are only rubicund, you may con-

---

* Peebles was about twenty-five miles fr m the spot in question.

tinue to enjoy the water, if it so pleases you. If you go in far enough to throw over the cast, that is sufficient; for, remember, it is not good to have a very long line when a short one will answer your purpose. You will not strike your fish so soon, and a sudden run of his might place you in an awkward predicament when your progress is impeded by wading.

It is really refreshing, and does one's heart good, to see how some that are green in the sport will, in the language of stag hunting, "take to soil." I heard of a very fat man from the precincts of Cheapside, who was encountered in the river Shiel, in Inverness-shire, by two gentlemen,—merrier ones than whom "I never passed an hour's talk withal." The corpulent man looked at the water for some time like a child that is going into a cold bath, and does not half like it; he then broke forth in the following guise :—

" I am convinced, gentlemen, that your waders catch most fish. I say, gentlemen, that those who wade are the most successful." His opinion being greatly encouraged, he put forth one foot in the pool ; and not finding the sensation very alarming, for the weather was warm, he walked soberly forward, saying at every step, "Ay, ay, —your waders catch the most fish." Now the rock shelving down near the bank, in progressing he was soon up to the hips—

"Tendebatque manus ripæ ulterioris amore;"

but he could not reach the desired spot even the n In this dilemma he looked wistfully at the shore for advice. "How deep should I go?" said the enterprising man. One said to the fifth button of your waist-

coat, and the other to your shirt-collar. He preferred
the fifth button; and soon treading on a faithless stone,
fairly toppled head foremost into the pool. His hand
relaxed its grasp, and away went the fishing rod down
the stream. He himself was soon placed out of danger
by the gentlemen,—an attention that, considering all
things, he was fairly entitled to; but his rod lay across
the river, the butt end opposed in its passage by one
rock in the middle of it, and the top by another; so the
weight of the stream bore upon the centre, and snapped
it in twain. The corpulent gentleman took all with the
greatest good humour; and as the water streamed
from him at all points, as it were from a river god, and
as he applied a brandy flask to his mouth, he said only
at the intervals between his potations, " I am not quite
so sure that your waders catch the most fish; gentlemen, I say, I have my doubts of it."

To the credit of my friends be it spoken, they waded
and swam after the two divisions of his rod, which
they spliced together for him, and set him going again;
not in the faithless water, but on the trusty shore,
which he now seemed to prefer.

I cannot in conscience recommend a course of wading to a sedentary man as a new experiment, or even as
an old custom revived after a lapse of years; and this
for the following reason.

General Gowdie was born on the banks of the
Leader-water, which falls into the Tweed about a mile
and a half below Melrose, near Fly Bridge. In his
youth he was an ardent and expert salmon fisher; in
after life he went out to India, and served honourably

9

there for forty years. At length, in the decline of life, he was seized with the Swiss passion—an unconquerable yearning to revisit the land of his sires. Night after night he heard in his dreams the murmuring lapse of the Leader as it glided down his native valley; again he reposed in the sunny dell, and thought of " auld lang-syne ; " then, when the cheerless morn broke forth, and he found himself on a vast continent, far away from the land of his fathers, he felt as one cast out of Paradise. Gone were the visions of his early scenes and companions ;—lost, long lost, but too well remembered. How distant, alas! from the bonny copses of Carrolside!—how far from the silver waters of the Tweed!

After honourable service he set sail for the shores of Scotland, determined to pass the remainder of his days in comparative privacy and tranquillity. I met him soon after his arrival, and gave him some salmon fishing. It was delightful to see how he enjoyed himself : he waded as deep as any of us. And I well remember showing him a favourite seat for a salmon near the point of a cairn : he cast his fly at once in the exact spot to an inch, and threw several times with the same adroitness ; not because he expected to raise a salmon, —for he well knew that if a fish did not come at the first dexterous throw, it was useless to cast a second time for him in the same place,—but because he felt great satisfaction at his renewed dexterity, and he was pleased that anyone should witness it.

Poor fellow! his happiness did not last long. The habit of wading at his advanced time of life brought on internal disease, which soon ended fatally ; and he only repassed the seas to lay his bones in the father-land.

CHAP. VI.

" I tell you more : there was a fish taken,
   A monstrous fish, with a sword by 's side—a long sword ;
   A pike in 's neck, and a gun in 's nose, —a huge gun ;
   And letters of mart in 's mouth from the Duke of Florence.
     Cleanthes.   This is a monstrous lie.
     Tony.   do confess it ;
  Do you think I'd tell you truths?"
                       Fletcher's Wife for a Month.

HAVING set forth the advantages, as well as the risk of wading, in a fair, and I hope a rational light, I will proceed to advise on other matters.

In primis, your rod should be proportioned to the size of the river you fish in; eighteen or twenty feet long. The longer the rod, the greater command you will have over your fish ; for being enabled to keep the line more perpendicular, you can lead him with more ease and security amongst rocks and eddies ; whereas with a short rod you cannot keep enough of your line clear of the water to prevent danger in such places. It is true that the late Lord Somerville, who was an excellent fisherman, used a one-handed trout rod for salmon. He did not, however, do so from choice, but from necessity ; for having once put out his shoulder, he could not manage to throw with a rod of the usual size. He once put this little rod into my hands when we were fishing together in his water ; but, for want of practice, I could make little or nothing of it, but I was astonished to see what a long line he himself could throw with it. It must be noted, however, that he fished from a boat in the upper and narrower part of the Tweed, where the channel is excellent, and where there are few bad rocks; in a large river, abounding in all those natural obstructions which its waters fight with, no human ingenuity could have saved him from being often cut with such Lilliputian tackle.

Your line should be about a hundred or a hundred and twenty or thirty yards, according to the breadth of the river you fish in, tapering, of course, towards the end. Your gut single, clear, and round. Of such you may make a casting line sufficiently strong for any salmon you will ever encounter in these degenerate days.

The colour of your casting line should depend upon the state of the river. Take some thought, therefore, to adapt it accordingly: in doing so, you may fancy that you and the fish have changed places. Whilst you are on dry land your object of comparison is the dark bed of the river, which misleads you of course; whereas the objects of comparison to the fish, who lies below, are the colour of the sky and the medium of water. If the water then be moss-stained, your gut may be very faintly tinged of the same colour,—very faintly indeed, as all dyes are overdone; but if the river be clear, do not on any account stain your casting line at all. The sky may vary in colour every minute: an attempt to match it, therefore, is out of the question. You may easily satisfy yourself of the superiority of white over dyed gut, in ordinary cases, by remarking the appearance of both when placed in a tumbler of pure water.

Whatever you do, have nothing to say to multiplying reels: they are apt to betray you in the hour of trial.

My first discovery of their insufficiency for heavy fish created some embarrassment at the time. I had a pet multiplier, which ran beautifully, and which I had long used for trout fishing. As it was sufficiently large to contain a salmon line, I employed it for that purpose also, till it began to get ricketty with the more heavy work. One day, the water being fallen in, and the morning also being sunny, so as to exclude the expectation of killing a salmon, I put some trout tackle at the end of my line, which was on the said reel, and began trouting in Bolside-water. In the course of the day a cloud passed before the sun; and at the same time, as is usually the case, a slight breeze arose and ruffled the surface of the water. I hastened to change my tackle, and substituted a small salmon fly in place of the trout ones: small, because, as I have said, the water was quite fallen in. Though many years have passed over my head since that time, I remember this fly well. His wings were of the clear brown feather from the bittern; his body of black wool, with a hackle of the same colour; and his tail of a very pronounced yellow, being made of the feather of a golden pheasant; red he was in the head, and altogether of a very commendable and alluring aspect. The curl on the water still continuing, I whisked him off gaily. At the very second throw, the pool being somewhat dead, I saw the water heave up, advancing in a wave towards me. I waited patiently for the break, which was a slight one, but pleasant and beauteous to behold. This

I knew to be the act of the *Salmo Salar ;* and as my line was short, I was, as I before recommended to others, in no hurry to strike ; but fix him I did in due season. He no sooner felt the hook than he began to rebel ; and executed some very heavy runs, which so disconcerted the machinery of my multiplier as almost to dislocate the wheels. The line gave out with starts and hitches, so that I was obliged to assist it with my hands. To wind up it resolutely refused ; so that I was compelled to gather in the line in large festoons when it was necessary to shorten it, and again to give these out as best I could when the fish made a run. Add to this embarrassment that the ground was distressing, there being alder bushes in my rear, which made it impossible for me to retreat and advance by land, by which means I could have humoured the fancies of the fish, so as to obviate in some degree the necessity of giving out and shortening the line. So I had no power whatever over the salmon, which was evidently a very large one.

In the course of an hour I made no impression upon him at all, my whole aim being to avoid a break. I never engaged with a more subtle animal. Sometimes he would make the tour of all the neighbouring stones, where he endeavoured, no doubt, to rub the hook out of his mouth ; then he would take a long rest, as if he cared nothing about it. From the cause I have mentioned my tackle was always in disorder, which kept me in great apprehension. Thus the matter went on for nearly two hours more, still with a very dubious result. At length a stone being thrown in by my attendant at a spot where I could follow along the bank, he put his head down the river peremptorily, and went off like a rocket. I ran with him down the channel, as he skimmed through the shallows and darted through the rough gorges, in evident danger, as I was, of losing him every moment. At length he fairly exhausted himself, and I was able to urge him to a sand bank, and lay him on his broadside.

The sand bank, however, had a few inches of water running over it, but not sufficient to cover the fish. My attendant, Philip Garrat, had the tact to place himself between the deep water and the fish. Then came the struggle. A Wiltshire novice, like the said Philip, could not hold a live salmon with his hands, so he tried to kick him forward on the dry channel. All this time I hallooed stoutly to him to take care of the line. My anxiety was extreme; for the fish was sometimes able to place himself in a swimming posture, and wriggle away near the deep water. In fact, had there been but one inch of water more over the sand bank, he would have had it all his own way. Philip, aware of the danger, set at him with redoubled activity, kicking his fastest and best. But the event being still doubtful, he knelt down and grappled with him; and finding him still slippery and elusive, he cast himself bodily upon him, and fixed him with his weight at once: "Toto certatum est corpore regni." So thought he of Macedonian appellation; but he did not express himself in such terms, being a man of no clerk-like capacity: whatever he might have thought, he only said, looking up with a grin of delight and with a Wiltshire accent, " I got un,—be hanged if I ha'nt."

A cold bath for a few minutes more or less is of no consequence; so I made him remain a space, like Ætna pressing upon the shoulders of Enceladus, till I came up and gripped the huge salmon by the tail, and walked to dry land with him, triumphant.

I was nearly three hours in killing this fish, all owing to the derangement of a multiplying reel; and as this contrivance, though useful enough in our trout rivers, will by no means answer with very large fish, I have mentioned the above occurrence in detail as a warning to others.

After this time I caused to be made some large single reels, nicely constructed, so as to give the line out evenly, and not run too slackly; and I directed that the cylinders should be of a very ample circumference, which gave me the same advantage that a multiplying reel has with the usual cylinder.

William Purdie at that time rented the Bolside-water, which runs by Abbotsford, and in which I caught this fish. His son, then a little boy, happened to pass by when I landed him, and I sent him home to his

father with the salmon; but it was with extreme difficulty that the little fellow got up the brae, as his load,
which was hung over his shoulders, frequently made
him stagger back down the rocks which he had from
time to time ascended. That little boy came into my
service as fisherman some seasons afterwards, and has
lived with me now about eighteen years. He is a
capital fly-maker and boatman, and a most valuable
servant. Some of his exploits appear in these pages,
he being the identical Charlie Purdie so repeatedly
mentioned in them.

A great deal of mystery is made on every river as to
the flies you should fish with. Thus when a novice arrives at his fishing station, he sends for the oracle of the
river; pulls out his book, crammed as closely as a pot
of pemmican, and displays before him the various
devices of an Eaton, an Ustonson, or a Chevalier.
Nothing dazzled, Donald much admires what one may
be, and what the other; this he rejects as useless, that
he laughs to scorn. At length, after having grinned
extensively at those tinselled animals called *kill devils*,
he examines some twenty dozen of your best flies; and,
pulling out one from the number, tells you that might
serve well enough if it had different wings, a different
body, and a yellow tail. Now all this is overdone;
but I would advise you to acquiesce in the predictions
of the said oracle, simply to save the trouble of argument. One thing you may be sure of, namely, that
you may as well attempt to make the Tweed run back
to its source as to shake his opinions.

Now, as there is no month in the year when salmon

flies are made by nature, so no distinction of species need be observed. My rule has been to adapt my fly, both as to colour and size, to the state of the water: a large fly with sober colours for deep and clear water; and a smaller one, equally unassuming, where it is shallower; in the throat of the cast, and as long as it continues rough, a large fly also; at the tail of it, where the water runs more quietly and evenly, a smaller one serves the purpose best. Thus you should change your fly in every stream once or twice. A large and rather gaudy fly is preferable when the river is full and discoloured, that the salmon, which lie at great depths, may see it; but I never had any great success with very gaudy flies, either in the Tweed or elsewhere, in clear and low waters. Salmon will rise at them, it is true; but those that have been long in the water will not take them freely when the river is in the state I have spoken of, though they excite their curiosity, and serve them for playthings. I believe it is the fashion now to think otherwise; so that in these days a golden pheasant's feathers are in as high estimation in Scotland as they always have been in Ireland.

In tying your flies, you may have some regard to the harmonic colours, as less startling and more natural. You may laugh, if you please, but I would fain think there is something in this. If you know them not, consult Sir David Brewster's table of spectral colours in his distinguished " Philosophical Magazine."

I have said that there is no animal in nature resembling our salmon flies; but I once caught a fish who was certainly persuaded that he was attacking an animal that he had previously seen flying. This event happened when I was a novice. Walter Ronaldson was attending me, and we were walking by the side of the *Elm-wheel* in the Pavilion-water. Walter was some way in advance, when I saw a white butterfly fluttering up and down over the water, and a salmon make a fruitless dart at it. It chanced that I had made some large salmon flies with white wings, in imitation of a pattern that was formerly the fashion for trout fishing, and was called, I know not why, *the coachman.* One of these I immediately looped to my line: the fish, no doubt taking it for the butterfly that he saw flitting above him, came at it at once, and I took him. When he was landed, Walter's astonishment was great when he saw the fly, and he made a dozen imitations of it before he laid his head on the pillow. I should not think that under other circumstances such a fly would be alluring.

When a man toils a long time without success, he is apt to attribute his failure to the using an improper fly; so he changes his book through, till at last, perhaps, he catches fish. The fly, with which he achieves this, is naturally enough a favourite ever afterwards, and probably without reason : the cause of success might be in the change of air and temperature of the water ; and the same thing would probably have occurred if he had persevered with the same fly with which he began. When the night has been frosty, salmon will not stir till the water has received the genial warmth of the day ; and there are a thousand hidden causes of obstruction which we, who are not fish, know nothing about.

As an instance, I once fished over a short stream above " The Webbs," in Mertoun-water, without having an offer ; being convinced there were fish in it, I went over it a second time with *the same fly* immediately afterwards, and caught two salmon and two gilse. Now if I had changed my fly, as is usual, the success would naturally have been attributed to such change. But, observe, I do not mean to assert that all flies are equally successful, for there must obviously be a preference, however slight ; but I mean merely to say that a failure oftener occurs from atmospheric variations than from the colour of the fly. Yet an occasional change is always advisable, particularly if you have had any offers ; since the fish in so rising, having, perhaps, discovered the deception, will not be solicitous to renew their acquaintance with a detected scamp. After all, the great thing is to give the appearance and motion of a living animal.

Once, when I was adjusting my tackle on Tweed side, I was accosted by a native fisherman in these words,— " Ye needna fash yersel the day wi' yer lang wand, for I wudna gie a pinch o' snuff for a' that ye'll get ; there are too many *pouthered lawyrs* aboot." Powdered lawyers ! I gazed around me, and did not see a single gentleman of the long robe. What on earth could the man mean? and what had a powdered lawyer to do with my sport? Upon explanation, I found out that he alluded to the numerous puffy white clouds above. Whether the likeness of these to lawyers' wigs was appropriate or not, I leave to those who are learned in similes to determine; but he certainly was right in his main position.

If your fish misses the fly in making his offer, wait awhile before you throw a second time ; and if he rises at all, he will come more eagerly for this delay. When he returns to his seat, after the unsuccessful sortie, he will say *mentally* (for thus do fishes and novelists discourse), "What a donkey I was to be so awkward! By St. Antonio, if he comes again, I'll smash him!" But if you keep lashing away at him immediately, as I have seen many fishermen do,—ay, and practised hands too,—he will probably treat you with contempt, and will have no intercourse with your gay deluders for the rest of the day. It is some time, perhaps, since he has taken up his seat in the water, without ever having seen an animal like that which you are so obliging as to tender him : all of a sudden come a swarm of locusts as it were, one after another over his *neb*, which astonish and alarm him exceedingly. Thus it is apparent, my most excellent, but too persevering friend, that you do not do justice to his sagacity, or instinct, or whatever you please to term it, if you set to work in such an intrusive manner.

As in all other rivers, so there are various flies made use of in the Tweed; but the variety consists more, I think, in size than in colour. A large fly, as I have said, for the heavy and deep waters, and a smaller one for the upper part of the river. That is the general system. More minute particulars I have already given. Here are six flies, which I have always found the most successful : I do not mean to say that they are the best that can be used, but only that they are such as I have most confidence in from experience. They were tried by my fisherman Charles Purdie, and in such a manner as to make them cut their way steadily through the water. They are known by different names; so that when I say to my fisherman give me this, or give me that, mentioning the patronymic, forth it comes, without the trouble of searching over the book myself.

Two of these flies are of the masculine gender, three of the feminine, and one of the neuter. The masculine are *Michael Scott* and *Kinmont Willie;* the feminine, the *Lady of Mertoun* or the *Flower of Yarrow, Meg with the Muckle Mouth* in her usual dress, and *Meg* in her bravery—or, Scotticè, *braws.* The fly of the neuter gender has been called *Toppy* from time immemorial.

No. 1.
Kinmont Willie.

Wings - -	- Mottled feather from under the wing of a male teal.
Head - -	- Yellow wool.
Body - -	- Fur of the hare's ear.
End of body -	- Red wool.
Tail - -	- Yellow wool.
Round the body-	- Black-cock's hackle.

I found this fly very successful in the Annan when I lived at Kinmont, from which place it derives its name.

No. 2.
The Lady of Mertoun.

Wings - -	- Mottled feather from under the wings of the male teal.
Head - -	- Crimson wool.
Body - -	- Water-rat's fur.
End of Body -	- Crimson wool.
Tail - -	- Yellow wool.
Round the body-	- Black-cock's hackle.
End of body -	- A little red hackle.

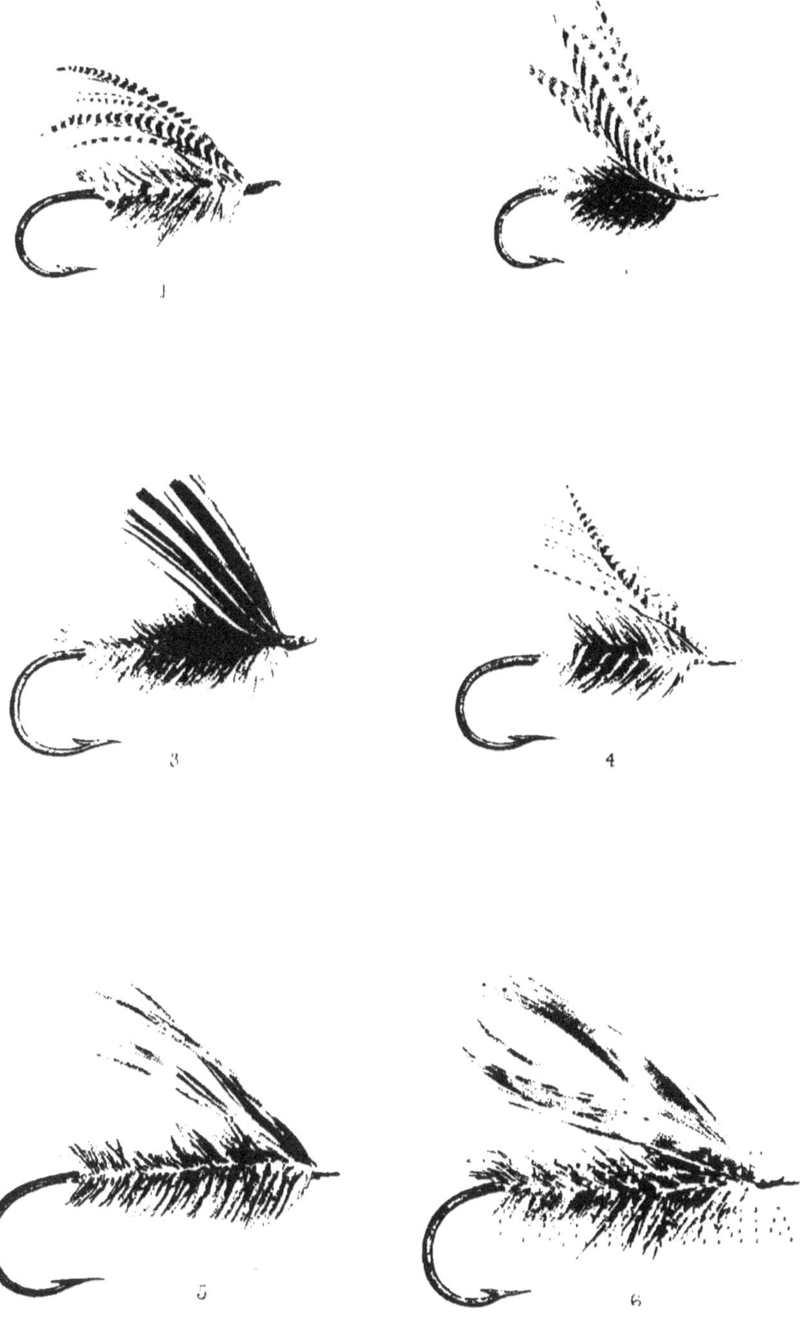

No. 3.

Toppy.

Wings	- - -	Black feather from a turkey's tail tipped with white.
Head	- - -	Crimson wool.
Body	- - -	Black bullock's hair.
End of body	- -	Crimson wool.
Tail	- - -	Yellow wool.
Body	- - -	Black-cock's hackle.
End of Body	- -	Small piece of red-cock's hackle.

No. 4.

I will now describe *Michael Scott*, a most killing wizard.

>———" Chi veramente
> Delle magiche frodi seppe il gioco."

Wings	- - -	Mottled feather from the back of a drake.
Head	- - -	Yellow wool, with a little hare's fur next to it.
Body	- - -	Black wool.
End of the body	-	Fur from the hare's ear; next to the hare's ear crimson wool.
Tail	- - -	Yellow wool.
Round the body	-	Black-cock's hackle.
End of the body	-	Red-cock's hackle.
Round the body	-	Gold twist, spirally.

No. 5.

Meg with the Muckle Mouth.

Wings	- - -	From the tail of a brown turkey.
Head	- - -	Crimson wool.
Body	- - -	Yellow silk.
End of body	- -	Crimson wool.
Tail	- - -	Yellow or orange wool.
Round the tail	-	Red-cock's hackle.
Round the body	-	Gold twist; over it hackle mixed with colour, as above.

No. 6.

Meg in her Braws.

Wings	Light brown, from the wing of a bittern.
Head	Yellow wool.
Next the head	Mottled blue feather from a jay's wing.
Body	Brown wool mixed with bullock's hair.
Towards the end of body	Green wool; next to that crimson wool.
Tail	Yellow wool.
Round the body	Gold twist; over that cock's hackle, black at the roots and red at the points.

Concerning these flies I will note one thing, which is, that if you rise a fish with the *Lady of Mertoun*, and he does not touch her, give him a rest, and come over him with the *Toppy*, and you have him to a certainty, and *vice versâ*. This I hold to be an invaluable secret, and is the only change that during my long practice I have found eminently successful.

Having now named all things necessary for the sport, I must now advise all fishermen, Cocknies in particular, to provide themselves with plenty of spare tackle before they go felicity hunting; for in the wilds of Scotland it is not easy to replace any loss that inexperience and ill fortune may occasion.

A friend of mine told me a circumstance, by which it appeared that a very worthy person was considerably embarrassed for want of this due precaution. This said friend had been fishing in the river Shiel in Invernessshire, and was seated on a bank with a large salmon before him that he had just caught. He was eyeing the fish with complacency, and smoking a cigar in all the enjoyment of success.   Whilst in this tranquil mood, a man suddenly vaulted over the wall of the Shiel bridge;

> " And when he had not the least suspicion,
>   Was with him like an apparition."

This man he described to me as fresh in his attire. Thin and new were his shoes,—new also was his jacket, new his waistcoat, and novel his pantaloons; but newest of all was his top-varnished salmon rod, turned out by Eaton; but he was shabbily thatched, his hat being worse than common.   His flies, to all appearance, were made by the Turks,—men forbidden by their religion to imitate any of the works of the Creation. As for the man himself, no one could look at him without being put in mind of Mantellini.

" Demnition fine pool, sir."

" Very fine indeed, sir; but you will never catch a fish where you are casting at present, because fish do not lie in that bare water."

Upon this our man faced round, put his fore finger to his nose, and, with an expression of sagacity and wisdom that I should in vain attempt to describe, said,

" Do you see any thing green in my eyes, sir ?"

It was evident such a person was not born to be instructed, but simply to be admired.   My friend, therefore, left his rod upon the bank, and walked after him, cigar in mouth, to get some insight into his tactics. Arrived at a better part of the pool, he hooked a fish; and here it was curious to see the difference of opinion between a Cockney and one who had been bred to the sport.   The Cockney was of a yielding disposition, and judged it advisable to let the fish have his own way;

10

the result of which was, that he ran out an exorbitant length of line, and was going to a sort of whirlpool amongst the rocks.

"Hold him in, hold him in; if he gets to that eddy, you are done."

"Fine fish, sir, fine fish: fast hooked, sir. Do you see any thing green in my eyes? I have an opinion of my own, sir."

"So has the fish. And now it is all over with you; for if you had nothing but a dried herring at the end of your line, you would never get it out of that mess. I hope you have another casting line, because you will never see that again."

"Fine fish, sir; fine rod, sir; fine line, sir; fast hooked, sir,—fast hooked. Do you see any thing green ——"

He was stopped short in the sentence by an alarming rush of the salmon, who shot forward up the stream, and took out the whole of the line of the consenting party to the tune of 120 yards. Now it is a wholesome rule to make fast the end of the line, by running it through a hole in the cylinder of the reel, and tying some knots at the extremity to secure it; and as this rule is wholesome, so it has been practised time immemorial by all sagacious persons, and even by some who are not very sagacious. But there are exceptions to all rules, and our man had neglected this caution; consequently, the line, being all run out, vanished at once through the rings of the rod, and streamed fair and ample below the surface of the water. The mermaid may, but that line shall no terrestrial ever see again.

"Demnition hard that, sir. What an extraordinary incident! Fish well managed, dexterously, artistically. Very odd indeed, sir: beautifully played;— fine rod, fine hand. Demnition hard, I must say. Now how far must I go to get a line?"

"If you mean to get the same, probably to the middle of the Irish Channel, or the mouth of the Shannon; but if you seek a new one, which I think would be the most prudent course, walk up to the road, and you will see a mile-stone, which says, 'To Inverness 120 miles,'—exactly a mile for every yard of line you have lost, and I am sorry for it."

Casting the fly is a knack, and cannot well be taught but by experience: the spring of the rod should do the chief work, and not the labour of your arm. To effect this, you should lay the stress as near the hand as possible, and make the wood undulate from that point;

which is done by keeping your elbow in advance, and doing something with your wrist, which, as Mr. Penn says, is not very easy to explain. Thus the exertion should be chiefly from the elbow and wrist, and not from the shoulders. You should throw clear beyond the spot where the salmon lie, so that they may not see the fly light upon the water; then you should bring the said fly round the stream, describing the segment of a circle taking one step in advance at every throw. In this manner the fish see your fly only, and not the line. It is customary to give short jerks with the fly as you bring it round, something in the manner of minnow fishing, but in a more gentle and easy way ; and I think this manner is the most seducing you can adopt : it sets the wings in a state of alternate expansion and contraction that is extremely captivating.

Salmon will often take your fly on one side of the river when they will not touch it on the other. In high water, the channel side, as a general rule, is the best, and at the cheek of the current; and you should not be in a hurry to pull your fly into the more bare and still parts of the channel, where the fish will come more cautiously and lazily. In low water it is best to throw over the channel from the rocky side, drawing at first rather quickly, that your fish may take your fly in the current, which is material. In very low water, indeed, when the fish may be said to give over rising, you may try your luck in the rapids by hanging your fly on them ; indeed, you should always let your fly dwell on this sort of water, or the fish will either lose sight of it, or not choose to follow where you may wish him. All these things are not easily explained in writing, nor, I believe, in conversation, as will appear from the following example.

A friend of mine went with two companions to fish in the river Mora, on the coast of Inverness-shire. One of these two comrades was a young Oxonian, and a novice; the other was an experienced fisherman. They were all three in one of those Highland shielings, redolent of peat smoke and whisky, which is absolute luxury to a thorough-bred sportsman, as being in keeping and character with the nature of his pursuit. The Oxonian was an excellent person, but, as I have hinted, knew nothing upon earth about salmon fishing; so Mr. E. C., who was an adept in the said art, set about instructing him by word of mouth. The third person of the party happened not to coincide with the excellence of the simple instructions he was giving, and laid it down as an axiom, that it was impossible to catch a fish, unless your fly was at right angles to your rod. This seemed not at all to be comprehended; and after a little arguing, the said oracle, by way of illustration, took a stick, tied his handkerchief to it, and gave a few throws on the table. "Now," said he, "these are very bad throws, and would never catch a fish." This assertion was applauded, and immediately carried by acclamation. "To make a good cast, and keep your fly in the rectangular position," continued the maestro, "you must furl your line thus." So saying, he gave the handkerchief a knowing whisk, which extinguished both the candles. Thus he argued with all his might, feeding the young Oxonian with scientific maxims, who promised that he would furl his line, and fish mathematically.

The next morning no one could start with a fairer prospect of sport than the said novice. He was accompanied by *Allan Beg*, or Little Allan, because he was told it was quite impossible for him to catch a salmon without his assistance; and he was taught how to kill his fish "par raison démonstrative." But throw as he would, furl as he might, he could by no means manage to keep his fly always at right angles to his rod, although he was a most excellent mathematician. At length, after having lost seven favourite flies, and two casting lines, he broke out in unqualified abuse of the system; which so enraged his "gentle brother of the angle," that high words arose, and they were on the point of committing the *duello* on those very sands where it is said Prince Charles drew up his forces. My friend was asked to act as impartial second to both parties, which he consented to, on condition only that they should stand and fire so that the balls might cross at right angles to each other. But "Etes-vous fou," said he to the Oxonian; " de l'aller quereller, lui qui entend les angles, et qui sait tuer un saumon par raison démonstrative?" At this good humour returned, and each party fished the rest of the day according to the angles that best suited his fancy, without let or argument.

Now in *holding* your fly on a rough stream you must advance your arms, and bring your rod straight across the river, consequently your line hanging straight down the stream may form a right angle at the point of your rod, and so you should work it in this instance; but in most other cases I prefer the obtuse angle. As to the argument, " Ils avoient raison tous deux."

In hooking a rising fish, it is best to strike a little sideways, that the hook may fasten in the fleshy part of the mouth ; whereas, if you pull straight up, you are apt to encounter the upper or bony part ; or if the fish has not closed his jaws, and fairly turned off, you may pull the fly away from him too soon, to the disappointment of both parties. As a proof of this, if it does not appear sufficiently obvious, I appeal to anyone who has tried it, to say whether or not it is an easy matter to hook a rising fish, the experimentalist being stationed on a high bridge.

Sometimes, however, when a salmon is clean run, and in high glee, you can scarcely miss him, strike which way you will.

I remember fishing at the Troughs, under the auspices of Rob Kerse, early in the spring, before a clean fish had been caught there that season. I stood over one of those gorges where an immense volume of water, pent up in a narrow passage, rolls furiously between its rocky barriers. Here I fixed myself for a few casts —the rocks being of such a nature that I could not go lower down the river either in a boat or by wading. This cast is called the Clippers, and is in Mackerston-water.

Here, with a line not given out above my rod's length, I hooked a clean salmon that rose close under me. I struck him as he was at the surface of the water: as soon as he felt the hook, he endeavoured to dig downwards. I gave him the butt of my rod, and he bent the whole of it in a way that I never saw before, making it in shape, with a slight exaggeration, nearly two-thirds of a circle. " Gie him line, gie him line," roared out Kerse and Charlie Purdie,—" od but he'll break ye, man." Now I knew that if he went down the Clippers amongst the rocks, I should be cut in a moment to a dead certainty; for, as I noted before, I could not follow. So I was determined not to yield at all events, and I held him firm at the surface of the water. In this position he had not half his natural power, and in less than a minute Charlie cleiked him, and brought him out before he could dig down. Thus he was taken by surprise. He proved to be a clean salmon of ten pounds, and the first that had been caught that season. Now this could not have been done, had not the line been short and the fish almost immediately under me. I remember Kerse (who had before been pressing the necessity of using *double* or *triple* gut in such dangerous water) saying, " Ay, that was canny enough; but if you had not been advised by me, it could not have been done at ony gait." I showed him my casting line, however, which, excepting the first length next the line, was of strong single gut. But he was certainly right in his assertion as to the necessity of very strong tackle in such a singular cast, especially as the river was very full, and the torrent so impetuous that nice tackle was by no means requisite.

In a low clear water you must be somewhat dilatory in striking: you often see the heave of the water and a break before the fish has actually seized your fly. Give him time to turn his head in his way back to his

seat, to which a salmon always returns after rising at
the fly. Tom Purdie gave me an account of a fish that
had perplexed him greatly by his non-observance of
this rule, as nearly as possible in the following words.
He might have used fewer certainly, but Tom was
not laconic.

"I had," said he, "risen a sawmon three successive
days at the throat of Caddon-water fut, and on the
fourth day I was determined to bring him to book; and
when he rose as usual, I went up to Caddon Wa's,
namely, the pool opposite the ruins of Caddon Lee,
where there had been a terrace garden facing the south;
and on returning I tried my old friend, when he rose
again without touching the heuck : but I got a glimpse
o' him, and saw he was a sawmon o' the biggest sort.
I then went down the river to a lower pool, and in
half an hour came up again and changed my heuck.
I began to suspect that having *raised* the fish so often,
I had become too anxious, and given him too little
law,—or jerked the heuck away before he had closed
his mouth upon it. And as I had a heavy rod and
good line, and the castin' line, which I had gotten thrae
the *Sherra*, had three fadom o' pleit gut at the end of
it, and the *flee* was buskit on a three plies o' sawmon
gut, sae I was na feard for my tackle. I had putten
a cockle-stane at the side o' the water fornent the place
where he raise; forbye I kend fu' weel where he was
lyin' : it was at the side o' a muckle blue clint that
made a clour i' the rough throat, e'en when the Queed
was in a brown flood, as she had been for twa days
afore. Aweel, I thought I wad try a plan o' auld

Juniperbank's when he had raised a sawmon mair nor
ance. I keepit my een hard closed when the heuck
was coming owre the *place*. Peace be here! I fand
as gif I had catched the branch o' an aik tree swingin'
and sabbin' in a storm of wind. Ye needna doubt I
opened my een! An' what think ye was the sawmon
aboot?—turnin' and rowin' doon the tap o' the water
owre him and owre him (as ye hae seen a hempie o' a
callant row doon a green brae side) at great speed,
makin' a fearfu' jumblin' and splashin', and shakin' the
tap o' the wand at sic a rate, that deil hae me but I
thocht he wad hae shaken my arms aff at the shouther
joints, tho' I said to mysel' they were gey firm putten
on. I never saw a fish do the like but ane i' the Auld
Brig pool in the Darnwick-water. I jalouse they want
to unspin the line; for a fish has far mair cunnin' and
wiles aboot him than mony ane wad think. At ony
rate it was a fashious plan this I fell on; for or he war
to the fut o' the pool I was tired o' him and his wark,
and sae was he, I'se warrant ye. For when he fand
the water turnin' shallow, he wheeled aboot, and I ran
up the pool as fast as I could follow him, gien him a'
the line I could at the same time; and when it was just
aboot a' off the pirn, and he was comin' into the
throat, he wheeled again in a jiffy, and cam straight for
my feet as if he had been shot out o' a cannon! I
thocht it was a' owre atween us, for I fand naething at
the wand as the line was soomin' i' the pool a' the
way doon. I was deid sure I had lost him after a' my
quirks; for whan they cast a cantrip o' that kind, it's
done to slacken the line to let them draw the heuck out

o' their mouths wi' their teethy tongue—an' they are
amaist sure to do sae.   But he was owre weel heuckit,
this ane, to work his purpose in that gyse, as ye sal
hear; for when by dint o' runnin' back thrae the water
as fast as I could, and windin' up the line I had
brought a bow on the tap o' the road, I fand the fish
had riestit in the deepest part o' the pool, trying a' that
teeth an' tongue could do to get haud o' the heuck; and
there did he lie for nearly an hour, for I had plenty o'
time to look at my watch, and now and then to tak'
mony a snuff too.   But I was certain by this time that
he was fast heuckit, and I raised him again by cloddin
stanes afore him as near as I durst for hittin' the line.
But when I got him up at last there was mickle mair
to do than I thocht of; for he ran up the pool and
doon the pool I dar say fifty times, till my feet wur
dour sair wi' gangin sae lang on the channel: then he
gaed owre the stream a'thegither.   I was glad to let
him change his gait ony way; and he gaed down to
Glenbenna, that was in Whitebank's-water, and I
wrocht him lang there.   To mak' a lang tale short,
before I could get at him wi' the gaff, I was baith
hungry an' tyrt; an' after a' he was firm heuckit, in
the teughest part o' the body, at the outside o' the
edge o' the wick bane.   He was a clean sawmon, an'
three an' twenty meal punds."

No creature is more capricious than a salmon.   One
of the Lairds of Makerstoun, many years ago, had a
fisherman named Robin Hope, who, like many of his
brethren on the Tweed, was an original.   Attending his
master on a day that was considered quite a killing

one, not a fish would stir. "What is the meaning of this, Robin?" said the Laird. "Deed, sir, I dinna ken," said Robin; "for sometimes they will tak' the thoom o' yere mitten, if ye would throw it in, and at ithers they wadna look at the Lady o' Makerstoun and a' her braws."

Salmon never take well when the weather is about to change; it is therefore useless to go out when the mercury remains at this point. When it first sets in for a continuance of dry weather the fish will rise about your hook, and only break the surface of the water; but before a flood they will spring clean out of it, for the purpose, perhaps, of filling their air-bladder before travelling.

These sportive fellows, however, sometimes get into a scrape by being hooked outside. A salmon of ten pounds was caught in the Skurry-wheel, at Sprouston, in the following curious manner. The fish were rising wantonly, but not taking the fly; in striking at one of them the line looped over its tail, and the hook catching the line on the upper side the fish was fairly snared, and at length killed, after showing extraordinary sport.

Sometimes, also, they will leap out for pastime, and at others from fear. Thus if a salmon had been once touched sharply with the hook, when he sees the fly above him on some future day he will often vault into the air. I once saw a marked instance of this.

A very young friend who was fishing with me saw a fish spring over his line in this manner, and he kept flinging at him with the same result, the salmon always moving forward, till he fairly chased him up the water

some hundred yards; that is to say, from " The Webbs,"
above Craigover Boat Hole in the Mertoun-water, half
way up to Maxwell Burn foot. Believe me, it was a
pleasant thing to behold. My friend would not be
denied. Master *Salmo Salar*, and he was a lusty one,
would not accept, but acknowledged the courteous
tender of *Michael Scott* at every cast, in the manner I
have described. Thus, they held correspondence with
each other a cousiderable time without coming in contact. At length piscator began to suspect that the
repulsive qualities were on his side, and the attractive
ones only on the part of the fugitive, who knew,

> ———" but how it mattered not,
> It was the wizard *Michael Scott*."

So he turned his back upon him reluctantly; but,
casting a lingering look behind, he could not forbear
returning and doubling his defeat. This fish had
probably been touched by a fly before.

That night, the hostel being full, we slept in a
double-bedded room. At the dead hour of twelve I
was awakened by loud cries of "I have him, I have
him!"—"Hold him fast then," said I, for I thought he
had collared a thief; but in truth he had not: he had
only got hold of the bell-rope, and was fishing away
with it in his dreams, with a salmon, of course, at the
end of it. Luckily he did not arouse the Maritornes
of the inn: no bell having ever been attached to the
pull, which was a mere matter of ornament.

The first thing to be considered in rod fishing is
the state of the water proper for the sport; and I beg
that it may all along be borne in mind that my obser-

vations relate to the river Tweed only : for it must be obvious that as rivers vary in their depth and volume of water, no general rule for their being in proper order for the fly can be laid down.

The waxing, as it is called, and the progress of a flood, has been already explained in a former part of these pages.

When the Tweed is not clear, but, as it is termed, *drumly*, salmon *that have been some time in the river* never take well; in such case, when there were no clean fish in the water, I have sometimes had fourteen or fifteen offers without taking above one or two fish. They do not see the fly distinctly, and therefore come at it slowly and with hesitation. One would think they had some particular method of holding it awhile by way of experiment, just within the point of their noses ; for I have often struck a salmon sharply, and felt as if my hook was firmly fixed in him, when in a moment afterwards it has come away quite easily; and this has happened two or three times in succession, the water being in the foul state I have mentioned. It must be noted also, that when the river is swollen and discolored, salmon travel in the daytime, particularly when there is a fresh wind to ruffle the surface of the water; and as they are intent on their journey, they are not apt to pay much attention to such food as we worthies offer them. Now as this uncertainty of hooking a fish that offers happens to me or to you, so the same thing will occur to every other fisherman that is out on the same day, these animals being all of the same mind; but I have heard good fishermen in the North say, that they always had the best sport before the river cleared. I suppose it was in shallow streams; because it is evident that salmon, who always lie at the bottom of the river, or on the edge of a rock near it, could not see the fly at any great depth when the waters were turbid. It must be observed, however, that in more shallow places, where they can distinguish it, there is a great difference between a newly run fish and one that has been some time in the river; the new one being wild and gamesome, and ignorant of the ways of the world, and the other the very emblem of prudence, and an admirer of the old adage, "*Always look before you leap.*" It is difficult to express by words the exact state of the water I wish to allude to: if it is only moss-stained good sport may be had with clean fish, but there must be a certain degree of transparency.

The upper parts of the Tweed come into order for being fished much sooner than those below, and this in proportion to the depth and volume of water.

It must be owned that fish may occasionally be caught in turbid, and even full water; but then it must be by a perfect change of system. At such a time the strong streams and usual salmon casts are useless; and you must throw in the easy checks near the land, and in the tails of the streams, where the fish rest in travelling. In this way I once caught five salmon in the Pavilion-water from off the shore, unattended even by a man with a cleik; whilst my friend, who fished above me in the finest streams in the water, with a boat and all appliances and means to boot, did not rise a single fish; not from want of skill—for it was Lord Somerville—

but simply because the salmon did not lie in their usual seats.

A word or two I will now say about the management of the cleik, which, although it seems simple enough, requires some address. Take care, most worthy attendant—for it is to you I speak—that in the effervescence of your zeal you steer clear of the line, and that after you have struck the fish you tow him steadily to the shore; and I beg, sir, to caution you, and just merely to hint, that if you attempt one of your flourishes, and try to do all at one rapid jerk, you will have decidedly the worst of it. There must be two motions,—a strike, and a haul.

By way of illustration, I must tell you of a gentleman who came to visit me whilst I lived on the banks of the Tay, and was desirous of seeing a salmon caught before he returned to the South; so I launched my boat and set to work. Now on these pressing occasions one has commonly a blank day, instead of a show off: not so, however, in the present instance, for in a short time I killed six fish. When I had subdued their strength, I gave up the rod to my companion, who finished them skilfully enough. These fish were from seven to twelve pounds each, as well as I can recollect. I next hooked a large and peremptory salmon; and when he got weak I could not land, on account of the alders which grew on the margin of the river.

"Give me the cleik," said my confident friend; "let me come at him. I should like to try my hand at that, as well as at the rod, though it is a savage affair. Do you think I can manage it?" "I have no doubt of it," said I,

—" tam Marti, quam Mercurio." But pray let me interrogate you a little. Can you swim ? "

" Swim ! no, not I ; why do you ask me that ? "

" Because assuredly, if you do not take care, that salmon will pull you into the water ; so be canny."

There was an open laugh at this, and a look of defiance at the fish. Rash youth ! you stretched forth your dexter, and executed a well-directed stroke at the animal, thinking to tuck him out of the water at one coup; but you had very considerably miscalculated your own powers, and the weight you were to encounter. There were two things decidedly against you ; one, that the salmon was three feet long, and lay with his broadside towards you, so that you had a heavy weight to lift, and a considerable column of water to displace ; the other, that you were standing in a boat, and had an unstable balance. Thus, you were tilted forward in a way with which your will had nothing to do ; so that had not I, even I, Harry Otter, laid hold of the skirts of your coat, we should have been fishing with the long net for you : as it was, the resistance only threw you prostrate in the boat ; and I was sorry to see you so much incommoded by the water which had not been ladled out of it : inheriting all the valour of your ancestors, you still grasped the cleik, and, as I pushed the boat ashore, struggled your very best, till you dragged your prey to firm land.

He was not a clean salmon, nor was he the cause of cleanliness in others ; but, as you may remember, exceeded twenty pounds.

The success of a salmon fisher not only depends upon

11

the weather, but upon the state of the river as it is affected by the rains; so that one may be weeks, and even months, on the spot, without the possibility of taking a fish with the rod. The water may be too low to admit of fish coming up, or it may be too full in flood, with diurnal waxings; so that sportsmen who come from a distance, and have not much time to spare, may be grievously disappointed. In the upper part of the Tweed, real good rod fishing lasts but a few days after a spate: indeed, the water there is not properly supplied with fish till there are two or three spates in succession.

The hills are now so well drained, that the flood runs off rapidly; and thus the river soon falls in, and becomes too low for the fly, except in the strong streams.

Before these complete drainages took place, the Tweed kept full a much longer time than it does at present; for the rains which fell remained in the mosses, which gave out the water gradually, like a sponge.

Now the hill sides are scored with innumerable little drains, which empty themselves into the burns, which burns soon become impetuous torrents; thus suddenly supplied, the Ettrick, the Yarrow, the Leader-water, the Ale, the Teviot, and the many other streams that empty themselves into the Tweed, come raving down from the mountains and from the lakes, and, with their united volume, raise that river to an alarming height in the space of a few hours, which then spreads over the haughs, and sometimes sweeps off corn and cattle, and levels the bridges in its irresistible course. In these awful spates, the water is too strong and turbid for fish to travel: the soil is washed away partially from the ploughed lands; and, as the practice of liming them is very prevalent, the waters are obnoxious to the fish. I have often wondered how the trout could possibly survive this state of things; but they do survive it, by keeping at the eddies and close to the banks amongst the grass, where the pout nets haul them out by dozens.

Though I have given the foregoing instructions with much pleasure, I would not advise any one who wishes to stand well with society to utter a word about his propensity for fishing. It is generally thought a poor, inanimate occupation; and so, indeed, it is in some cases; and yet the passion is so strong, that I believe the sedentary angler who catches a roach or dace, worthless though he be, and weak and diminutive withal, has as much pleasure in his way, as the proud conqueror of a twenty-pound salmon.

I was once rowing on the Thames when a friend hailed me from afar, and beckoned with joyous and eager solicitation. Though I was pressed for time, I pulled up to him against the wind and stream, for I thought he had something of great moment to impart; but it was only to say, "that I would be glad to hear he had caught two dozen gudgeons that morning." But I do not think I was glad, at least not particularly so, though he was a very worthy man.

As for myself, if I am ever so indiscreet as to utter a word about fishing, I am always asked, "if it does not require a great deal of patience." Now, these sort of interrogators are in Cimmerian darkness as to the real thing. But I tell them, that to be a first-rate salmon fisher requires such active properties as they never dreamed of in their philosophy. It demands (salmon fishing at least) strength of arm and endurance of fatigue, and a capability of walking in the sharp streams for eight or ten hours together, with perfect satisfaction to one's self; and that early in the spring season, when the clean salmon first come forward. In after life, people are considerably addicted to boats, and to go about attended like admirals; that is what we must all come to. But your real professor, who has youth on his side, should neither have boats nor boots, but be sufficient in himself. No delay, no hauling the boat up the stream, but in and out, like an otter; even like we ourselves in the time of our prime, Fahrenheit being below zero. We then pitched our tent under Craigover rocks, on Tweedside, and slept in it, that we might go forth, rod in hand, at five o'clock each morning to our aqueous pastime. It is true that the late John Lord Somerville objected to our tent, as being a white object, and therefore likely to prevent the fish from passing by it to his upper water. But we proved to him, by mathematical lines adroitly drawn, that it was not within the range of a salmon's optics. So our tent stood, till a violent storm assailed us one night with barbarous fury, tore up the pegs to which the ropes were fastened, and gave up all our canvas to the winds. Thus, we got an ample soaking in our bed, in which we cut a pretty figure, no doubt, when disclosed to public gaze; but we were not blown into the Tweed; so that, upon the whole, we were uncommonly fortunate. But we discard ourselves for the present.

I say then, and will maintain it, that a salmon fisher should be strong in the arms, or he will never be able to keep on thrashing for ten or twelve hours together with a rod eighteen or twenty feet long, with ever and anon a lusty salmon at the end of his line, pulling like a wild horse with the lasso about him. Now he is obliged to keep his arms aloft, that the line may clear the rocks,—now he must rush into the river, then back out with nimble pastern, always keeping a steady and proper strain of line; and he must preserve his self-possession, "even in the very tempest and whirlwind of the sport," when the salmon rushes like a rocket. This is not moody work; it keeps a man alive and stirring. Patience indeed!

It is indispensable to have a quick eye, and a ready hand: your fly, or its exact position, should never be lost sight of; and you should imagine every moment of the livelong day that an extraordinary large salmon is coming at it. No man can do any thing properly unless he is sanguine, and his whole heart and soul is in the business. "Remember, my good people all, I do not wish to press this laborious sport unfairly upon you: excuse me, but it may be you are not exactly fit for it,—' *non cuivis homini*,'" &c. You may saunter about with a gauze net and two sticks, if you prefer it, and catch butterflies. Every man to his vocation; but "what is a gentleman without his recreations?"

There is a speculation in angling that gives great zest to the sport. You may catch a moderate-sized fish, or a distinguished one; or mayhap, a monster of such stupendous dimensions as will render your name im mortal; and he may be painted, and adorn some fishing-tackle shop in London, like Colonel Thornton's pike, which threw *Newmarket* on his back as he was landing him,—a lad, says the Colonel, so called from the place of his nativity. Of course you expect the latter phenomenon every cast. You see him in your mind's eye eternally following your fly, and you are ready to strike from second to second. It is true he does not actually come, as experience teaches. But what of that? he may come in an hour—in a minute—in a moment; the thing is possible, and that is enough for an angler.

A friend of mine (sacred be his name!) of great repute for his dexterity with the rod, and celebrated for his agreeable and amiable qualities, as well as for his intelligence and various accomplishments, had this poetical facility of seeing what did not really exist in substance. A curious instance of this popular talent occurred at a friend's house in the country with whom he was staying. There was a fine piece of water in the park, well stored with fish, where he used to spend most part of the morning, rod in hand; so that his perseverance excited considerable admiration from the host, as well as from his guests. Not having been very successful, his ardour at length began to flag. It was a pity, for it is a pleasant thing to be excited. What was to be done? You shall see. A report was raised that there was an enormous pike seen in the water, about the length of a decent-sized alligator. He was said to have maimed a full-grown swan, and destroyed two cygnets, besides sundry ducks. At first he was no more believed in than the great sea snake, which encloses at least half the

world in his folds. But after the lapse of a few days,
the keeper came to the private ear of my friend, and
told him that a *mortal* large pike was basking amongst
some weeds, and could be seen plainly. " You are sure
to cotch em, sir." He was rewarded for this intelligence, and exhorted to keep the important secret from
the other visitors at the mansion.

When piscator, cunning fellow! thought that all were
out of the way, employed in hunting, shooting, or some
other occupation, he and John Barnes the keeper glided
down secretly to the awful spot, and they there descried
the semblance of a fish so enormous that it was doubted
if any thing less than a small rope could hold him. The
sportsman was astounded—the keeper was not; for the
said awful animal was nothing more than a large
painted piece of wood, carved deftly by himself into
the shape of a pike, painted according to order, and
stuck in the natural position by means of a vertical
prop, which could not be discovered amongst the weeds.
It was too bad, really a great deal too bad; but
tolerably ingenious, and beautifully deceptive. The
gentleman approached with tact and caution, and the
eyes of the fish glared upon him; as well they might,
for they were very large and dazzling, being made of
glass, and originally designed to be inserted in a great
horned owl which the keeper had stuffed.

" What a prodigious fish, John!"

" Very perdigious indeed, sir."

" What eyes he has!"

" So he has, sir."

" I'll try him with a roach.—There,—it went in
beautifully, and he did not move."

" No, he won't take it no how. Give him a frog; he seems a difficult fish."

Piscator did tender him a very lively one in vain; in short, he offered him every bait he could possibly think of, running through all the devices and temptations he was master of. Cautious in his approaches, that the supposed fish might not see him, he always advanced to make his cast upon his knees, to the no small merriment of his friends, who were looking at him through a telescope from the windows of the mansion.

Well, thus he spent the whole morning; waiting, however, at times, for a cloud to intercept the sunbeams, and a breath of air to ruffle the surface of the water. When these came, he would set to work again with renovated hopes; till at last, tired and discomfited, he bent his steps homewards. On his arrival there, he was accosted on the very threshold by some of the guests.

" Oh! you have been fishing all the morning, I see; but what could make you stay out so long, and get away so cunningly with the keeper ?'

" Why, to tell you the truth, Barnes (you know what a good creature he is) told me of an immense pike that was lying amongst the weeds at the end of the lake; he must be the same that swallowed the cygnets. I never saw so enormous a monster in fresh water."

Omnes.—" Well, where is he—where is he ? let us look at him."

Host.—" John, tell the cook we will have him for dinner to-day.—Dutch sauce, remember."

Piscator.—" You need not be in such a hurry to

send to the cook, for I am sorry to say I did not catch him."

Host.—"Not catch him—not catch him! Impossible, with all your skill, armed as you are to the teeth, with roach, bleak, minnows, frogs, kill-devils, and the deuce knows what. Not catch him! Come, you're joking."

Piscator.—"Serious, I assure you. I never was so beat before, and yet I never fished better; but though I did not absolutely hook him, *he ran at me several times.*"

An universal shout of laughter followed this assertion, which made my friend not a little suspicious; but he never again touched upon the subject. Some time afterwards, wandering near the scene of his operations, he saw an immense carving of a pike placed upon a pole near the margin of the water, and painted beautifully: he guessed he had seen him before.

Let us now return to the Scotch rivers.

The Tay, which rises from, and is approximated by, vast and desolate regions of moss and moor, preserves its volume of water much longer than those rivers that have their sources in a more pastoral and agricultural country, and of course is much longer in good order for fly fishing. But when the black clouds burst over the vast wilderness of mountains, a hundred torrents gleam on all sides, rush down the rocky ravines, and change the burns into turbulent rivers, which pour their floods into the mighty channel of the Tay: thus this river probably carries more water to the ocean than any other in Great Britain.

I have read much of the rapids of the great rivers in

America, and the difficulty of steering and shooting down them in safety; and the accompaniments of the scenery, and the descriptions of these cataracts, have always appeared to me singularly wild and picturesque. They made so great an impression upon my mind that, to form a more correct idea of the sort of thing, I meditated a voyage down the Tay when, filled with her countless tributaries, she goes raging to the ocean. Besides this inducement, I had some small boats which I wished to take to Perth by water, instead of land carriage; for I was changing my quarters from Meikleour on the banks of the Tay to the Pavilion on those of the Tweed. These boats were built on Tweedside for fly fishing in small waters, and in warm weather were held for the fisherman by a man who waded in the water, lest the salmon should be scared away by the motion or appearance of the oars, or canting pole, as it might be. Being, therefore, of a very light and diminutive construction, they were not exactly calculated to endure the buffets of large and tempestuous waters: one is not apt, however, to be over nice about such things, and accordingly I resolved to put them to the proof. Nor was an opportunity long wanting. After a night of heavy rain, the Tay, which flowed through the park of Meikleour, rose to a fearful extent. This was exactly the sort of thing to suit me; so I proposed to my fisherman, Charles Purdie, to go down the flood to Perth, a distance of about twelve miles by water. We did so; and I here insert the particulars of our voyage, as they may serve to give an idea of a Scottish spate.

We were standing at the foot of the sloping lawn before my house; and as Charlie Purdie bent his regards on the frightful violence of the flood, I thought he did not half like to embark on it. In fact, he did not only disapprove of the general conduct of the river, but also of the peculiar rocky nature of the channel in which it was its pleasure to gallop along to the ocean. Moreover, he knew there was an obstruction in the river at a place called the Linn of Campsie, about four miles below the proposed starting-place, where at the arrival of his little boat he did not anticipate much pleasure. In fact, neither Charlie or his master conceived it would be possible to pass the falls into the Linn, since no boat could do so in the ordinary state of the water without being upset, or dashed to shivers. They would see how things looked, however, on their arrival at the spot, and act accordingly.

" Now then, loosen my boat, Charlie : I will go first ; and take care you do not run foul of me."

The boats being unmoored, we shot down the river in a moment, and were soon at the end of the park where the Isla comes into the Tay. This additional volume of water increased our velocity ; we guided our boats into the main currents, and away we went with the swiftness of a steam-engine. Rocks and woods opened to our view in an instant, and in an instant vanished behind us. Thus we were driven along with great fury till we came within the sound of the great falls of the Linn of Campsie : soon we descried before us the awful barrier of rocks which rose up right athwart the stream, extending from bank to bank.

The waters had worn their way in some places through this barrier, and tumbled madly through the rocky gorges; down they went, thundering with stunning sound into the enormous cauldron below. Then arose the strife—the dashing of the spray—the buffeting against the banks—the swirling of the eddies, crested with large masses of foam—all was in hideous commotion.

This state of things threatened to put an end to our projected voyage. To go right onwards through the centre gorge was to pass to certain destruction: as well might one hope to shoot in safety down the falls of Schaffhausen.

I was prepared for all this, and was quite aware of the impediment before I began my voyage; so I did as I had made up my mind to do before I started. I pulled towards some alder trees which grew on the bank above the fall, and held my boat fast by the branches; I then told Charlie to secure his boat also with a rope, and to land and reconnoitre. We were enabled to do these things without much difficulty, as the water was in some measure arrested in its course above the fall, being slightly bayed back by the barrier of rocks. Being on terra firma, my hero looked ruefully at the torrents: one alone appeared something like being practicable; and it was one that, in the mean state of the river, was nothing but a dry channel. Whether our small craft could shoot down it without foundering or not was by no means evident to the eye, though a practised one, of the explorer. He was, however, somewhat encouraged by two fishermen who were mending their nets. They thought, they said, that we " might possibly descend in safety, if we managed our boats well." Charlie looked, and sighed, and looked again : the thing was evidently not in harmony with his ideas ; for he could not swim himself, and he doubted whether his boat would either, when it arrived at the bottom of the fall. However, I decided that I would try the thing alone ; and if it should prove a failure, the example was not, of course, to be followed. So I brought my little boat some way above the cataract, with her head up the stream, and by rowing against it let her fall by degrees stern foremost, by which means I had a clear view before me, and could therefore steer to a nicety. She went down most agreeably, though in nearly a vertical position, but pitched upon a rock below the fall ; but before any harm happened, I swung her off by inclining my body to and fro. My fisherman followed successfully ; and having passed the wide-spreading Linn, the channel of the Tay became more contracted, and we resumed our former pace, shooting down the rapids like an arrow, and by occasional swift snatches of the oars avoiding the breakers around us. So we passed amongst the hanging woods and impending rocks of this romantic river, till we arrived at Stanley, where groups of people were assembled on the hill-top, who shouted to us with all their might, and made signs and gestures, the meaning of which I could not comprehend, but they seemed to be warning us of some impending danger : I could not catch the import of their words, as the sound was but faintly heard amidst the din of the waves. So I did not perplex myself with attending to them, but thought it wisest to trust to my own discretion, which fortunately carried the boats safely to their place of destination. I learned afterwards, that seeing our boats were mere insignificant cockle-shells borne down by the flood with great impetuosity, they were fearful that we should be carried down the mill-dam, and come in contact with the machinery. But a better fate awaited us than such a Quixotic one; and after a little rough work, in which we shipped a reasonable quantity of water, we at length approached the vast bleaching grounds of Perth, where the river swept swift and ample in an even channel under a wooded bank studded with villas; we then darted through the middle arch of the beautiful bridge in the town, and hauled up our boats on a wharf below it.

CHAP. VII.

" Whate'er Lorraine light touched with softening hue,
Or savage Rosa dashed, or learned Poussin drew."

EXPLORING one morning the upper parts of the river,
with my trout rod in my hand, I came to a little meadow
in a vale where the stream played in mazes beneath
hanging coppices. In this sequestered spot, I espied a
gentle angler—I may say particularly gentle. His
mode of fishing appeared so novel, that I was induced
to pry a little into it; so I ventured to approach him,
and asked what sport he had been having.

"Oh, glorious, glorious,—perfectly enchanting! All
Paradise is around me!"

I took notice, however, that although he held his rod
pretty much in the usual piscatorial position of altitude,
his fly was by no means on the water, but lay very
comfortably dry upon the furzes on the bank side, and
that, whatever his hand might pretend to be doing, his
mind was not at that moment particularly bent upon
a capture. Whilst he stood entranced, I took the
liberty of lifting up the lid of his basket, in which I
descried nothing but a pair of gloves—not a fish reposed in it. It was clean, new, and Cockney-like, and
I ventured to give him a hint to this effect.

"Well now I declare, sir, that is very singular;

because I certainly caught two trout, and put them into my creel. But I daresay you are a little absent, and did not notice them; I am somewhat absent myself occasionally."

He examined the basket, and found only gloves by themselves,—gloves.

" Where can I have put them ?"

" Indeed I can't guess, sir."

He then began to shuffle about and examine his waistcoat pockets and those of his pantaloons, nay, actually his fob.

" Perhaps, sir, you did not find quite room enough in your fob, and put them into your coat pocket for fear they should soil the basket."

" Bless me ! so I did; and here they are, truly. I see now how it is; in a hurry, and whilst I was wrapt in admiration of the scenery, I put the gloves where the fish should have been, and *vice versâ*,— nothing could be more natural."

This he said with a simplicity worthy of the golden age. But he declared that although he was not at that moment very intent on the sport, he did like fishing exceedingly. "Because," said he, "it requires no parade of attendance, like other field sports; it leads to the most beautiful spots; and I take up my rod and my painting box at any hour I please, and saunter over the flowery meads, in a state of tranquil enjoyment amidst all the most pleasing images of rural life."

I observed there was considerable excitement in fishing occasionally, as well as tranquility. " For instance, now," said I, " there is a sea trout in that run of water

that will make your heart dance, if you should happen
to hook him; I saw him put his head up at the cheek of
the current, and he had a wilful look, and is likely
to make most pernicious runs when hooked; for these
sort of fish are very active and strong. If you will
give me leave, I will change your trout fly for a
larger one, and instruct you how to proceed, as from
the nature of your tackle I conclude you are not accustomed to fish of this description. There now—
go a little higher up the stream; throw above him,
and bring the fly gently round; and if he comes at it,
do not strike him too hard, or you will break your
slender tackle. If you get hold of him, we shall see
how he is to be managed; he will put your tranquillity
to the test, I promise you."

He grasped the rod, and held it aloft; then, after a
considerable pause, "He is exactly in the right spot,"
said he. "Precisely," I replied.

"What a rich red tone of colour he has,—how well it
tells in the shadow! He will come in capitally."

"He is not red, I assure you, but clear as silver, and
I wish he *may* come in capitally."

"Bless me! he looks red to me, and I must take him
immediately; he is exactly the thing I wanted."

So saying, to my amazement, he dropped the rod, and
pulled out a sketch book, in which he began painting a
red cow in water colours that was reposing under a
hawthorn bush on the opposite bank, just beyond the
stream where the fish was lying, and which had been
the real object of his remarks. When he had done with

12

the cow, however, I put the rod once more into his hands, and reminded him of the fish.

"Now throw a few yards above the spot where you see the water boiling around that large blue stone· Very well; advance a step every time you throw. Capital! Now you are precisely at the fish. Strike him gently if he rises. Well done!—by Paul Potter you have him! Hold up the top of your rod, and keep an even steady pull upon him."

"How can I keep a steady pull upon such a wild animal? Why he springs out of the water, and whizzes about in it, like that fire-work called a serpent."

"Be steady—be steady, or he will whiz you about with a witness. Shorten your line; get into the water, and follow him."

"What a cruel speech! Why I never learned to swim. You are exceedingly inconsiderate indeed, sir."

"Swim! why the water on this channel is scarcely over your ankles, and I will help you if you should happen to stumble."

"Then we should both meet a watery grave together. I have often read of such calamities."

"In with you,—in with you, I say, or he will be off. There, I told you so; he has broke your line; and, pray pardon me, but pretty work you have made of it with your tranquillity."

"Well, as it seems to make you so uneasy, I will go a little way into the water, though I shall not enjoy it."

"Why, what is the use of wetting yourself, now you have lost the fish?"

"True, true,—I did not sufficiently consider that;

so now I will go back, and see if I can improve my cow."

This was abundantly philosophical; but intelligible enough to me, who being very much addicted to painting myself, know how absorbing a passion it is.

The cow was a good cow,—drawn in a clean and decisive manner, with a correct knowledge of the anatomy of the animal. I praised accordingly, and we began naturally enough to talk upon the principles of landscape painting; and as we both agreed pretty well as to those principles, so we both laid down the law with as much confidence as if we were the lineal descendants of Zeuxis or Appelles,—a fashion, I must observe, most particularly prevalent at the present day. I fear it is not worth while to notice our remarks. I will write them down, however, at a venture; and here they follow.

" View-taking," said the cow limner, " I consider as of a distinct character from landscape painting. The interest of the first, as a work of art, in all highly cultivated countries, must in a great measure depend upon accidental causes. Trees in hedge-rows, and most other positions, have been planted or removed by the hand of man for profit or convenience, so that they are rarely found in the most natural or effective situations; other objects share the same fate, and even the vivid verdure is produced by artificial means. Still it is right for the view-taker to copy every thing before him just as it really presents itself. This may be desirable as a remembrance, or an exact illustration of the scenery of a country, and indeed occasionally, by some happy accident, as a work of art; it may also have great interest as representing passages in rural life. But it is obvious that, in a country highly cultivated, a scene very accurately delineated represents the materials only, and not the composition of nature, strictly so called.

"On the other hand, the landscape painter should aim much higher; he should get all his materials from the most striking and characteristic specimens in nature, and study such forms and combinations as may make an interesting impression on the mind. Trees, rocks, water, mountains,—all his materials he should arrange upon the same principle that an historical painter observes in composing from living models. He should address the imagination rather than the eye, and endeavour to convey to his work some prevailing character, which may awaken a corresponding sympathy and interest in the comtemplative beholder.

"As to colour and effect, every tinge of light that is beautiful and striking, every varied appearance that the change of the hour and seasons may bring forth, should be marked down and coloured on the spot. This should be the unremitting practice of the artist, that his works may bear the impress and truth of nature.

"Taking care to lay his emphasis upon those dominant objects that give beauty, character, or sublimity to the landscape, he should keep all the rest subordinate, though intelligible; always bearing in mind that the eye sees those objects only *in detail* upon which it is immediately fixed. If, on the other hand, he copies from nature every individual thing before him exactly as he sees it, when his eye rests upon that individual object alone, he does not represent the scene such as he saw it in nature at one general and comprehensive view, but as it appeared to him by examining separate parts one after the other, each part having a distinct focus. If then he adopts this method of proceeding, he will paint upon a false, though a very prevalent principle, and his picture cannot fail to have an unpleasant and irritating effect.

> " Infelix operis summâ, quia ponere totum
> Nesciet."

He paused a little to take breath, as well indeed he might; so I took the opportunity to lay down the law also, and to remark that he must have arrived at his conclusions from a study of the paintings of those eminent masters whose works are sealed with perfection, and sanctified by time,—productions that elevate us above the level of common thought, and carry us into the regions of poetry and romance.

"In the pictures of Claude, by a happy treatment of his subject you see more than the bare materials of common nature. There the glow of Italy lies radiant before you : the eye passes from the flowery foreground, with its tall trees just moved by the zephyr, and wanders from distance to distance over clustering groves, and classical ruins, amidst the quiet lapse of waters, and all the pastoral beauty that poets have delighted to feign.

" Directly opposite to the blandishments of this great master, but true to itself, is the genius of Salvator Rosa. Little recked he of Arcadian scenes. Mysterious and elevated in thought, he delighted to stalk over the wilds of Calabria; and there, in regions desolate and dolorous, by the side of some impending rock, amidst the din of torrents plunging down to the horrid gulf below him, he formed a style original, savage, and indomitable. Nothing entered into his pictures that was commonplace or mean. His figures were banditti, forlorn travellers, or wrecked mariners. His trees the monarch chesnut, forming impenetrable forests, or blasted and riven by the thunderbolt. All his forms were grand; even his winged clouds had a stern aspect, and partook of the general character. Titian, Claude, Poussin, Salvator Rosa,—these, and some others of the good old times, drew the poetry and soul of landscape, and not its mere dead image—and this is the triumph of art."

I fancy my new friend the artist paid very little attention to my remarks, which I am not at all surprised at; for he began to soliloquise in an absent manner about Poussin, whom he said I should have placed between Claude and Rosa; and as he seemed to threaten rather a long encomium, I pretended to see a fish rise, and glided away quietly: for I thought enough had been said on the subject of painting already. As I stole off, however, I caught a few unconnected expressions; such as "dark groves and solitude, — storms, — tempests, — and alpine ridges." Then he grew somewhat classical, and began to recite from Virgil—

> " Tot congesta manu præruptis oppida saxis,
> Fluminaque antiquos subterlabentia muros."

At this I walked faster and faster, till I got totally out of hearing. Not through dislike of the subject did

I make my escape, for it was one after my own heart; but my rod was in my hand, and "*hoc age*" has always been my maxim. Besides, the day began to alter, and a fine fresh breeze arose, which came up the river; clouds appeared over the horizon, which kept gathering, and brought on slight showers and passing shadows, with occasional bursts of sunshine that glittered on the curl of the water. Now, as far as my experience goes, this is the best sort of weather for sport. The prejudice, notwithstanding, I believe, runs in favour of a grey day; but such a one has often deluded my expectations; at which time I have found the fish dull and sulky, when I was in hopes they would be up and stirring. It is not meet that they should study Zimmerman.

It was now the month of September, and I was expecting to catch some of the grey scull that come forward at that season. These fish are of a goodly shape; but though fresh from the sea are not quite so glossy in their scales, or so rich in flavour, as your brown-backed salmon that comes up early in the spring. They are altogether of a greyer colour than that beautiful fish, and derive their name from that circumstance.

So soon as I had changed my tackle, my enthusiastic companion came sauntering up to me. I am not quite clear that he was fully sensible of my presence, for his heart seemed still to be amongst the Apennines with Poussin. I made an attempt to dislodge him, and bring him down to the level of my own ideas.

"You know," said I, " that Gaspar was a great sportsman, though it is not probable that he ever caught a salmon, which is a northern fish; but if you will condescend to transport yourself from the banks of the Arno to those of Tweed, and to walk an hour or two with me, I think I can promise that you shall see such a feat performed."

Stranger (abstractedly):

> " Fluminaque antiquos subterlabentia muros."

" Come now, sink Virgil and the artist a little; put your sketch-book in your pocket, and let us see what can be done with the salmon. Your quotations, my dear sir, with your permission, will keep, as they have kept, for ages—

> ' Adde tot egregias urbes.'

No, no; there are no eminent cities or towns here, only Melrose and Gattonside; and if you call these 'egregias urbes,' you are egregiously mistaken."

He made no reply, but looked at me with a smile that seemed directed at the simplicity and absence of his own character.

" Now," said I, " as you seem to have descended from your stilts, which I beg to say are very becoming, though somewhat out of season, I will tell you how all people are not exactly of our way of thinking, as to the triumph of art and these classical illusions; imagining, on the contrary, that painting is a sleight of hand, and comes by intuition.

" I was lately sauntering with my painting-box in the romantic glen beneath the towers

> ' Where Roslin's chiefs uncoffined lie;
> Each baron, for a sable shroud,
> Sheathed in his iron panoply.'

As I went along I traced the mazes of the river, in some places brawling among the rocks, and at others gliding silently through the mossy stones. I was thus endeavouring to find out such points of view as had most interest, and to investigate the peculiar character in which the charm of the scene consisted.

"Having at length settled all this to my satisfaction, and marked in the outline of a scene with a piece of white crayon, preparatory to colouring it in oil, a very respectable-looking lady came sailing up to me, and begged to look at my canvas. The day being somewhat advanced, she asked me how many sketches I had made that morning; and upon my telling her that the one she was looking at was the first, she replied with very perfect exultation that her daughters had not been half an hour in the glen before they made nearly a bookful of drawings; but then, indeed, there were very few people so gifted as her daughters. I acquiesced in good faith; for I really knew no human beings that could do the same thing in the same time, and perhaps I might add in the same manner; so I concluded that the talent of these young ladies, like Madame Laffarge's genius for pastry, was 'colossal.'

"'Then they never learned,' continued the lady; 'it was all pure genius. Indeed Maria showed a singular facility for taking likenesses at three years old. Sir Thomas Lawrence had admired them very much.'

"I bowed, and did not doubt it. In a short time the young ladies themselves, and very pretty and sprightly ones they were, came tripping up.

"'Oh, mamma, we have been here only an hour, and have brought away all the scenery of the glen!'

"'Only forty minutes, upon honour, Maria.'

"'There, sir, you see my daughters do not throw away their time like some people.'

"I was not quite so sure of this; but a look of admiration on my part followed of course. The young ladies then began to discourse on art, and to ask what was my peculiar method of getting up sketches.

"'Pray, sir,' said the accomplished Maria, 'do you make your trees in twos, or in threes?'

"As I did not comprehend the exact meaning of these terms of art, she was pleased to illustrate by favouring me with a sight of one of her recent performances. The trees she particularly alluded to, I found, were those which represented a distant mass of wood. In executing a tree in such situations, I was instructed that a sort of flourish should be made, consisting of two segments of a circle, just as birds are drawn in prints; and this is doing trees in *twos*—in *threes*, another segment was added; and thus the mystery was solved,—the whole was executed in a running flourish with admirable facility. I cannot conscientiously aver that any one of the leaves of the sketch books of these intelligent young ladies contained what might be termed a drawing, but still there was something about them that might put a person of imagination very much in mind of drawings."

Thus, having beguiled the attention of Mr. Tintern (for that was the stranger's name) from the summits in which he had been soaring, I found him quite ready to receive an impression of a more humble kind, and he attended me in my walk, nothing loth. I was very much gratified with his company; for, besides his talent and simplicity of character, there was such an appearance of benevolent feeling in much of his conversation, which I have not thought it necessary to mention, that no one could avoid being taken with him.

I commenced operations at the Carry-wheel, which is nearly at the head of the Pavilion-water, and had not made four casts before I hooked a fish. He was evidently diminutive; but, dwarf as he was, he thought a good deal of himself, and was prodigal of the little strength which nature had given him. I thought him conceited, and so hauled him on shore at once without any ceremony. He proved to be a river trout of four pounds,—a silly-looking creature enough.

Well, I went forward and caught a few gilses and salmon in the upper Pavilion-water, not worth mentioning, except as the sport had the effect of rousing my new friend from his abstraction; indeed I met with nothing remarkable till I came to the Kingswell Lees. Now everyone knows that the Kingswell Lees, in fisherman's phrase, fishes off land; so there I stood on *terrâ durâ* amongst the rocks that dip down to the water's edge. Having executed one or two throws, there comes to me a voracious fish, and makes a startling dash at " Meg with the muckle mouth." Sharply did I strike the caitiff; whereat he rolled round disdainful, making a whirl in the water of prodigious circumference: it was not exactly Charybdis, or the Maelstrom, but rather more like the wave occasioned by the sudden turning of a man-of-war's boat. Being hooked, and having by this turn set his nose peremptorily down the stream, he flashed and whizzed away like a rocket. My situation partook of the nature of a surprize. Being on a rocky shore, and having a bad start, I lost ground at first considerably; but the reel sang out joyously, and yielded a liberal length of line, that saved me from the disgrace of being broke. I got on the best pace I was able, and was on good ground just as my line was nearly all run out. As the powerful animal darted through *Meg's Hole*, I was just able to step back and wind up a few yards of line; but he still went a killing pace, and when he came near Melrose Bridge he evinced a distressing preference for passing through the farther arch, in which case my line would have been cut by the pier. My heart sunk with apprehension, for he was near the opposite bank. Purdie seeing this, with great presence of mind took up some stones from the channel, and threw them one by one between the fish and the said opposite bank. This naturally brought Master Salmo somewhat nearer; but still for a few moments we had a doubtful struggle for it. At length, by lowering the head of the rod, and thus not having so much of the ponderous weight of the fish to encounter, I towed him a little sideways; and so advancing towards me with propitious fin, he shot through the arch nearest me.

Deeply immersed, I dashed after him as best I might; and arriving on the other side of the bridge I floundered out upon dry land, and continued the chase. The salmon, "right orgillous and presumptive," still kept the strength of the stream, and, abating nothing of his vigour, went swiftly down the *Whirls;* then through the *Boat shiel*, and over the shallows, till he came to the throat of the *Elm-wheel*, down which he darted amain. Owing to the bad ground, the pace here became exceedingly distressing. I contrived, however, to keep company with my fish, still doubtful of the result, till I came to the bottom of the long cast in question, when he still showed fight, and sought the shallows below. Unhappily the alders prevented my following by land, and I was compelled to take water again, which slackened my speed. But the stream soon expanding, and the current diminishing, my fish likewise travelled more slowly; so I gave a few sobs and recovered my wind a little, gathered up my line, and tried to bring him to terms. But he derided my efforts, and dashed off for another burst, triumphant. Not far below lay the rapids of the *Saughterford:* he would soon gain them at the pace he was going, that was certain;—see, he is there already! But I back out again on dry land, nothing loth, and have a fair race with him. Sore work it is. I am a pretty fair runner, as has often been testified; but his velocity is surprising. On, on,—still on he goes, ploughing up the water like a steamer. "Away with you, Charlie! Quick, quick, man,—quick for your life! Loosen the boat at the Cauld Pool, where we shall soon be." And so indeed we were, when I jumped into the said craft, still having good hold of my fish.

The Tweed is here broad and deep, and the salmon at length had become somewhat exhausted; he still kept in the strength of the stream, however, with his nose seawards, and hung heavily. At last he comes near the surface of the water. See how he shakes his tail and digs downwards, seeking the deep profound—that he will never gain. His motions become more short and feeble; he is evidently doomed, and his race well nigh finished. Drawn into the bare water, and not approving of the extended cleik, he makes another swift rush, and repeats this effort each time that he is towed to the shallows. At length he is cleiked in earnest, and hauled to shore : he proves one of the grey scull, newly run, and weighs somewhat above twenty pounds. The hook is not in his mouth, but in the outside of it ; in which case a fish being able to respire freely, always shows extraordinary vigour, and generally sets his head down the stream.

During the whole period of my experience in fishing, though I have had some sharp encounters, yet I never knew any sport equal to this. I am out of breath even now whenever I think of it. I will trouble any surveyor to measure the distance from the Kingswell Lees, the starting spot, above Melrose Bridge, to the end of the Cauld Pool, the death place, by Melrose Church, and to tell me how much less it is than a mile and three quarters,—I say I will trouble him to do so; and let him be a lover of the angle, that he may rather increase than diminish the distance, as in good feeling and respect for the craft it behoves him to do. I will likewise thank my contemporaries and posterity to bear in mind that the distance about to be measured by this able surveyor was run at an eclipse pace, always allowing for some slight abatement in speed pending our immersion.

Whilst I was taking a rest on the greensward, the heated face of my excellent new friend appeared through the alders. He could not, however, be fairly said to be in at the death ; the *coup de grace* having been already given about five minutes. He expressed the greatest astonishment at the swiftness and result of the race, and at the power of the fish, who had been able to distress two full-grown men so completely. He owned he was much excited, but thought fishing for salmon would be too turbulent an amusement for him; though perhaps he might have kept up with a good pony, had the ground been passable by such a beast. Poussin, Virgil, the Apennines, all were forgotten; and he began to enter warmly into the spirit of the present, and was curious to know by what particular tactics one can contrive to get the better of such a large furious monster, as he expressed it, with such apparently inadequate means, when a small sea trout broke *him* with all the ease imaginable. As I now reckoned upon his attention, I told him, as follows—how to manage a large salmon, and how a large salmon may manage us :—

"When you get hold of a *monstrum horrendum, ingens* of a fish, say of some five and forty pounds, you must anticipate a very long and severe battle. If, therefore, you have a disposable Gilly with you, despatch him instantly for some skilful fisherman, as well to assist you when you are exhausted with fatigue, as to bring your dinner and supper; not forgetting a dark lantern, that you may not be beaten by the shades of night,—a circumstance by no means improbable. At the first onset you will probably be obliged to keep your arms and rod aloft, in order to steer clear of the rocks. This action, with a heavy rod and large fish on your line, is very distressing, if continued even for a short time; and it will be necessary to repeat it often, if the channel is not very favourable; and in that case your muscles will ache insupportably, if they at all resemble those of other men. The easiest position, when it is safe to use it, is to place the butt of your rod against the stomach as a rest, and to bring the upper part of the arm and the elbow in close contact with the sides, putting on at the same time an air of determination. If your leviathan should be superlatively boisterous, no one knows what may happen. For instance, should you be in a boat, and he should shoot away down the river, you must follow rapidly; then, when he again turns upwards, what a clever fellow your fisherman must be, to stop a boat that has been going down a rapid stream at the rate of eight miles an hour, and bring it round all of a sudden in time to keep company with the fish, who has taken an upward direction! And what a clever fellow a piscator must be, if he can prevent twenty yards of his line, or more, from hanging loose in the stream! These sort of things will happen, and they are ticklish concerns. All I can do is to recommend caution and patience; and the better to encourage you in the exercise of these virtues, I will recount what happened to Duncan Grant in days of yore.

"First, you must understand that what is called 'preserving the river' was formerly unknown, and every one who chose to take a cast did so without let or hinderance.

"In pursuance of this custom, in the month of July, some thirty years ago, one Duncan Grant, a shoemaker by profession, who was more addicted to fishing than to his craft, went up the way from the village of Aberlour, in the north, to take a cast in some of the pools above Elchies Water. He had no great choice of tackle, as may be conceived; nothing, in fact, but what was useful, and scant supply of that.

"Duncan tried one or two pools without success, till he arrived at a very deep and rapid stream, facetiously termed '*the Mountebank:*' here he paused, as if meditating whether he should throw his line or not. 'She is very big,' said he to himself, 'but I'll try her; if I grip him he'll be worth the hauding.' He then fished it, a step and a throw, about half way down, when a heavy splash proclaimed that he had raised him, though he missed the fly. Going back a few paces, he came over him again, and hooked him. The first tug verified to Duncan his prognostication, that if he was there ' he would be worth the hauding;' but his tackle had thirty plies of hair next the fly, and he held fast, nothing daunted. Give and take went on with dubious advantage, the fish occasionally sulking. The thing at length became serious; and, after a succession of the same tactics. Duncan found himself at the Boat of Aberlour, seven hours after he had hooked his fish, the said fish fast under a stone, and himself completely tired. He had some thoughts of breaking his tackle and giving the thing up; but he finally hit upon an expedient to rest himself, and at the same time to guard against the surprise and consequence of a sudden movement of the fish.

"He laid himself down comfortably on the banks, the butt end of his rod in front; and most ingeniously drew out part of his line, which he held in his teeth. 'If

13

he rugs when I'm sleeping,' said he, ' I think I'll find him noo ;' and no doubt it is probable that he would. Accordingly, after a comfortable nap of three or four hours, Duncan was awoke by a most unceremonious tug at his jaws. In a moment he was on his feet, his rod well up, and the fish swattering down the stream. He followed as best he could, and was beginning to think of the rock at Craigellachie, when he found to his great relief that he could 'get a pull on him.' He had now comparatively easy work ; and exactly twelve hours after hooking him, he cleicked him at the head of Lord Fife's water : he weighed fifty-four pounds, Dutch, and had the tide lice upon him."

Thus Duncan Grant has instructed us how to manage a large Salmon. Let us now see how a large Salmon may manage us.

In the year 1815, Robert Kerse hooked a clean Salmon of about forty pounds in the Makerstoun Water, the largest, he says, he ever encountered : sair work he had with him for some hours ; till at last Rob, to use his own expression, was " clean dune out." He landed the fish, however, in the end, and laid him on the channel ; astonished, and rejoicing at his prodigious size, he called out to a man on the opposite bank of the river, who had been watching him for some time.

" Hey, man, sic a fish !"

He then went for a stone to fell him with ; but as soon as his back was turned, the fish began to wamble towards the water, and Kerse turned, and jumped upon it ; over they both tumbled, and they, line, hook, and all went into the Tweed. The fish was too much for

Rob, having broke the line, which got twisted round his leg, and made his escape, to his great disappointment and loss, for at the price clean Salmon were then selling, he could have got five pounds for it.

Thus you see how a large fish may manage us.

I must tell you that the above-mentioned Robert Kerse has long been a distinguished character on the Tweed. At a secluded spot, where the woods and rocks dip down to the margin of the river, and where its current is opposed by a rocky barrier through which it has worn its way in frightful gorges, the gaunt figure of auld Rob of the Troughs has been seen any time these forty years. He is very tall and bony, and when working his boat with the canting pole amongst the rapids, or looking down on the water from a jutting rock with his leister aloft ready to strike, he cuts a most formidable Salvator Rosa-like appearance. Rob is now highly seasoned with the saltness of time, being nearer eighty than seventy years old; drinks whisky like water, his native element; and to this day runs after the hounds, when they come near, like a boy of fifteen. He is a genuine lover of all sports, and has begot numerous sons and daughters: of the former four are gamekeepers, and fishermen on Tweed, Teviot, and Ettrick, to the Duke of Buccleuch, Lord Lothian, and Lord Home. They are remarkable as claiming a regular descent from Saxon ancestors in the most remote times, and are an active, athletic, clean-limbed race of men, keen of eye, and swift of foot, of good pluck, and altogether amphibious, loving the heather and mountain flood better than the street and servants' hall. Stalwart men would they have been in a Border Foray had they lived in the time of Johnny Armstrong. Such and so great are the Kerses; but they will not go down to posterity like the Purdies, "carent quia, Vate sacro;" neither could the old river god Rob himself contend with the otter so valiantly as Charlie Purdie. Whether it was that he had a sort of fellow-feeling for an animal that was amphibious like himself, and followed the same profession, or from what other cause I cannot say, but Rob did not particularly shine in a fair stand-up otter fight, as you shall hear.

In the latter end of September, 1839, Kerse had set a cairn net at the Clippers, "a little below Makerstoun House, but on the bank of the river opposite to it; and on going to the cairn to examine the net he saw a young otter sitting on, and entangled in it; he threw more of the net over it, whilst drawing it to the land, and when he had caught hold of the tail, and was carrying it off, a large otter which he described "as a she ane," five feet in length, jumped out of the water, ran up the bank after him, to use his own words, "like a mad bear," and commenced a furious attack upon him. Rob had nothing to defend himself with but his hat; and as he was holding the young one with one hand, he found he was likely to have the worst of it, and to be bitten by the one animal or the other. So he threw the whelp to the old one, saying, "Aye, ye she devil, he may get her, twac to ane is odds." They both swam away; that is, the two otters, not Kerse.

On looking after them he saw two other young ones

trying to make past the point of the cairn, which, owing to the strength of the current, they seemed unable to effect: Kerse thought he would try the thing again, so he laid hold of one of them, and pulled it out also by the tail. Scarce had he done this, and had begun to take to his heels, ere out again jumped the old one, and attacked him; but this time Rob had provided himself with a large stone, and hit the old beast on the back, when he again set off, and carried the young one with him, which was afterwards given to Lord John Scott. During the whole contest, says Rob, "the auld beast keepit squeeling, and makin' a noise something like a horse when he gi'es a snore."

How Charles Purdie contended with an otter will be seen hereafter.

CHAP. VIII.

> " Of Scotland well, the friers of Faill,
> The limmery lang hes lastit ;
> The monks of Melros' made gude kaill
> On Fridays when they fastit."

Spec. Godly Songs, page 87.

IN rambling by Tweedside, one never loses sight of the Eildon Hills, within many miles of Melrose, which, together with the river and abbey, are the dominant features of the country.

Of the legend touching them there are two versions: the poetical one given us in "The Lay of the Last Minstrel"—

> " And, warrior, I could say to thee
> The words that clove Eildon hills in three,"

comes, as all the world knows, from a very high authority ; and, besides being extremely probable in itself, has good classical conformity to the magician in Ariosto, who produced marvellous visions in the air which astounded the beholder ; but he having a glass given him by a more powerful enchanter, which enabled him to see things in their true semblance, saw only the magician sitting on a cloud, reading his book ; thus in both these cases wonderful things were done by cabalistical words, which art is called *Glamour.*

Now as to the Eildons, I do not exactly see what motive the wizard could have in cleaving them in three; I therefore rather lean to the story, which is still current in the country, especially as it is very circumstantial, and most agreeable to sober reason. It runs as follows :—

Old Michael Scott, the wizard, whose fame as a powerful magician had spread over most part of Europe* (the same alluded to as having cleft the Eildon Hills in three), was at continual feud with the holy monks of Old Melrose, and constantly playing his cantrips on them. They on their part were assiduous in using exorcisms, and such means as put Michael Scott's power in some danger; so the wizard resolved that they should not have the light of the sun during vespers, but that they should either abstain from them altogether, or be put to the expense of oil or candles.

To effect his purpose, he summoned a spirit or imp, or something very like a real devil, who was subject to his bidding, and for whom he was obliged to find constant employment.

Him he commanded to place a mountain to the west of the monastery, so as to intercept from it the rays of the setting sun. The imp being ingenious, and strong withal, looked around him, and found his affair in the Cheviot Hills. Thither he hied, and with an iron shovel, he took away from them at one scoop a

---

* " Quel' altro Michele Scoto fu, chi veramente
Delle magiche Frodi seppe il Gioco."   DANTE.

quantity sufficient to form one of the hills, which he deposited where he was commanded, and in two more journeys formed the other two hills, just as we see them now, only that they were bare of verdure. In his passage a part fell out of the shovel, which is now called Ruberslaw, which slovenly slip accounts for the inequality in point of size of the Eildons. At this slip Michael was exceeding wroth, and pursued his imp towards Tweedside, to punish him. The imp had a good start, and Michael lay rather out of his ground; when the evil spirit came to old Melrose: he saw a brave company of monks in the haugh, who had made a *kettle of fish,** and were carousing with goodly flagons of ale. It is said Thomas the Rhymer of Ercildoune was with them, and that the prior, who threw a long line, had been very successful with it that morning, having had good sport in the Gatcheugh streams, and caught two clean fish in the Holy-wheel, now called the Hally-wheel, a stream which he himself tabooed upon the same principle that the Italians write "Rispetto" on the walls—namely, to keep off intruders.

At the sight of so many pious men, the little imp skulked behind a tree, and Michael himself was taken aback, and ran cunning, making a cross cut over the peninsula, in order to come in upon the imp below; the latter being hardly pressed, made for the river, well knowing that his task-master was not only a bad boat-

---

* It is still a custom to make parties, and dress the salmon on the spot immediately after their capture, which is called *having a kettle of fish.*

A PRETTY KETTLE OF FISH

man, but that no enchantment could subsist in a running stream. Arrived there, he formed the scoop of his shovel into an iron boat, in which he sat and launched himself, using the handle as a rudder, round which he twisted his tail that he might steer with the greater nicety—*tali* auxilio—Michael forgetting, in the heat of his wrath, his impotence of enchantment in a river, got into a fisherman's boat above Dryburgh, and gave chase. Now, this boat being more buoyant than the imp's iron one, he gained fast upon him, and just got hold of his tail in a long reach above Mertoun, called ever after from that event " the *Doup Roads.*" As to whether the said usual appendage to a devil was greased or not, tradition has left us in ignorance ; but it eluded the grip, and the imp shot down a cauld, through so rapid a gorge, that the warlock hesitated to follow.

And now a new scene presented itself ; a third boat came sweeping under the scaurs in their rear, and joined the chase, its crew consisting of Thomas the Rhymer, and two zealous fathers, who pursued the wizard with bell, book, and candle ; and they would have ran into him a little below Craigover, but that he shot ashore; and then being on dry land, threw up by his art a bay behind him to obstruct their passage, and thus jocky* them ; but Thomas of Ercildoune, who was also a powerful magician, opened a passage on the south side of the river, and the monks only received a slight check. In the meantime Michael launched again ; but

* This spot still goes by the name of Jocky Bay, and is a good salmon cast.

the devil beat them all hollow at Little-Dean stream, which, being swift, rocky, and shallow, suited his style of navigation admirably. Now there was, and still is, a witch dwelling on the craigs near Makerstoun, at the *Corbie's Nest*, who, by a deception in magic called *glamour*, assumes the semblance of a crow. She was a sort of ally of Michael Scott, and flew forth, croaking her hoarsest and best upon the occasion. How far her power extended, and what she did, I have never heard; but certain it is that the wizard landed that his magic might have effect, and with or without her assistance, endeavoured to "bridle the Tweed with a curb of stone;" but his left foot insensibly touching the running stream, the work was imperfect and disunited, so that the whole volume of the river gushed through the rocks in gorges with such appalling violence, that neither he of Ercildoune or the Frati thought it prudent to follow.*

Michael now, seeing the pursuit after his familiar was vain on the water, remained ashore, and summoned another spirit who was subservient to him, in the shape of a coal-black horse, and springing on him, said, as was his custom, "Mount, Diabolus, and fly;" but he was scarcely firm in his seat before the little devil got down to sea, where he sunk his boat, and vanished to the bad place from whence he came. There is still a dan-

---

* These rocks are called the "troughs," or in Scotch, "trows," and are under the beautiful grounds of Makerstoun. A very active gentleman, who resides a few miles higher up the river, has in very low water leaped from rock to rock, and thus crossed the Tweed without wetting his feet.

gerous sandbank over the spot where this curious iron boat is deposited ; and, as the mode of dissipating shoals and blowing up sunken vessels is now well known, I trust some effort will be made, either by government or a joint-stock company, to recover this valuable curiosity.

Thus terminated a race, singular for the skill that was displayed under embarrassing circumstances, and wonderful as to the persons and powers that were engaged in it.

> " When next these *wights* go forth to *sail,*
> May I be there to see !"

CHAP. IX.

IF I were to write an account of half the poaching
stories that are common to all Salmon rivers, I should
produce a book, the dimensions of which would terrify
the public, even in this pen-compelling age.

In times when water bailiffs in Tweed had very small salaries, they themselves were by no means scrupulous about the observance of close time, but partook of the good things of the river in all seasons, lawful or unlawful. There is a man now, I believe, living at Selkirk, who in times of yore used certain little freedoms with the Tweed Act, which did not become the virtue of his office. As a water bailiff he was sworn to tell of all he saw; and indeed, as he said, it could not be expected that he should tell of what he did not see.

When his dinner was served up during close time, his wife usually brought to the table in the first place a platter of potatoes and a napkin; she then bound the latter over his eyes that nothing might offend his sight. This being done, the illegal salmon was brought in smoking hot, and he fell to, blindfolded as he was, like a conscientious water bailiff,—if you know what that is; nor was the napkin taken from his eyes till the fins and bones were removed from the room, and every visible evidence of a salmon having been there had completely vanished: thus he saw no illegal act committed, and went to give in his annual report at Cornhill with his idea of a clear conscience. This was going too near the wind, or rather the water; but what would you have?—the man was literal, and a great eater of Salmon from his youth.

People who are not water bailiffs have not always so delicate a conscience. Let us examine the style and bearing of such marauders as have fallen under our notice.

In the first place, there is your man with a pout net,

which resembles a landing net, only that it is very considerably larger, and is in shape only half of a circle ; with this he scoops out foul salmon during floods, when, from weakness, they are unable to stem the current, and get close under the banks. This he transacts very snugly, under pretence of taking trouts; so indeed he does, and welcome too, if he would stop there ; but this he is perfectly averse from.

Next in consequence comes your Triton, who walks the waters with a long implement in his hands, namely a leister, alias a waster ; with this weapon, "quocunque nomine gaudet," the said deity, quick of eye and ready of hand, forks out the poor fish that are spawning on the streams ; and this in close time. Vile, vile Triton !

Then comes your lawless band of black fishers, so called from their masks of black crape with which they disguise themselves : these men come forth in the darkness of the night to burn for salmon. When the winds are hushed, you may sometimes hear the dipping of oars and the clanking of a boat chain, and see at a distance a small light, like a glow-worm. In a little while the light blazes forth, and up rise a set of Othellos who are about to take a private benefit. These minions of the night are generally men of a desperate character, and it is not easy to collect water bailiffs sufficient in number or willing to encounter them ; but if water bailiffs would fight, how very picturesque the attack would be ! The rapids,—the blazing,—the leisters,—the combatants driven headlong into the river. Why, the battle of Constantine and Maxentius, and the affair of the bridge, as seen in the famous fresco, would be nothing to it. The only thing I should apprehend would be, that the bailiffs would eventually sport Marc Antony and run.

In contradistinction to these illuminati comes your plausible poacher, a sort of river sneak. This man sallies forth with apparent innocence of purpose; he switches the water with a trout-rod, and ambulates the shore with a small basket at his back, indicative of humble pretensions; but has a pocket in his jacket that extends the whole breadth of the skirts. He is trouting, forsooth; but ever and anon, as he comes to a salmon-cast, he changes his fly, and has a go at the nobler animal. If he hooks a salmon, he looks on each side with the tail of his eye to guard against a surprise; and if he sees any danger of discovery from the advance of the foeman, he breaks his line, leaves the fly in the fish's mouth, and substitutes a trout one;— said fish swims away, and does not appear in evidence.

I once came upon one of these innocents, who had hold of a salmon with his trout-rod in a cast a little above Melrose bridge, called " *The Quarry Stream.*" He did not see me, for I was in the copsewood on the summit of the bank immediately behind him. I could have pounced upon him at once, I and my fisherman. Did I do so? I tell you, no. He would have broken his line as above, and have lost the fish; and I wanted a salmon, for it is a delicate animal, and was particularly scarce at that time.

So I desired Charlie to lie down amongst the bushes, and not to stir till the fish was fairly landed, and was in the capacious pocket, which has already been described. Then I counselled him to give chase, and harry the possessor. Judging, however, that if the man crossed the river at the ford a little below, which he was very likely to do, that he would have so much law of Charlie before he could descend the steep brae, that he might escape: I drew back cautiously, got into the road out of sight, and passed over Melrose bridge, taking care to bend my body so as to keep it out of sight behind the parapet; I then lay concealed amongst the firs in the opposite bank. Thus we had Master Sneak between us. I was at some distance from the scene of action to be sure, and somewhat in the rear, as I could advance no further under cover; but I had the upper ground, and was tolerably swift of foot in those days, which gave me confidence. I took out my pocket glass, and eyed my man. He was no novice: but worked his fish with great skill. At length he drew him on the shore, and gave him a settler with a rap of a stone on the back of his head; he then, honest man, pryed around him with great circumspection, and seeing no one, he took the salmon by the tail, and, full of internal contentment, deposited it in his well-contrived pocket: he then waded across to the south side of the river, with an intention, as it seemed, of revisiting his household gods and having a broil.

Charlie now arose from his lair, and scrambled down the steep. The alarm was given, but he of the salmon had a good start, with the river between him and his pursuer. So he stopped for a moment on the haugh to make out what was going forward on all sides, much after the fashion of an old hare, who runs a certain distance when she apprehends any thing personal, then rests for a moment or two, and shifts her ears in order to collect the news from all quarters of the compass. Even so did our friend, and having satisfied himself that he was a favoured object of attraction, he was coy, and took to flight incontinently; I now sprang up from the firs, the game being fairly afoot, and kept the upper ground. The pursuit became close and hot, but as the fugitive, like Johnny Gilpin, carried weight, I soon closed with him.

"You seem in a hurry, my good friend; your business must be pressing. What makes you run so?"

"Did ye no see that bogle there by the quarry stream, that garred me rin this gait, haud on for yer lives, sirs, for if he overtakes us, we are deid men."

"Why, the truth is, Sandy, that I do not choose to haud on at present, because I came forth in quest of a bonny salmon, and cannot go home without one; could you not help me to such a thing?"

At this Sandy took a pinch of snuff from his mull, and seeing my eyes fixed upon the length and protuberance of his pocket, answered quaintly enough,—

"Aye, that can I, and right glad am I to do ye a favour, ye shall no want for a salmon whilst I have one."

So saying, he pulled forth a ten pounder, which occupied all the lower regions of his jacket. "How the beast got here," said he, as he extracted him gradually, "I dinna ken, but I am thinking that he must have louped intill my pocket, as I war wading the river."

"Nothing more likely, and I will admit him to have done so for once, but, mark me, I will not admit of any salmon doing so in future without my permission in

14

writing.   You have been trouting, it seems, pray what sort of a fly do you use?"

"Whiles I use a wee ane, and while a muckle flee, ane for rough and deep water, and the ither for shallow streams.   That is the way to trout, both in loch and river."

"True! I see you have some bonny little flies in your hat; take it off carefully, Purdie—you understand me,—and let me admire them."

Charlie advances, and taking off the man's hat with great care so as to keep the crown undermost, he pulls out from the inside six well tied salmon flies of the most approved colours, which he transferred to his own pocket.   I actually saw "*Meg with the muckle mouth*" amongst them.

"Aye, ye are as welcome to the flees as ye are to the sawmont, and I am proud to do ye a good turn at ony gait."

"Well now, bear in mind, that I will never permit you to throw a fly wee or muckle in the Pavilion-water again; and if you darken the shores with your presence a second time, I will have you up at Melrose."

"I'm thinking I shall tak' your advice, for ye seem a sensible chiel.   Will ye accept of a pinch of snuff?"

"Good morning, good morning, get home to Selkirk as quick as ye can; we know ye well for a souter of that town.   Run, run, the bogle is after you!"

"Run, aye that will I, and the deil tak' the hindmost," said he, and off he went at his best pace; leaving this blessing and the salmon to solace us.

Perhaps I shall best give a general idea of what was

going on formerly in close time by a recitation of the
confessions of my departed friend Thomas Purdie ; and
let it be borne in mind in his behalf, that at the time
of his cantrips salmon were not valuable, and, consequently, little cared for, so no great harm was done ;
but it is clear from his own showing, that Tom in his
early days was a sort of *Donald Cuird*, for he had no
right to be " bleezing up," where he did.

For the better understanding of his narrative, I shall
give a description of the clodding, or throwing leister,
or waster, as he was used to term it, the instrument
with which he performed his sleights. It differs ma-
terially from the one in common use ; a description of
which latter will be given hereafter.

This throwing leister is used chiefly on the upper
parts of the Tweed, and its tributary streams, where
the water is not deep. The spear has five prongs of
unequal, but regularly graduated, length. Those which
are nearest the fisherman, and which come to the ground
first in throwing being the shortest. The entire iron
frame of the spear is double the weight of that in common use. An iron hoop is bound round the top of the
pole, as a counterbalancing weight ; and the pole itself
has a slight curve, the convex part being the outermost
in throwing: a rope made of goats' hair, called " the
lyams," is fastened to the top bar of the spear just above
the shortest prong ; this rope is about twelve yards
long, and is tied to the arm of the thrower. The spear
is cast like a javelin ; and, if thrown by a skilful hand,
the top of the shaft, after it has pierced the fish, falls
beyond the vertical point towards the opposite bank of

the river; then the fish is pulled to land by means of the aforesaid rope or lyams, so that there is little chance of his escaping in his struggles for freedom.

The accompanying engraving represents the iron of the clodding waster; that in general use will be given hereafter.

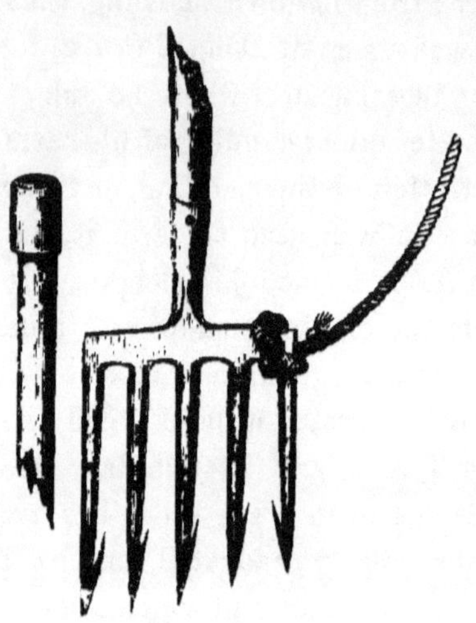

Now for Tom Purdie. I should miss the nice points of his character were I to deprive him of his own peculiar way of communicating his feats, though it is but too true, that when he got upon a favourite sub-ject, he was most inhumanly elastic.

TOM PURDIE'S MUCKLE FISH.

" While I was with Mr. Anderson, and shepherd at West Bold, one Sunday," says Tom, "I didna go up to Traquair to the kirk, but took a walk by the river side: there were a vast o' fish in the water, and I saw ane or twae great roeners turning, a sure sign there

were mickle kippers too. I had dandered down too
near the burn fit, and had a pair of good stilts aye
lying there. My first wife was then a lass, and lived
at Caberston ; and the stilts were ready to cross the
water at an orra time. I took a thought that I would
like to see what was steering on Caberston throat ; and
sae I lap on the stilts, and went through at the rack ;
and when I was on the other side, I thought I might
as weel tak' a keek at the *throat*. I keepit weel aff
the water-side, until I was down aneth where the fish
began to work. I ken'd by a clour in the water a gey
bit afore me, that there was a big redd there, and drew
cannily forrit. 'Odd, sir, my vera heart lap to my
mouth when I gat the glisk o' something mair like a
red stirk than ought else muve aff the redd, and hallans
down the water and make for the south side. I fand
my hair creep on my head. I minded it was the Sabbath, and I should not ha'e been there. It might be a
delusion o' the enemy, if it wasna the deil himsel'. I
stuid and considered. I had never seen the deil i' daylight ; and, forbye, there was just then a great brown
rowaner slade aff the redd after him. If it was the
deil, what could he be doin' wi' the rowaner ? The
water was breast deep at the least ; it might be a fish
after a', and I had heard the auld folk speak o' vera
muckle anes. I lookit up the brae to the toun. Peggy
aiblins hadna likit my hankering aboot the throat *on
sic a day* and she had slippit into the house, and didna
come oot again. Sae when I saw it was sae, I held up
the water side for my stilts, keepin' for a' that an e'e to
the redds. Heaven forgi'e me ! I never saw sic a water

o' fish! If it wasna the deil I had seen, I was sure he wasna far aff. I saw eneuch to tempt a better man than me; and I began to think I had better be at hame reading a chapter o' the guid book, if no a leaf or twae o' 'The Fourfold State;' sae I took the stilts and cam' through again by the rack, and wan hame just a wee thought afore the master and the mistress, honest woman! cam' hame thrae the kirk. I haflins wist I had been there too;—but yet I was only lookin' at the warks o' the creation, and couldna say I had done ony great wrang; an' if I hadna seen Peggy come oot o' the byre at Caberston, I aiblins hadna stiltit the water after a'. But I fand I couldna read a styme; for, dae as I micht, I couldna get the appearance that I had seen oot o' my mind; an' yet whan I consider'd aboot *the mickle rowaner*, that I was sure eneugh was a yeithly thing, I couldna help believing that it was, after a', a fish I had seen; but I never saw sic another.

"Weel, a' the time the master was at the readin', I couldna keep the glisk o' the awesome mickle fish oot o' my heid, and whan we raise thrae the prayers, I popit the shouther o' the nowtherd callant, and said quietly, 'Sandy, if I raise ye aboot twal o'clock, ye needna wonder; sleep as fast as ye can till than, an' tak' nae notice to Jamie when ye rise.' I had aft ta'en this lad wi' me afore to haud the licht; for he was a stout loon o' his age, and could haud a licht weel enough: having a natural cast rather bye common for a kin-kind o' mischief an' ploys, an', I believe, was sound asleep in five minutes.

"As for mysel', I need hardly say I never steckit an e'e. I ken'd fu' weel, that if we warna at Queedside by the first o' the Monanday morning, the hempies oot o' twae or three o' the touns o' the north side o' the water wad be bleezin' up afore us; and some *devilrie* cam' o'er the cock that sat on the byre balks aside us, for he never miss'd to skirl every ten minutes thrae the time I lay doun; sae I was as aften grapin' the hands o' my watch, which I had gotten in a coup thrae Geordie Matheson three weeks afore.

"At last, whan I had a guid guess it was drawin' near to twal o'clock, an' nae fear o' breakin' the Sabbath, I gat up an' shook Sandy by the shouther, wha was oot o' bed in a giffy. We went to the barn, an' tied up twae prime heather lichts, frae a bunch or twae, which I had gae'd the miller lad to dry on the kiln ten days afore. They may talk o' *ruffies* and birk bark baith, but gi'e me a good heather licht, weel dried on the kiln, for a throat o' the Queed. However, I got the lichts on my back, Sandie carried a weel-dried *bairdie*, an' I took in my hand my cloddin' waster. I had gi'en the Runches o' Yarrowford seven white shillings for her; but nane could make a waster wi' the Runches,* nor track an *otter* either; they had clean the best terriers in the hale country side; and they

---

* The Runches (Runcimans) of Yarrowford were two celebrated smiths, probably brought to Selkirkshire by Murray of Philiphaugh. They were famous for a peculiar art in tempering edge tools. Their otter hounds and terriers also were capital. Singular stories were told of their sagacity. Rob Runchy as a forlorn hope, once threw his clodding leister at a drowning man floating down the Yarrow in a high flood, and hauled him out with the lyams unharmed.

had an art o' their ain in temperin' the taes o' a waster that they took to the grave wi' them. I could ha'e thrawn mine aff the heid of a scaur; an' if she had stracken a whinstane rock, she wad ha'e been nae mair blunted than gif I had thrawn her on a haystack.

"On oor way to the water, I was nae little fashed wi' the unsonsie callant blowin' up the bairdie every now and than, to mak' sure that it wasna oot, an' I had ance or twice to shake him by the neck, for I wasna sure that the Gabberston folk—wha were aye devilish yaap when there war mony fish in the water —mightna be lying at the side of the throat, ready to blaw up when it passed twal o'clock; and guid truly, if they had gotten a blink o' oor bairdie, they wad ha'e ta'en that instead o' the hour. At any rate, there was little use in warnin' a' the north side o' the water that Tam Purdie was gaun oot to the fishin'; an', to tell the truth, the Sabbath-day was little mair than owre.

"But some had clippit the wings o' the Sabbath closer than us after a'; I saw the twinkle of a coal every now and then comin' doun Caberston peat-road, an' I weel ken'd it was jist the Sandersons o' Priesthope bent for the same place wi' oursel's. It was ill bein' afore them on a Monanday morning wi' fair play, when the water was in good trim. Faith I lost nae time when I saw the twinkle o' their peat-coal (there was nae strae for bairdies at Priesthope) in tying the lights on the callant's back and thrawing him, and the clod-waster on my shouther and stilting the water as I had done in the daylight. I kent fu' weel the place where

the big redd was, and blew up about thirty step below,
sae that the light might be at the best when we came
fornent it. Sandy held the light weel: his een were
glenting in his head wi' eagerness; and just when we
cam' to the tail o' the redd, I saw the muckle kipper
lyin' like a flain wedder. I had, as I thought, the advantage on my side, for the brae was three or four
feet aboun the water, and I strack him wi' a' my pith.
Whether the mid grain had stracken him on the back
lin, I took nae time then to consider; but the fourteen
pund waster stottit off his back as if he had been a
a bag o' wool.

"A cauld sweet cam' owre me, an' I believe every hair
on my body crap. I was dead sure it was the *deil
himsel'* that had been permitted to throw himsel' in
my way for breaking the Sabbath! For I had begun
to tie up the lights as soon as I shook up the callant;
an' it was hardly twal o'clock. I pu'd the burnin'
licht out o' his hand, and dash'd it in the Queed, threw
him on my back as fast as I could, an' was hardly able
to stilt the water again for vera dread.

"I needna say we were soon in our beds; and I took
the callant in aside me, for he was to the full as feard,
poor fellow, as I was,—an' mair. For when I got
time, an' turn'd calm enough to consider, I began to
see it couldna weel be *auld clootie*, for I could mind o'
seein' the vera een, an' gib an' teeth and the gapin'
mouth o' the kipper. And by and by, I cam' to be
certain sure it was neither mair nor less than the big
monster I had seen i' daylight. Sae wi' that settle-
ment there cam' the question : how could I get another

chance ?   A weel, I lay still till just afore sky-break, which I kent baith by my watch, and the cock that had been through the night as quiet as the kye aneath him. I waken'd Sandie wi' muckle ado this time, and he had nae grit broo' o' the business; but, however, be that as it may, we tied up another light and set off again. But there was still a hankering i' the callant's mind anent ga'in' back to the same place, where he had gotten sic a fleg.   He was like a colt that has been scar'd wi' a grey stane, an's no willing to venture back to see that it's nae bogle. 'But is ye *sure*, Tam, it wasna the deil ?' '*Deil a bit* o' Satan *it was*, Sandie, ma man,' says I, ' for I saw him afore you ; an' the deil darena show himsel' in daylight on sic a day.'   Weel, we gat through the Queed again, an' kindled up the auld place. When we cam' up to the muckle redd, the fiend a haet was there but twae or three rowangatherers whidden about ; sae we cam' up the water-side for the light was only at the best, when, gonshens ! there was the great brute o' a kipper, that, when he had gotten a glint o' the light, had minded the dunt he got on the back, an' was glidin' up the side o' the water within three step o' the channel.   I scraucht to Sandie to haud up the light, and keepin' clear o' the back fin this time, I strack him atween the back fin an' the gills, at the same time shakin' the lyams off my arm.   Peace be here ! if he didna stem the throat four feet deep wi' the waster sticking straight up in his back as if he never fand it, wi' the lyams about him !   I durstna draw, however. I had nae fear o' their breaking, for they were spun of the hair o' the grey auld buck that gaed for mony years on the Plora craig;* but had I pu'd at the lyams, the kipper behooved to turn, an' he might ha' ta'en down the throat tap water, an' I wad ha' lost my waster an' lyams, or pu'd it out o' his back. That I had nae mind to do.

"I never was fear'd for drownin' in my life; at ony rate never in the Queed. I strack into the water breast deep, an' wonder sin' syne how I keepit my feet; but I had on a pair o' guid cloutit shoon. The kipper tired o' the trade o' gaun against the strength o' the throat, an' tralin' the lyams, turned down the deep side of the water atween me an' the brae. I got haud o' the shaft o' the waster, but to try to grund him was needless, sae I keepit down the shank, an' that made the force o' the water raise the fish to the tap, an' I push'd him to the side, following as I best could, an' pressed him to the brae, when I lifted him out. Wi' the help o' Sandie (who had, when he saw the blood, gotten rid o' his fear o' the deil), I carried him to the head o' the rack, and when I got him on my back, my certie I was a massy man! I was aye vext I didna weigh him, but my belief was he was forty guid pounds, Dutch weight. As I waded the water wi' him, leadin' Sandie by the hand, his neb was above my head, an' his tail plash'd in the water on my heels.

---

* I know not the derivation of *lyams;* the word is only used, as far as I know, to denote a small twisted rope usually made of goats' hair, for the sake of elasticity, and fastened to the bow of the clodding leister: it is coiled on the left arm at the other end in such a manner as to go freely off when the leister is thrown. Jamieson in his Dictionary derives the word from the French *lien.*

" My father was than miller o' Bold Milln, an' I took him down to be reisted in the kiln; but we were a' sae thrang wi' talkin' about his size, that we forgot to lay him on the broads, and that, as I was sayin', vexes me to this day."

GLOSSARY.

Clour—a heaving up of the water.
Hallans—slanting.
Thrae—from.
Haflins—partly.
Styme—none at all, in the least.
Popit—tapped.
Steekit—closed.
Hempies—scamps—rogues.
Balks—cross beams.
Skirl—crow.
Coup—a swap.
Ruffies—old pieces of tarred sacking.
Bairdie—a straw rope to keep the light in.
Yaap—alert.
Flain—flayed.
Broo—liking.
Rowangatherers—meaning trout.
Massy—proud.
Meal stone—containing 16 pounds.
Reisted—dried.
Broads—scales.
Lyams—rope of horse-hair used with the throwing leister.

CHAP. X.

> " And doun the stream, like Levin's gleam,
>   The fleggit salmond flew ;
>   The ottar ynap his pray let drap,
>   And to his hiddils drew."
>
> *Border Minstrelsy.*

WHILST the Pavilion* was getting ready for my reception, I took up my quarters at an inn at Melrose, and, at my instigation, Mr. Tintern came there also, and thus we soon got intimate. The river had been falling in for some time, and was now too low for fly-fishing ; and as the sky had lately been pretty clear, and as the evening promised a calm and sunny day for the morrow, I promised to show him the manner in which we speared salmon by the light of the sun, should the weather prove as good as I anticipated.

My expectations for the time, at least, were fulfilled ; for on waking I found the whole expanse of heaven serene and glowing ; not a cloud to be seen ; not a breath of air to ruffle the water ; so I sent to awaken my companion. Breakfast was prepared, but no Mr.

---

* Having often mentioned the Pavilion Water, I should have explained before that it belongs to Lord Somerville ; and I have thus called it from the name of his house, which I rented for some years, and which is about two miles up the river from Melrose. The chief scene of my operations, however, was some miles lower down the river from Dryburgh, as far as Makerstoun.

Tintern. A little while after I heard a languid voice say, "Want some hot water." A quarter of an hour elapsed, when I heard the same words again; after about a similar interval of time I heard, "Want a stocking;" and then, after a long pause, "Want a stocking" again. I was out of all patience; so I went up to entreat the man of wants to use more expedition, as we were losing a very fine morning.

I did not find him in his room, but sitting down half dressed on the upper stair near it, looking at his sketch-book. He had not shaved, as his hint for hot water, having been uttered in a mild tone, had not been taken. He did not so much care about shaving, he said, but he could not go out with only one stocking on, and he could not find the other, and unluckily he had sent his dirty ones to be washed. It certainly was true that one of his legs was bare; and, after a fruitless hunt, we had nothing left for it but to send into the town and buy a fresh pair. After they arrived, however, he discovered that there was no particular necessity for such a step, as he had favoured one leg at the expense of the other, by putting *both* stockings on it.

I had already breakfasted, and my impatience increased; so it was agreed that my friend should take our host's little pony, and join me above Melrose Bridge. When I got to the spot, Tom Purdie, who was usually very forward on these occasions, was not arrived; but I descried Mr. Tintern at a distance, not upon the inn-keeper's pony, but walking down hill; and I went to meet him that he might not miss us at the river. I came up to him precisely at the turnpike by Newton, and overheard the following little dialogue between him and the turnpike woman :—

" Here's twopence for you, good woman."

" What for do ye gi'e me this ?"

" Why, for my horse, to be sure."

" And whar may your horse be ?"

" Where ? why here, behind me, my good dame."

" It must be a gey piece ahint then, I'm thinking, for I canna see the beast."

At this he began to pull the bridle rein which he had in his hand, and, upon finding it very particularly obedient, he looked round and found, true enough, that the pony whom he fancied he had been leading down hill, and was at the end of the said bridle, had slipped out his head, and trotted back the way he came. At this incident, he seemed almost as much amused as we were; though I thought I saw a lurking appearance of distress in his countenance, too, as having further to walk than he had bargained for.

Let us now see what the fishermen were doing. Charles Purdie and Thomas Jamieson, whilst sitting on a rock by the water-side, at length descried Tom Purdie making up to them with his leister.

" Well, Tom," said Jamieson, " I never knew ye keep ahint afore, when there was any wark for the leister. What makes ye so late, man ?"

" Why, I couldna get awa' from Abbotsford; there was a gentleman wi' Sir Walter; but wha he was I dinna ken, but I think he was English. Sir Walter gaed out to tak' a walk, and cried to me to follow him. When we war juist gaen up near to the turn before we cum to the Boor,* *Pepper* and *Finnet* were hunting the woods, and Maida was gaen ahint us ; and, to my great astonishment, when I lookit a wee piece among the trees, DI, who was wi' me, war standing, and pit out her muckle tail like the handle of a cleik. Or ever I wishes, out gets a dirty beast of a hare, and bangs right on to the walk afore us. Sir Walter and the other man war going side by side ; or over I kent, *Maida* pit his muckle nose past me, when *Pepper* barkit and set up his great lugs ; and as the gentleman walked rather wide at the knee, he saw the hare through atween his legs, and made a great brush all at aince, and lifted him off his feet. The gentleman, thinking he was going to fa', cotched a firm grip o' Maida's rough hair as he sat stride legs on his back. Maida wanted to follow Pepper, and ran awa' wi' him aboot thirty yards, when he coupit him off, and he fell owre the brae among the bushes on the under side o' the walk ; and Sir Walter gie a laugh ; and I couldna behave mysel' ava, for I was nearly fawd doun wi' laughing too. Hey, man, I never was so takken by the face in aw my life ; and when the gentleman got up, his breeks were riven at the knee ; and when he cam' out from among the bushes, he lookit sae soor, that Sir Walter turned round and flate on me for laughing ; but if I was to dee for it, I couldna help it ; and Sir Walter turned his back to the gentleman and laughed himsel', juist as bad as me ; but the gentleman never laughed a bit. Aweel, we turned to gang hame again, and a' the way doun the walk the

---

* A moss house or rustic seat.

gentleman he keepit looking at Maida, and when he got to Abbotsford, he ordered his carriage and gaed awa."

" Well, that was better sport than we are likely to have to-day, Tom, for the clouds are beginning to rise, and the wind is getting up; more's the pity, for it was the finest morning I ever saw, and now we are late, and have lost twae hours. But here comes the maister and the strange gentleman with him, he that does not know a fish from a cow, and who was broke by ane of thae whitlings."

The little party being now entirely assembled, agreed that, as the day was beginning to alter, it was a pity to disturb the water till they saw clearly how it would turn out; so the fishermen remained with the boats and leisters at Craigover boat-hole: and, in the meantime, I, Harry Otter, thought I could not do better than explain the operation of sunning to my friend Mr. Tintern, as there was now some chance of gaining his attention; so we sat down, and I commenced as follows :—

Sunning, as I have told you, is a mode of taking salmon with a spear by sun light; and vast numbers are captured in this manner, particularly in the upper part of the Tweed, where fish are more easily seen than in the lower, from the comparative shallowness of the water in which they lie.

This sport does not begin till the river is quite low and clean, and useless for the fly. To succeed perfectly requires a bright and calm day. You cannot see a fish lying even at a very moderate depth when the surface

15

of the water is ruffled by the wind. As soon as the river is thus fairly in order, take the first good day that occurs; you may not have many more; and if you have, you will not mend the matter by waiting too long, as after a continuance of hot weather a green vegetable substance rises from the bottom, which lessens the transparency of the water.

If you have a man sufficiently clever with the leister, let him stand in the water at the head of the stream whilst you are trying below, that he may strike the fish which endeavour to pass out of it into another cast. If you have no such man, and there are very few who can see a fish pass up a rapid gorge, you may hang a net in the stream; but you must not bar the river by stretching it quite across, as that is illegal. If you sun a large pool where there is deep water, and various runs and eddies in it, it is advisable to place nets in such situations as are most favourable for fish to strike into when they are disturbed by the boats, and the other means in use for frightening them. The pass being thus in part secured and all prepared, the next thing is to rout about, and endeavour to frighten the fish by every means in your power, so that they may hide themselves under the rocks and stones, or even lie, as they sometimes do, half stupified beside them, when you may strike them with the leister. To effect this, it is usual to begin by rowing your boat or boats over the pool with some white object hanging in the water from the stern: the skulls of horses are in high repute for this service; and I dare say a stuffed otter would be excellent, though I never tried it.

When you think you have created sufficient terror
by these means, you may look about for the fish, and
the sport begins. You may manage your boat with
the leister, as in burning by night, of which hereafter :
but you do not, as in that case, necessarily work her
broadside in front; and one artist is sufficient for the
amusement, though more may partake of it. If the
leisterer knows the water well, he puts the boat gently
over the rocks and stones, where the fish endeavour to
conceal themselves. Sometimes they get under a large
stone and are entirely hidden; generally they are
partially concealed under smaller stones, part of the
body and tail only being seen; so that it requires some
dexterity to strike them properly, or indeed at all.
Some will lie under the shelf of a rock quite open to
the view; in which case you must be careful, when
you strike, that a prong of the leister does not rest upon
the ledge of a rock above, instead of on the salmon.
Others I have seen lying fair and open in the bare
channel; but these will not lie to the leister so well as
those in the situations I have mentioned. If you do
not strike a fish near the centre of his body, you are
never very sure of lifting him. The late Staffa, before
he came to his title, was once sunning the Pavilion-
water with John Lord Somerville, and perceiving that
the fisherman in their boat had struck a salmon that
was likely to get off the spear when he might attempt
to lift him; in the true spirit of a Highlander, and
without saying a word to any one, plunged at once into
the Tweed with his clothes on, dived down to the fish,
and brought him into the boat with his hands. "A

Highlander can never pass a seal, a deer, or a salmon, without having a trial of skill with him."

To take a fish whose tail alone is seen projecting from the hiding place, provide yourself with a small steel harpoon, the barbs of which shut into the shaft when the point enters and makes the wound, but which spread laterally when you pull it back; tie a line of small whip-cord to this weapon, and fix the butt of the harpoon itself in the point of a rude rod made for the purpose. You may then push it into the tail of the fish, when the little spear will come from the rod; and you may pull out your salmon with the line attached to it.

There are some very large stones in the Tweed, sometimes two or three lying together, under which salmon can totally conceal themselves; but you will easily discover if there are any underneath them by the air-bubbles which they cast up to the surface of the water when you poke with your leister shaft. My method of taking these fish was to throw a casting net over the stone or stones that concealed them, and then to poke them out with the pole of the leister. The net should be strong, or they will swim clean through it, as if it were a cobweb; in throwing the net, you must cast above the hiding stone, allowing for the current, which will take it down some little distance before it sinks to the bottom, according to the depth and strength of the water. Of course this method may also apply to fish *partially* concealed.

In sunning, as in burning, begin at the lower part of the river that belongs to you, so that you may again come across those fish that escape upwards, and may not go beyond your water; and you will have a more successful day of it, if you wait till your neighbour below has sunned his water. If the river continues low for some time, disturbed fish will be continually coming forward, and you may go over your water two or three times at different periods, till you have caught nearly every fish that takes up his seat in it.

If a salmon gets off your leister wounded, being weak, you may be sure he will go down the river; and the eels will come out instantly, if it be hot weather, and follow the blood: if the fish is badly wounded, although not dead, the said eels will soon settle the matter, and eat out his flesh, leaving the skin alone for speculators to make mermaids with.* You will see the eels by dozens hanging thick on him like the sticks in a bundle of faggots; but they are too small to be taken with a salmon spear, and do not resemble the fine silver eels in the Kennet and some of our English streams, but are browner in colour, and have large heads. The Scotch have a strong antipathy to them, and never use them for food. But they should be removed from the river if possible, as they make great havoc in the spawning beds.

This information having been briefly given, Mr. Tintern went up the river with his fishing-rod, as the sky was not yet clear enough for the main sport: after

---

* Some people will remember an exhibition of this sort many years ago in St. James's Street, in London. It was very ingeniously constructed, though far from alluring. It was placed under a glass, and created some sensation amongst the naturalists, as mermaids ought to do.

having absented himself for a considerable time, he returned to the party with a fish, which, being too large for his basket, he held with his handkerchief, a corner of which he had passed through the gills. This fish he lifted up before Tom Purdie, with an air of success that I never saw him assume before, saying, "Now, Mr. Purdie, I have conquered a sea-trout at last, and here he is!"

Tom was all aghast, for before the fish was laid on the ground he thought he saw what he called "a very nice new-swoomed gilse;" but, upon a closer inspection, his practised eye soon descried the difference; for it was a real river trout, of above four pounds weight, and unusually bright in colour. Tom turned him over and viewed the other side, then turned him over again, and viewed both sides with great seeming interest; he then examined his teeth and gills, and uttered a short groan; pulling out his snuff-box from his pocket, and having solaced himself with a pinch, he took a still more minute survey, looking alternately at the fish and Mr. Tintern: at length, casting a reproachful glance at the animal, he said, pithily, "Od, and to be ta'en by the like o' him!"

The sky was now clear again, and the wind, which had only been brought on by a few rising clouds, had subsided. Mr. Tintern, however, being too good-humoured to take Purdie's sarcasm to heart, was so charmed with his success that he would not join the leisterers, but preferred fishing with the fly; at the same time he delicately hinted to me, that he thought there was something a little sanguinary in the use of such a

SUNNING AT CRAIGOVER.

weapon, though he owned that the invariable custom of knocking the fish on the head immediately they were lifted made their sufferings very short, and certainly, he thought, not exceeding those of sheep and other animals in the way they are commonly killed for the table.

He then seceded, and I promised to join him at Melrose. We went over the *Webbs*, and Craigover boat-hole, setting nets and using various devices to make the fish conceal themselves, in the way that has been mentioned above. Upon the whole, we were tolerably successful; but having already described the process of sunning, and being of a compassionate disposition, I will trouble no one with a relation of the particulars of our transactions, especially as I mean to give a flaming description of what is called " burning the water " towards the end of these pages.

I went home from Mertoun by Melrose Abbey, to take Mr. Tintern along with me, according to agreement. As he was in the habit of fishing and sketching alternately, I surmised he would establish himself in the churchyard, and fall to work with his crayons: nor was I deceived; for when I came to the wicket gate, I descried him very busy indeed; whilst a corpulent little gentleman in a snuff-coloured coat, with a cane in his hand, was looking over his shoulder. As I thought some amusing contrast of character would take place, I listened to what was going on; in fact, the little man's gestures were so grotesque that I was willing to enjoy them as long as possible. He would stand still and look over the artist's paper with a scrutinising expression; then he would draw back a little, and stamp his cane on the ground with all the force and dignity of a bailie.   In the meantime our friend was so absorbed in his work that he seemed wholly unconscious of this person's presence, till he was aroused by the little man himself, who said, in a loud tone, and with an air of consummate consequence, stamping a tombstone at the same time with his staff of office,—

"Weel, friend, what may ye be doing here?"

Tintern, looking back over his shoulder, said, in his absent manner,—"I think he must have been buried at the eastern end of the Abbey; am I right, my good sir?"

"Aye, aye—I thought so,—I ken weel eneuch what ye're after; ye are ane o' thae chiels that gang aboot to raise the dead bodies o' the departed corpses;—Od, that's a guid ane!"

Tintern (still sketching, and speaking abstractedly), "I'd give something to see old Michael Scott's tomb."

"Nae doot ye would; but I'll tak' guid tent to hae a sure hand or twae to watch yer howking tricks the nicht."

So saying, "the little round fat oily man" marched off with great dignity, muttering, "Od, that's a guid ane! disturbing the dead bodies o' the corpses! He shall gang afore the Sherra'."

It seems my unlucky friend was doomed to a continued interruption of his studies; for no sooner had the man in office departed than some old women came and stood over him for a very considerable time, and occasionally interrupted his view; one of them at length said pithily to her companions,—"Hech, sirs, this is idle wark! let's awa' to the praaties."

Such interruptions, though trivial in themselves, are sometimes a little troublesome to a studious man, and happy had it been for Mr. Tintern had he met with no other; but in a short time afterwards the churchyard was full of all the idle boys in the town, who fairly hooted him, and compelled him to leave the place, which he did under the best protection I was able to afford him. He called them "naughty boys," and they shouted amain, "Corpse lifter! corpse lifter!" having been previously so instructed, as may readily be guessed.

This disagreeable attack annoyed Mr. Tintern so seriously, that he resolved to leave Melrose the next day, which I was sincerely sorry for. I could not, however, change his resolution, as he seemed to think that he was a marked man, and that he should enjoy tranquillity no longer in that country.

I got up early the following morning to bid him farewell, and just in time to prevent his going into the Glasgow coach instead of the London mail. He seemed sorry to part with me; and, as he was getting into the carriage, he begged the mail-coachman not to drive fast, or to whip his horses.

I felt a blank at his departure; for he was a most agreeable and clever gentleman, and not the less entertaining for his eccentricities, which appeared only from time to time, and interfered with no one's humour.

TROLLING.

In the Tweed, and indeed in some other rivers, they have a method of fishing which is called *Trolling* in

Scotland, but *Cross Angling* in England, where it is practised with the natural May-fly for catching trout. In trolling for salmon, two men stand opposite to one another on either side of the stream, each with a rod in hand; their lines are joined together, and from the bow which this junction creates about half-a-dozen flies are suspended vertically. Of course there can be no casting of the line; but the flies are hung in the stream, and passed over it, the fishermen trailing them, and acting in concert; thus, by means of the number of flies, and the saving of time by not having the line to throw, a great quantity of water is gone over in a short space of time. But this sweeping method has its drawbacks, and very serious ones they are. Out of the number of fish that offer, very few are taken; many get only a touch of the hook, and escape, and are thus entirely lost to the proprietor of the part of the river where this occurs; for, generally speaking, fish so alarmed quit the water the same night, and travel upwards. I remember a singular instance of this occurred to me in the Pavilion-water.

The river was very low and clear at the time; so much so, that it was in good order for sunning, and therefore in no state for fish to travel in. I chanced, however, to hook a salmon with a fly, which, after being played a little, got off the hook : there was a cairn just above the spot where this occurred, and I told my fisherman to set the net belonging to it that night; he did so with a very bad grace, assuring me that it was perfectly useless; or, as he was pleased to express himself, "just perfect nonsense." Nevertheless the fish, having started from his stream, was caught in it that night.

John Crerar mentioned to me another instance where a salmon, having broken a fisherman's line, went down the Tay for a mile, and then up the Tummel three miles, and was there caught the day following by the same fisherman, who thus regained his fly with two or three fathoms of line attached to it.

On the other hand, I know of three well-attested instances of salmon having been caught almost immediately after they had broken the fisherman's line; but I conclude these fish were touched at first in a part that was scarcely sensitive. A very curious circumstance of this sort occurred in the Isle Isla, where a gentleman was broken by a salmon, which he caught immediately afterwards. Upon landing it, he found, to his amazement, that he had not touched the fish itself the second time, but that his hook was linked in the one left in his mouth previously. This was a very delicate affair; for had not the pull upon the fish been moderate and even, he must inevitably have escaped. As for my own practice, I never recollect having risen a fish a second time that had touched my hook previously.

What I have said regarding the number of fish lost or set down in trolling is so universally acknowledged, that this style of angling is seldom practised, except, indeed, in fishing for kelts in very full waters, when no one can throw completely over the casts without the use of a boat. In this state of the river the flies are drawn down the stream; but when the water subsides, they are trailed up it. It is practised also a day or two before close time, when the loss of fish off the hook is immaterial, as far as regards future sport.

In the Tay, and some other large rivers, there is another method of fishing with a fly in full water, which is called *Harling*. Two rods are laid in the bottom of a boat, and hang over the stern, with a large fly attached to each line. The boatman then rows against the stream to the right and left of the river, in a zigzag direction, but still letting the boat fall gradually down the river, so that he passes over no fish that have not previously seen the flies. The rower judges his pace by the objects on the banks. When fish rise they hook themselves. Those who practise this method are generally fishermen who have been working the previous night, and like it because they have not the fatigue of holding or throwing the rod. They fancy, also, that having two flies, they have a double advantage; but this is a deception, because both flies follow each other in the same direction. Without much fear of contradiction, I pronounce this same harling to be a most prodigiously stupid method of proceeding, and little superior to setting night lines. I tried it once in the Tay; but no more harling for me. To do the Tweed folks justice, I never saw it practised there; and I can only recommend it to those liberal persons who wish to drive the salmon from their own waters to those of their neighbours above.

What, alas! becomes of the beautiful wielding of the rod, thrown (albeit heavy, and difficult to manage) with a grace and dexterity that indicates no exertion, the fly not falling like a four-and-twenty pounder, but just kissing the surface of the water, and moving to and fro in a manner so seducing as to beguile the most wary salmon of every atom of prudence!

FISHING WITH BAIT, MINNOW, AND PARR'S TAIL.

When the water is too low for the fly, and quite clear, then begins the bait or worm fishing in Tweed. The tackle consists of a large hook at the end of your line, and a smaller one above it, placed like the lip-hook in minnow tackle. These are threaded with worms. The manner of putting them on will be better learnt from the fishermen on the river side than it can be explained in writing. When the water is in right order, that is, low and clear, as I have said above, and the weather fresh, a clever fisherman may glean the river of almost all the fish that are left in the streams. Tolerably large shot being fixed towards the end of the line, and the worms themselves being heavy, it requires some dexterity to throw a good distance without accidents. To obviate these, and to effect your purpose, begin with a line of moderate length, and tuck out a few folds of the reel, holding them fast with your hand when you bring your rod back, but letting them go just as you have discharged your throw. Thus the line is short at first, but the weight of the shot and worms carry out the folds to the extent required. Having thus cast beyond the run of the salmon, let the stream carry round your bait easily, without any jerk on your part whatever, or any further motion than humouring it towards the shore. Contract the line as the bait comes near you, by gathering it up in folds with your left hand, and holding them fast against the rod with the fingers of your right, letting them go again at the proper time when you cast, in the manner I have before described. Thus you may throw a very long line without endangering its safety by coming in contact with the ground, or any objects in your rear.

You may fish to any depth you please merely by elevating and lowering the point of your rod according to the run of the water. When the weather and water are quite fit for the sport, the fish seizes the bait briskly, and returns with it to its seat or elsewhere : you must give him the line by pulling from the reel with your left hand, and letting it run smoothly between the fingers of your right. A check at this time may lose him ; but let him alone a few seconds, and he will have gorged the hook ; then strike and kill him as soon as you can : he is safe enough. Fresh open weather is the best for this sport ; but fish will sometimes take well even in a frost.

Many excellent and credible fishermen have informed me that they have had good sport with the worm in northern rivers, and in those of Ireland, when the water was thick. Their testimony I do not doubt ; I only say fish are not caught with the worm, or bait as it is called, when the water is in a foul state *in Tweed.* I remember a gentleman applying to me for leave to take a day's salmon fishing, which I granted. There had been rain the day before, and a spate came down in the morning. I thought this unlucky ; but he was of a contrary opinion, and rejoiced in the change ; "for," said he, "if I sit on the point of a cairn, I shall catch every travelling fish that

passes with a worm, as I have often done in Ireland."
This was a new light to Charles Purdie and myself.
Worms were given him in abundance; an excellent
cairn selected for the sport; and there my gentleman
sat the livelong day without having an offer. Old
Richard Wilson could have introduced him into the
landscape with effect, for he was picturesque and well
placed; but as a fisherman, says Charlie, "he is useless
a' thegither." However, the cairn is a laudable monu-
ment of his patience and perseverance.

FISHING WITH MINNOW AND PARR'S TAIL.

Salmon do not take the minnow or the parr's tail so
well in the Tweed as they do in the Tay, nor so well
in the upper parts of Tweed as they do in the lower.
The minnow, in low water, is preferable to the parr's
tail; and it should be worked in the same manner as
in trout fishing, only not quite with so quick a motion.
It is not necessary to use more than two hooks; namely,
the large hook that passes through the minnow, and
the lip hook. Shot should be put on the casting line
about a foot and a half from the bait—fewer or more
according to the strength of the stream.

What is called the parr's tail is a pretty liberal
allowance of the said little fish, consisting of a diagonal
cut from the shoulder to the anal fin; so that in fact
you have all the firm part of the fish, discarding the
head and the stomach. In full water I think this bait
is preferable to the minnow; and it has the advantage

of a much firmer hold of the hook, not breaking like the soft parts of the minnow.

Clean salmon will take this bait whenever the river is in order for the fly, or perhaps a little before it is so, even when the water is slightly discoloured, or, as the fishermen call it, *drumly*. But foul fish, including kelts, never take it well in the upper parts of the Tweed, unless the water is clear, though they will take it in a drumly water in the Tay; nor can any sport be expected with it in very warm weather.

The best state of the water, and the most convenient time, is between the fly and bait fishing; that is, when it is rather too low for the one, but not low enough for the other. The best weather is a fresh day, with wind to act upon the surface of the deep pools. In summer the proper hour is early in the morning. After a night's burning, salmon take the minnow, small parr, or parr's tail, particularly well in the streams.

The best way of casting the minnow is precisely that which I have indicated in my instructions for fishing with the worm.

As in a deer forest, however extensive, every burn, rock, glen, moss, and mountain has its distinct appellation, so that you can describe with the greatest accuracy where a hart has been slain, or any signal event has happened; so in a salmon river, every stream and pool in which these delectable fish lie is called by a name that either distinguishes its character, or relates to some event or circumstance which tradition has not always preserved. Some casts are called after the names of persons who were drowned in them: there is one such, yclept "Meg's Hole," some little distance above the Melrose bridge. I wonder who Meg was; but Charles Purdie, who is coming up the river, is right sure to tell me some nonsense or another anent it, so I will sound him.

"Well, Charlie, I see you have been putting all the boats in place, so sit down upon the bank here and rest yourself: pulling a boat up a strong stream is hard work, and pulling several over is harder. Now, tell me why the pool I fished the other day is called Meg's Hole; but stick to truth, mind, and do not let me hear any of your foolish tales."

"Aweel, then, I'll tell ye the hale truth. Ye'll hae heard o' Thomas the Rhymer, him that in days lang gaen by lived at Earlston,* and was ta'en awa' by the fairies, and is wi' them at this day; we hae Sir Walter's word for it. Black Meg of Darnwick lived wi' this Thomas, who, ye ken, was an enchanter; and Meg learned some awfu' words of him, and also power as a witch. Ae time she was seen sitting upon ane of the towers, aboon the Elfin Glen, in the shape of a raven; at anither, she came doun to the Tweed at the gloamin' in the likeness of a lang-craiged heron, flappin' her muckle wings, an' utterin' dreidfu' shrieks; and again she was a cormorant, perch'd upon a blastit tree on the muir. I have seen her mysel' mair than ance."

"Seen her, man! why you said she lived with Thomas the Rhymer; and it is some centuries since he was taken away by the fairies."

"Aweel, aweel, that may be; but as sure as deid, I

* Formerly Ercildoun.

aince saw her in her ain proper shape; and she had a lang neb, and a muckle mouth, and a red petticoat on, and she held a leister under her oxter, as if she waur gaun to the burnin'; and wha kens but she may live till this day? for her deid body was never found, nor the corpse-light* seen. There are three towers on the muir a long way aboon the Elfin Glen; ye'll hae seen them yersel'; an' Meg used to live in ane o' these towers by turns: no one kent in which she was, an' nobody cared to speer. At nightfall she would come doon the glen to seek thae grey stanes† that the fairies cast their cantrips with, and muckle scaith she wrought rottin' the sheep of ae body, and takin' the milk frae the kye o' anither; so the lads waylaid her wi' flails, and pitchforks, and sic-like gear. They chased her a' the nicht in the glen, up an' doun the braes an' thickets, and through the water; but they could never grip her, an' they cam' back at skreigh o' day wi' torn plaids an' broken shins, all covered wi' mire; an' some o' them had a sair sickness afterwards, and repentit that they ever meddled wi' her."

"Oh, of course; but what became of her at last, Charlie?"

---

* When a dead body was lost, it was supposed that a light appeared over it at night, to indicate its position.

† These *fairy stones*, as they are called, are to be found in the Elfin Glen, where the Maid of Avenel is said to have appeared. This romantic spot belongs to Lord Somerville, and is in the ornamental grounds belonging to his house called the Pavilion. The stones are of a grey colour, and of various curious shapes, sometimes closely resembling articles in common use, such as tea-cups, saucers, etc.; they are supposed to contain some charm, and are constantly sought for to this day by all sorts of people.

"Why, then, when she persistit in her foul ways, some o' thae freebooters, who feared neither witch, warlock, nor deil, made a raid into her country, and pit a fire round each of the towers,* and made the ane she was in too het to haud her, and out she ran wi' awfu' yells, skelping owre the muir, and so doun to the Elfin glen, where ane o' these three reivers, who had a flaming firebrand in his hand, wounded her ahint wi' it; and the deidly nightshade still grows in the place where her blood was spilt. Then they drave her through the glen, and so doun the brae above a deep pool in Tweed, and pushed her in wi' a pole and a firebrand; so she cam' to her end by wood, fire, and water.

"The pool was draggit in the mornin', but her body was never found; and many people watched all night for a lang time, and the corpse-light never appeared; nor was her wraith ever seen, except by mysel' and my faither at Trequair, and Walter of Darnwick, who saw it howking a grave wi' many ither wicked spirits round it on the tap of Eildon Hills.

"So the pool goes by the name of 'Meg's Hole' to this day; and when ye hookit the muckle sawmont that ran ye doun to the Cauld pool, ye ken that her spirit tried to drive him through the farther arch of Melrose Bridge, but ye were owre canny for it."

The earliest method of taking fish, previous to the invention of either hooks or nets, was that used by the Egyptians, by means of a spear resembling a trident. A sculptured stone, excavated at Chester in 1738, and

---

* The three towers are still standing in the place indicated.

engraved in Lyson's history of the county as a Roman remain, represents a fisherman with his spear and basket.

I will now describe the salmon spear at present in use. It was formerly called *waster*; but that term is nearly out of use, except by the old fishermen, and it is now better known by the name of *leister*. It resembles

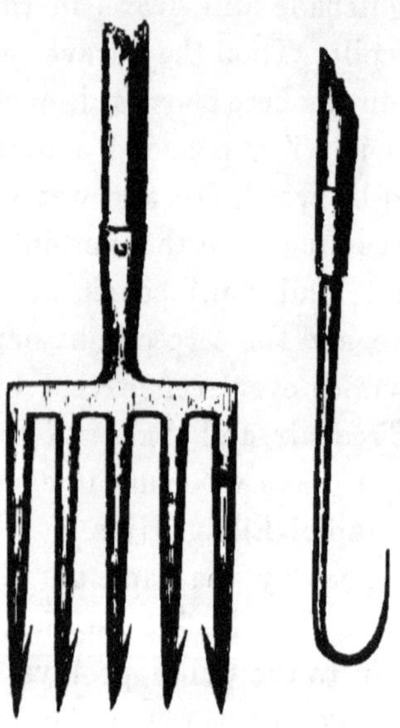

a trident in its general appearance; but has five prongs instead of three, made of very stout iron : there is only one barb to each prong, as two would tear the fish too much in extricating them. This weapon is fastened to the end of a pole more or less long, according to the depth of the water in which it is intended to be used ;

sixteen feet is the general length, and it is not easy to see or strike a fish at a greater depth; but in sunning I have sometimes tied a light rope to the top of the pole, and gone deeper than this with success, but then it was when the river was unusually clear. The opposite woodcut represents the cleik and the leister: the latter is rather narrower, and altogether of a neater make than those in general use.

In burning, the boat is managed with this leister; but no one can make use of it in this way who has not learnt to work it with a pole,—which art is termed *canting*, and is, I believe, little understood except in the Tweed—in the Tay and the Annan they know nothing of the matter. Now the pole is not used as in punting; but the man who manages the boat, instead of shifting his place, stands up or sits down at the stern; he keeps his eye upon her head, and forces her straight up the rapids, pressing the pole in the direction in which he would steer with a rudder. This is in a great measure effected with a twist of the body. If he does not keep her straight in her course, the current takes her at the side, whips her round in an instant, and down she goes, the deuce knows where, head foremost; nor can you resume your position till you again bring her head up the stream.

In forcing your boat up very strong water, at every fresh thrust you must catch up the pole and put it in again very quickly; for when you are not pushing the boat will recede if the rapids are heavy, and thus you may lose way. This, I think, can be done better by sitting than standing, as you are nearer your work.

In this manner you may thrust your little craft where no oars could take hold of the water.

To perform this requires vast practice, and accordingly it was a considerable time before I mastered it completely, although I had been accustomed to punting on the Isis in my younger days. The rapids had it all their own way for months, or more. As you use the canting pole, which is shod with a heavy iron spike, so you must use the leister; only with more caution, lest you should injure the prongs.

As a proof of the difficulty of this operation, I will mention that I once put the canting pole into the hands of an English gentleman, who was a good rower, and, as he asserted, a good punter also. We were sunning a strong stream called the Carrywheel, and I had placed Charles Purdie at its gorge, to leister such fish as might attempt to pass up it from the fright given by the disturbance below. In a few seconds the head of the boat, not being held straight up the stream, went round like a shot, and so down the river. My friend was perfectly confused, and did not know what on earth should be done; so, as we were losing way rapidly, I took the pole and brought her head up again. Still he would not give in, and was determined to have another trial. Well, he pushed here, and he pushed there, and with these strenuous efforts succeeded in describing pretty accurately in his course what in Gothic architecture is called the zigzag moulding, losing way, however, at every angle.

Not having taken any notice of the objects on the banks, he did not precisely know whereabouts he was;

but his exertions, simply as exertions, were highly laudable. When he had permitted the boat to fall down into easy water, he had some little command over her, and of this he was right proud. As time was precious, I resumed the command, and put the boat up again with my leister. When we came up to the fisherman, my novice said, with considerable exultation, " Charlie, did you see me cant?"

" Hoot, toot, man, you canna cant ava; she was aye ganging doun," was the uncourteous response.

Having described our method of managing the boat, I will endeavour to explain the manner in which we strike the salmon. The leister should not be held firm in the grasp, but sent loosely through the hands, as its own weight in falling will be more effective than any force you can give it with a thrust.* You may think otherwise, perhaps. Well, then, take your own way; hold the weapon firmly and determinedly; you are going to do great things, you fancy. But what happens? The water proves deeper than you had calculated upon, and, not touching the bottom with your spear as a support, in you go, your head taking the lead, and the rest of your members following the playful example.

---

* The *Droit* lately contained the following :—" At the moment that an omnibus was passing on Friday through the Rue Montmartre, under a house, No. 63, that was undergoing repairs, a pole more than thirty feet in length slipped from the scaffolding at the fourth story, and fell perpendicularly on the omnibus, passed right through the body, and entered so deeply between the stones of the pavement that the horses were stopped on the moment, the vehicle being literally nailed to the ground ; by a providential chance none of the passengers were injured ! !! "

Strike your fish over the shoulders if you can, and bring your boat in such a position as to make the stroke as vertical as possible. When you have fixed him, hold him to the ground a space; then run your hands down the pole, making the distance between them and the fish as short as you conveniently can; lift the animal with his head uppermost, by which means he will come out lighter, and such action as he may make with his tail will assist you rather than himself.

If you do not bear in mind this instruction, and choose to have a go at a salmon at a little distance from you, as having a way of your own, I will tell you what will probably happen from this freak also. The stroke will drive back the boat, and you and the fish will part company. You may have struck him, perhaps,—not impossible that; but your intended victim twists off in a moment, and says as plainly as a salmon can speak, "levrò l'incommodo."

I should observe, that in burning the water by night there is no time to fix every fish to the ground, and that they are then most usually lifted quickly; indeed, as the boat falls gradually down the stream, it generally comes over them conveniently enough.

To these various methods of taking fish, I must add the destruction by means of rake-hooks. The tackle is very simple: it consists of two strong hooks, about two or three inches long, tied back to back, and fastened to twisted gut, on which are put five or six large shot, at equal distances from each other. The fisherman, with a strong rod, throws the line, with these bare hooks attached to it, about a foot beyond

any salmon that he may discover lying, and then with
a sudden jerk draws the hook into him if he can, and
gets him to the land if he is able.

Clean fish are sometimes taken in this manner, and
most fishermen are provided with the tackle. In a very
low water in the summer, when fly-fishing might have
been said to be over, I once hooked a good salmon in
the Quarry stream above Melrose Bridge. As a fish
was at that time a great rarity, I was particularly
cautious in leading him; nevertheless, with all my
care, the hook, not having a firm hold, came away from
him after I had played him a considerable time.

Purdie saw him lying in rather an exhausted state
in the same stream, which was shallow, and, without
saying anything to me, to my great surprise, seized
hold of my casting line and broke off the lower end of
it; opened my book; took a pair of rake-hooks from
it; tied them on to the line, and, at the second throw,
tucked them into the salmon; put the rod into my
hands, and I killed the fish after all.

All this to the Southern ear sounds like poaching of
the most flagitious description; but a salmon is a fish
of passage, and if you do not get him to-day he will
be gone to-morrow. The Tweed used to let for above
£12,000 a year; judge, then, in what a wholesale
manner these fish are caught by long nets and other
sweeping modes; yet in what profusion they continue
to be found! You may just as well think of preserving
herrings or mackeral as these delicious creatures; and
there would be no objection to your taking 337S
salmon at one haul, if fortune would so favour you, as

Commander Ross did at Boothia Felix on the 26th of July, 1831.

Keep *Close time* strictly; kill no spawning fish; tamper not with foul ones of any sort; preserve the fry; send the black fishers to Iceland; but catch as many salmon as you can, *recte si possis* (meaning with a rod), *si non, quocunque modo,*—that is, with a net or leister, and so forth.

CHAP. XI.

> " 'Tis night, dread night, and weary Nature lies
>   So fast as if she never were to rise ;
>   Lean wolves forget to howl at night's pale noon ;
>   No wakeful dogs bark at the silent moon,
>   Nor bay the ghosts which glide in horror by
>   To view the caverns where their bodies lie ;
>   The ravens perch, and no presages give,
>   Nor to the windows of the dying cleave ;
>   In vaults the walking fires extinguish'd lie ;
>   The stars, heaven's sentry, wink and seem to die."
>
> LEE.

BEFORE I describe what is called "burning the water," I will make an observation that may be of service to the rod fisher. It is, that salmon which have been disturbed in the night with boats and lights will draw into the streams above, and take the fly all the better for this disturbance the following morning ; and as burning always takes place when the water is very low, they probably will not be found far from the place of the nocturnal operations.

Trout also will take better for having been routed about, and for change of situation ; a remarkable instance of which I witnessed a few years ago at Castle Combe. A hole under some hatches by a mill was emptied of its water, that the trout might be caught and taken lower down the stream, more out of the way of poachers. This was done by means of buckets, and in doing it the water became thick and white, and the fish partook of the same colour. I sent thirty-five brace of these fish, all similar in size, a considerable distance lower down the stream, when they were put under a bridge near my house. Many of them died. But in three hours after the removal I caught eight of the others with a fly without moving from the spot: neither the size nor the colour of the fish could possibly be mistaken.

THE BURNING.

"Charlie Charlie," cried Thomas Jamieson, "there's fine sport going on the nicht; our maister's minded to burn the water, for she is low enough, ye ken; so ane o' us will hae to gang and split the twa auld tar barrels for lichts, an' the ither mun slidder up to Abbotsford and tell your uncle Tam what's ganging forrat, and say that he has to meet us at the Carrywheel at eight o'clock prececsely. Charlie, ye'd best do the lichts yoursel', and I'll hae to win to Darnick, and get the wasters a' new sharpened. Sandy and Rob will come nae doot, and we should hae auld Wat too; but if he has been fou yestreen, he'll no be worth a bawbee."

"Ye needna fash yoursel' aboot the like o' him, for he had a wee drap. I saw him this mornin' riddling a cart fu' o' sand lyin' again the house end, which he said he was making ready for biggin; and as I was coming awa' auld Janet gied me a wag wi' her finger, and I juist steppit in. 'What do ye think?' says she; 'the auld vagabun was fou yestreen, and he gaed out as he thought unseen by ony; I watched him, and he hid his siller amang the sand, for he aye thinks I graip his pouches for it. After he was awa' I sliddered out and fun' his purse; there war seeven shillings and a groat in it; so I gaed to auld Mary Butler's, and bought yetmeal for the bairns' parritch wi' it, and ye see the auld cuffer is riddling the sand, thinking to find his purse. He'll no be worth a rigmaree the nicht for fishing.'"

"Aweel, Charlie, Janet says true; but wha maun we hae to lead hame the fish? Tam Hardy or Rob Colyard would mak' guid fun. Tam, he'll tell us that lang story aboot the scramidge, and the muckle fish he killed in Leader-water, that misured nine inches atween the een; and if we hae Rob, he'll get a stick and be gaun through his braidsword exercise, and tell us how he did wi' the twa Frenchmen on the field of Waterloo; so Rob may meet us wi' his cart to tak' hame the fish, when we come to Brig-end pool. We maun now tak' up the twa boats to the Carrywheel, where they will bide our coming at night;—and look here, man: when we are in a sweet wi' pu'ing them up, we will tak' a wee drap out o' this black bottle."

The boat in general use for burning at night is larger than the rod fishing boats, as more room and steadiness is required. In the centre of it, close to the side on which the leisterers strike the fish, is a pole fixed vertically, with a frame at top of it formed of ribs of iron to contain the combustibles. Three men are sufficient to man the boat; one at the head, another at the stern, as boatmen and leisterers, and the third at the centre to kill the fish and trim the fire. But it will contain more men, if necessary.

The remainder of the day having been spent in

making the arrangements, and the proper hour being now come, Harry Otter and Charlie Purdie went out from the Pavilion to meet the party, who were to assemble at eight o'clock about a mile and a half up the river. The night was most favourable, it being utterly dark, and not a sough of air stirring. With caution and with difficulty they felt their way step by step at the rocky base of the Scaur, where it dips into the river, till they descried the boat which was to take them across it at the Brig-end pool. The clanking of the chain as it was loosened and flung on the planks sounded harshly in the silence of night; the oars dipped duly, and they were soon on the opposite side of the river, by which means they cut off a great sweep of the haugh, "a huge half moon, a monstrous cantle out," and proceeded in a more direct line to their mark. They went on in darkness through the chilling dews, now and then stumbling into the patches of furze which were scattered over the haugh; soon they begin to hear the rushing of the waters through the gorge of the Carrywheel: now it breaks full and loud upon the ear, for they are arrived at the base of the wooded brae that overhangs the cast.

Two groups of men, but dimly seen, here await their arrival; one consists of spectators lying on the ground with their plaids thrown athwart their bodies, and the other of the heroes who were to figure in the grand operation: these latter were sitting on the boats, and on the masses of rock beside them on the water edge.

All being now ready, a light was struck; and the sparks being applied to rags steeped in pitch, and to fragments of tar-barrels, they blazed up at once amid the gloom, like the sudden flash from the crater of a volcano. The ruddy light glared on the rough features and dark dresses of the leisterers in cutting flames directly met by black shadows—an effect which those will best understand who in the Eternal City have seen the statues of the Vatican by torch-light. Extending itself, it reddened the shelving rocks above, and glanced upon the blasted arms of the trees, slowly perishing in their struggle for existence amongst the stony crevices; it glowed upon the hanging wood, on fir, birch, broom, and bracken, half veiled, or half-revealed, as they were more or less prominent. The form of things remote from the concentrated light was dark and dubious; even the trees on the summit of the brac sank in obscurity.

The principals now sprang into the boats. Harry Otter stood at the head, and Charlie Purdie at the stern. These men regulated the course of the craft with their leisters; the auxiliaries were stationed between them, and the light was in the centre by the boat side. The logs, steeped as they were in pitch, crackled and burned fiercely, sending up a column of black smoke. As the rude forms of the men rose up in their dark attire, wielding their long leisters, with the streaks of light that glared partially upon them, and surrounded as they were by the shades of night, you might almost have fancied yourself in the realms below, with Pluto and his grim associates, embarked on the Stygian lake. But as the sports began, and as the Scotch accent prevailed, the illusion passed away; for no poet, that I am aware of, has made the above swarthy and mysterious personages express themselves in the language of Tweedside; nor could one fancy salmon in the Styx, though they might well disport in the streams of the happy fields beyond.

"Now, my lads," says the master, "take your places. Tom, stand you next to me; Sandy, go on the other side of Tom; and do you, Jamie, keep in the middle, and take tent to cap the boats well over the rapids. Rob, do you and Tom Purdie keep good lights and fell the fish. Hulloo, Tom, you have smuggled a leister into the boat for your own use."

"Aye, aye, that have I, juist for mine ain deversion, ye ken."

"Well, well, you may just keep it, for you are a stout chiel, and it would be hard work to get it from you; besides, no one can use it more dexterously than yourself. Now, then, we will push the boat up the cheek of the stream till we come to the head of it. That will do. Now shoot her across the gorge, and down she goes merrily, broadside foremost, according to rule. Cap, Charlie, cap, man; we are drifting down like mad; keep back your end of the boat."

"Aweel, aweel, she gangs cannily now; look, uncle, a muckle fish before ye, or ever ye kent; the maister's leister gaed through him, and played auld dife. That side, that side, Jamie; he's rinnin up to get past. Od, ye have him; and I ha'e anither, and anither. Keep a guid licht, Tom. Now let us tak' up the boat to the head of the stream, or ever we look the stanes, for there war a muckle fish gaed by that nane o' ye gomerils ever saw. There, we are high eneuch now; haud yer hand, an' let her fa' doun again : hey, but I see him the noo afore me ;—ou ! what an awfu' beast !"

So saying, Charlie drove his leister furiously at him; but whether one of the prongs struck against the edge of the rock above him, which prevented its descent to the bottom, or from whatever other cause, the stroke was unsuccessful, and as he lifted the barren weapon out of the water, there arose a merry shout and guffaw from the spectators on the shore.

" Cap! cap !" cried Charlie, "now haud yer hand; gie me up the boat ;—od, but I'll hae him yet; he's gane amangst thae hiding stanes."

So saying, Charlie brought the head of the boat to the stream, pushed her higher up, and pulled her ashore ; he then landed, and seizing a brand out of the fire, put it into Jamieson's hand, who preceded his eager steps like a male Thais, or one of the Eumenides in pantaloons. He now stood upon a rock which hung over the river, and from that eminence, and with the assistance of the firebrand, examined the bottom of it carefully. His body was bent over the water, and his ready leister held almost vertically ; as the light glared on his face you might see the keen glistening of his eye. In an instant he raised up his leister, and down he sprang from the rock right into the river, and with that wild bound nailed the salmon to the channel. There was a struggle with his arms for a few seconds; he then passed his hands down the pole of the weapon a little way, brought himself vertically over the fish, and lifted him aloft, cheered by shouts of applause from his friends on the shore.

17

Two or three more fish were taken amongst the stones at the tail of the cast, and the sport in the Carry-wheel being now ended, the fish were stowed in the hold of the boat, the crew jumped ashore, and a right hearty appeal was made to the whisky bottle. It was first tendered to the veteran Tom Purdie, to whom it was always observed to have a natural gravitation, but to the astonishment of all, he barely put his lips to the quaigh, and passed it to his nephew.

"Why, uncle, man, what the deil's cam' owre ye? I never ken'd ye refuse a drappie afore—no, not sin' I war a callant; I canna thole to see ye gang that gait."

"Why, I'll tell ye what it is, Charlie. I got a repreef from Sir Walter for being fou the ither nicht."

"Eh, uncle, hoo was that?'

"'Why,' says Sir Walter, 'Tom,' says he, 'I sent for ye on Monday, and ye were not at hame at eicht o'clock; I doubt ye were fou, Tom.' 'I'll juist tell ye the hale truth,' says I, 'I gaed round by the men at wark at Rymer's Glen, an' cam' in by Tarfield; then I went to Darnick, and had a glass o' whisky wi' Sandy Trummel at Susy's, and I war juist comin' awa' when Rob steppit in, and cried for half a mutchkin. I wasna for takin' mair, but the glasses were filled, an' I didna like to be beat wi' them, so I tuk mine.' 'And is that all you had, Tom?' said Sir Walter. 'Aye, indeed was it,' said I; 'but, Heaven have a care o' me, I never was the war o't, till I was gangin' up by Jemmy Mercer's by Coat's Green; and when I cam' up by Kerr side, I wanted to see Mr. Laidlaw, but I thocht I durstna gang in: and hoo I gat hame I dinna ken, for I never

STARTING FROM AN EMINENCE

mindet it nae mair; but our wife war in a terrible bad
key the morning, because I war sair wanted last nicht.'

" ' Well,' said the maister, ' ye maun never do the like
again, Tom.' We then gaed to the woods, and thinned
the trees; and I laboured with the axe at thae that
Sir Walter marked.

" ' Now Tom,' says he, ' you will go home with me,
for you have been working very hard, and a glass of
whisky will do you good;' and he ca'ed to Nicholson
to bring Tom a glass of Glenlivet. I tuk it doun; and,
man, if ye'd found it, it beat a' the whisky I ever tasted
in my life. ' Well, Tom,' said Sir Walter, ' how do ye
feel after it ? Do ye think another glass will do ye
ony harm ?' I said naething, but I thocht I wad like
anither, and Nicholson poured out ane, and I tuk it.
Then the maister said, ' Tom, do you feel ony thing the
war o' it?' 'Na', na',' said I, 'but it's terrible powerfu,'
and three times as strong as ony whisky I ever drank
in my life.' ' Then, Tom,' says Sir Walter, ' never tell
me that three glasses o' Susy's whisky will fill ye fou,
when ye have drank twa of mine, which you say is
three times as strong, and you feel all the better for
it.' Hey, man, I never was so ta'en by the face in a'
my life! I didna ken where to luk. The deil fa' me
if ever he cotch me so again!"

Tom Purdie's forbearance, however, was not of an
enduring quality; his eyes glistened as he followed the
course of the bottle; three times was his arm extended
to make a grip at it, and thrice did he draw it back
with modest confusion. At length when all were served
he could hold out no longer, but elongating his dexter,

he laid fast hold of the bottle, and filling the quaigh to the brim, " Here goes," said he, " to the lousy stranger." After he had drunk, and mended his draught, he kept the bottle in his own custody with a pretty smart allowance in it, in the character of residuary legatee. I had an account, however, to settle with him ; for being the only stranger in company, I fancied his toast meant a reflection upon my cleanliness. What did he mean by the dirty and degrading epithet? This I demanded, advancing with a warlike countenance, and leister in the rest; and had not Tom been in a very benign humour, this book might never have been inflicted on the public, for the man was well armed and resolute, and might have leistered me according to art. But putting on his sweetest smile, he assured me that by the " lousy stranger " he meant a newly run fish with tide lice on it, " which," said he, " are far the best ye ken." This I well knew, though the application did not occur to me at the moment. And here, by the way I beg to observe, however odd it may seem, that you may know the best *clean* fish, by their having tide lice upon them.

" All hands to the boat again. Come, Rob, give us a merry blaze; never spare the tar barrel : well done, Vulcan! Now we have a splendid light on the water, and can see well enough to read small print at the bottom of it."

" Sandy Trummel, ye great bear, what gars ye stamp and scream at that rate ? "

Sandy in fact not only stamped and screamed, but swore that he was dreadfully *brunt* with the pieces of charcoal and drops of flaming pitch which insinuated themselves between his shirt and cape of his jacket behind; whereat Tom Purdie, who was a considerate and humane man, took up the scoop which was used for ladling out the boat, and filling that capacious utensil with water to the extent of its capacity, came behind the aggrieved, and emptied the whole contents down his back. "An' noo, Sandy, man," says he, "I hae made ye quite comfortable, and ye owe me a guid turn." But who would have thought it? The blood of the Trummels was up, and seizing a firebrand in a style that did little honour to his gratitude, the diluted one rushed forward intent on vengeance. Grim looked Tom Purdie, and charging with his leister, he held the foeman at bay. Who can say what Homeric deeds might not have been done, had not Charlie, first whispering to the master to *stand fast*, given the boat a sudden whirl round with the stroke of an oar, which laid Tom Purdie flat upon his back at the bottom of the boat, and canted Sandy Trummel fairly overboard? He fell in rather a picturesque attitude, for which I cannot in candour give him much credit, as the affair seemed to be quite involuntary and too sudden for him to study effect. His right hand held the torch aloft for a moment, Marmion fashion, which soon fell and hissed in the current with a train of smoke which trailed along the surface of the water. Sandy's feet were actively employed in kicking his best, by which means he agitated the water in such a manner that, with the assistance of the light, it made a very brilliant and imposing appearance. The stream here being very shallow, he soon began to emerge, and about two-thirds of his fair proportions rose up from the channel; his mouth seemed full of water and abuse; he soon got rid of the one; but before he could vent the other, he was anticipated by the boat's crew, who all shouted out shame upon him for his awkwardness, and for having nearly upset the boat in his fall, and endangered the lives of several worthy individuals. Thus a sort of balance was struck between faults on both sides, and Tom Purdie himself assisted him to regain the boat; "and Sandy, man," said he, as he lifted him in, "I shall be always willing to dae ye some guid service when ye need it; sae ye'll let me ken when the burning pick gets aboard ye again."

They now passed over some bare streams where no salmon would lie; the navigation amongst the rocks was somewhat intricate, there being barely room for the width of the boat in some of the rapids; but Charlie Purdie hit the thing off to a nicety. They then burned the *Glass-wheel Pot*, the *Oak Tree*, and the *Noirs*, in all of which they got a few fish.

"Rob," said Charlie, "wale out some o' yer sticks that they may be weel kinelt afore we get into Brig-end Pool; now lads we mun cap weel here, for she will gang owre the stream wi' a terrible flee; od, I see them glancin' doun the pool as thick as herrin'. Sandy, man, but ye're dancin' again; what's come owre ye? ye'll be wantin' Tam Purdie's big ladle again, I'm thinkin'."

"The deil may hae Tam Purdie and his muckle ladle; for as he knockit off a bit fish in the boat, he dung yin o' the taes o' the waster intil my leg; he is aye sae camsteric."

"Ye canna blame me, Sandy, for the mischanter, for

ye are aye stammering among the fish like a haveril as ye are, and half fou into the bargain. Halloo, Sandy, ye'll no crack o' yer deeds the nicht, for yer waster's aye clanking against the stanes, whilst the maister is striking the fish afore ye by dizens; and see, muckle Tam has lifted in yin amaist as lang as himsel."

"Come, come, lads," says the master, "hold your clish-ma-clavers, for we are just going into Brig-end Pool; so keep back the boat as well as you can, or we shall go fiery fast over the stream."

As the boat neared the pool, the men shouted out, "Auld Michael! auld Michael! the charm for auld Michael Scott: trim the boat, and take care the muckle wizard doesna loup intil her." "Od, lads," cries Tom Purdie, "pit yer best fut foremost; they are lying afore us like sacks, and will be as thick as you can dab them up. Mind the licht, Sandy, and take care that kipper doesna wallop out o' the boat. See what a muckle fish Charlie has got!"

In fact the men were making a great slaughter; and when they had gone over the pool two or three times, had half filled the boat with the spoil; so as they found they were well laden, they called to Rob Colyard to come forward with his cart and take them home.

"Shove the boat to the shore; Colyard, come forrat wi' yer cart; that'll do, man; a' hands to wark, coont the fish as ye pit them in; Charlie, how many hae ye coonted?"

"There's juist a hunder and twa, great and sma', whitling, bull-trout, saumonts, and a'thegither."

The men passed round the whisky bottle, and we

resumed our sport; I, Harry Otter, stood as before at the head of the boat, and the other men in their allotted places; we passed pretty swiftly down the streams, broadside in front, striking many fish, till we came near the Elfin Burn, when, observing that the water-break in the centre of the river, caused by a concealed rock, was more gentle than usual, I thought the boat would strike, so I called out to Charlie for caution.

"Hoot, toot, he mun let her gang; there is plenty of water to take her over."

Charlie Purdie was never more mistaken in his life; the stream drove us downward at a rapid race, notwithstanding we in some measure moderated it by capping our best with the leisters. Bang went the boat's broadside right against the rock, to which she stuck fast till the stream above poured into her in the most effective possible style, and down she went of course. The water, however, was by no means deep; but those fish, which we had taken since the load went home, found their way again into the river and began to vanish down the streams. Being deprived of life, they went passively along, followed by all the boat's crew, who rushed about and charged with their leisters, " hurry, hurry, splash, splash," till they fished out most of them, the remainder being left to solace the eels. This in common parlance would be called a disaster; a sort of shipwreck in miniature; but judging from the merriment it excited, it might be deemed the best sport of the night.

Whilst these gambols were carrying on, and the men were rolling about in the waters, after the guise of sea calves, Charlie Purdie and I had got the boat to the shore, and heaving her upon her side, had poured the water out: "And, now, Purdie," said I, "whilst these clever fellows are catching dead fish, do tell me what you all meant by shouting out 'auld Michael!'" and calling for the charm at the Brig-end Pool?"

"Why, ye maun ken that Michael Scott, who lived in bygane times, was a warlock, and I could tell ye mony wonderfu' cracks aboot him, for the hale country rings wi' his foul deeds. Mony years syne there was a brig at yon cast, but the spate ran away a' but the middle pillar, which stood up in the water as high as ever; and as the fishermen o' thae days were burning the *Noirs*, they saw a muckle man sitting a tap o' the pillar, wi' a flaming brand in the tae hand, and a lang leister in the tither; he had a hairy cap on his heid, made, perhaps, o' the fur o' the tod, or some sic like beastie, and a long gown on, wi' a linen dress aneath it, a' doun to his knees, tied roond wi' a queer girdle, which was written aboot wi' magic words, and a lang whinger stuck intill it; we hae Sir Walter's word for it, ye ken. Aweel, the fishermen wha war in the boat were sair frightened, and in ganging doun the water, got as far frae him as they could, and, as they thought, out o' reach o' him; but he louped frae the pillar intill the boat from an awfu' distance, and doun she went so soon as he set foot or hoof in her; and a' the men war drooned, and left the bonny banks o' the Tweed wi' all their sins on their heids. Then the foul wizard, Michael Scott, was seen by some folks on shore to rise up and loup on a muckle black horse that cam doun frae the clouds, and he fleed awa' on it till he became inveesable. The folk at Darnick pu'd doun the pillar; they didna leave ae stane on anither. Aye, aye, ye may laugh and call this clish-ma-claver if ye please, but it's true what I tell ye; I have seen auld Michael mysel'."

" Where, Charlie, where?"

" Why, aince on Cowden-knowes I saw his wraith, and his torch a tap o' the hill, and his muckle black horse feeding below on the muir, as plain as I see ye the noo; and though he is not in life at this day, for he war killed by drinking the kail made o' a breme sow, yet his spirit is abraid, ye ken, and it war that which sent our boat to the bottom, for ye hadna a fairy stane;* but ye'll be wiser, I'm thinkin', afore ye burn that cast again."

" Aye, that will I; but courage, man; all is set to rights, so let us have the whisky, for with that and the blazing brands we shall be warm both within and without, and fear no wizards. But if wizards ever visit rivers, I hope they will open a slap in every cauld where there is no local act, so as to admit of the free run of fish; for there are many fine-looking streams that are ' bridled with a curb of stone.' I do not wish to hurt the property of mill-owners; but how easy it would be in such cases to accommodate all parties by making an opening at every barrier, and a proper slope constructed with rolling stones at the back of it; a hatch to be put in at the opening, and drawn only when there was a superfluity of water for the mill. This

---

* See note at page 246.

plan would answer perfectly; for in very low water fish do not travel, and in a very high one, when they do, the miller would suffer no loss."

"Weel, I wadna say but ye are perfectly richt, and I am thinking that a river, like a road, should be open for all passengers."

Most of the dead salmon having been at length forked out of the river, we all got afloat again, and passed down those rapids above Melrose Bridge called "*the Quarry Stream,*" "*Back Brae,*" and "*Kingswell Lees,*" snatching out a fish occasionally in our course; then the flame soon gleamed upon the bridge, struck upwards on the roof of the vast arch as we shot through it, and revealed the dark pines below, which shelved down to the margin of the river.

We were now in a salmon cast called "*the Whirls,*" which runs deep and solemn, and we had scarcely set our leisters in the rest ere we found that a fisherman had been to work before us, and an excellent hand he was at the sport; he had neither light nor boat, and, being tolerably hungry, I suppose, was devouring a twelve-pounder, all raw as it was, in the dry channel of the river.

"See! the otter, the otter! he has got into the water. Bring round the boat,—quick, quick. Now keep her on the edge of the deep current, and we shall leister him to a certainty." No such thing. He had not yet made up his mind to be leistered; and, being of a solitary disposition, rather shunned our society than otherwise; so, instead of attempting to gain the main stream, he went insidiously down the shallows, where no boat could swim. He was thus out of the reach of being speared in the usual manner; but Charlie Purdie had a go at him by flinging his leister from a distance—

> "Nequicquam patrias tentasti lubricus artes,
>   Vane Ligur."

It was a complete failure. Charlie followed up the thing, however, by leaping out of the boat; nothing could be fairer or more honourable, as he thus gave the amphibious animal the advantage of element. The men were all eager and in commotion; so what with boat and lights, to say nothing of the dreadful tridents, the beast was fairly confused, and almost surrounded. Purdie, who had sent away his leister upon a vain errand, albeit unarmed, continued the chase on foot, and at length gripped the brute by the tail; there was pulling and splashing, till at last he held the otter up aloft triumphantly. Now as this position, though not precisely vertical, did not happen to suit the brute's convenience, the subtle animal managed to twist round, and to fix his teeth on the captor's arm. This was rather disagreeable to Charlie, as the teeth of the otter abound in practical experiments. The posture of affairs then, you see, was as follows:—the tenacious Purdie had hold of the vermin with his dexter, and was loth to relinquish his grip; the foe, nothing behind in tenacity, fixed his teeth in Charlie's sinister with equal perseverance; thus both his arms were fully occupied. Nothing daunted, Charlie cried out with Spartan endurance, "Hey, lad, but twa can play at that!" So, extending his jaws, he fixed his grinders in the animal's throat and worried him exceedingly. In fine, after a very ludicrous struggle, he shook off my excellent namesake and flung him on the shore, where he was despatched with the leisters before he could regain the river. Thus ended the "Battle of Otterbourne," and thus ended also our sport for the night; for the beast, no doubt, had disturbed that cast, which, together with the lower water, was set apart for another night's amusement.

We now marched home with our spoil, triumphant: —Sandy in front, with the blazing beacon over his shoulder to light our steps, as has been practised from time immemorial; the others with the fish and leisters. One of the spectators began a *concordia discors* with his bagpipe, but bade us adieu at Melrose Bridge, and the dulcet sounds died away among the pine woods and furze brakes of the Eildon Hills. Then it was that we had the good fortune to meet my most humorous and excellent friend Sir Adam Ferguson, who made rare amends for the loss of our piper, by singing the following strains in his richest style, which, as they are not very well known in the South, I venture to subscribe.

> " The Laird o' Cockpen he's proud an' he's great,
> His mind's ta'en up wi' the things o' the State
> He wanted a wife his braw hoose to keep,
> But favour wi' wooin' was fashous to seek.

> " Doon by the dyke-side a leddie did dwell,
> At the head o' his table he thocht she'd look well,
> Macleish's ae dochter o' Claver's Ha' Lee,
> A penniless lass, wi' a lang pedigree.

" His wig was weel pouther'd, an' maist guid as new ;
His waistcoat was red, his coat it was blue ;
A ring on his finger, his sword an' cock'd hat,
An' wha could refuse the laird wi' a' that ?

" He mounted his mare, an' rode cannilie,
An' rapp'd at the yett o' Claver's Ha' Lee ;
' Gae tell tell Mrs. Jean to come speedily ben,
She's wanted to speak to the Laird o' Cockpen.

" Mrs. Jean she was makin' the elder flower wine ;
' An' what brings the laird at sic a like time ?'
She threw aff her apron, threw on her silk goun,
Her mutch wi' red ribbons, an' cam' awa' doun.

" An' when she cam' doun, he bowed fu' low,
An' what was his errand he sune let her know ;
Amazed was the laird when the leddie said ' Na' !'
An' wi' a laigh curtsy she turned awa'.

" Dumfoonder'd was he, nae sigh did he gie,
He mounted his mare, an' rode cannilie ;
An' said to himsel', as he gaed through the glen,
' She was daft to refuse the Laird o' Cockpen !' "

It had been my intention to give an account of the burning of the water from Melrose Bridge to the Cauld Pool, and so on to Cow's Hole, but the description, if faithful, would be so similar to the one already given, that it would be lamentably tiresome, and I have been ultra tedious already. Besides, it must be considered that I have been out of my bed most part of the night; that I am to the full as sleepy as any of my readers can possibly be ; and, moreover, that my back is half-frozen, whilst my front is scorched with the firebrands.

Farewell, then, dear brothers of the angle ; and when you go forth to take your pleasure, either in the mountain stream that struggles and roars through the narrow pass, or in the majestic salmon river that sweeps in lucid mazes through the vale, may your sport be ample, and your hearts light! But should the fish prove more sagacious than yourselves—a circumstance, excuse me, that is by no means impossible; should they, alas—but fate avert it—reject your hooked gifts, the course of the river will always lead you to pleasant places. In these we leave you to the quiet enjoyment of the glorious works of the Creation, whether it may be your pleasure to go forth when the spring sheds its flowery fragrance, or in the more advanced season, when the sere leaf is shed incessantly and wafted on the surface of the swollen river.

APPENDIX TO NEW EDITION

COMPRISING

THE TWEED FISHERY LAWS AT PRESENT IN FORCE

BEING

THE ACTS OF 1857 AND 1859.

*[The Appendix to the First Edition consisted of the 1830
Act which is now Repealed.]*

THE 1857 ACT.

WHEREAS an Act was passed in the Eleventh Year of the Reign
of His Majesty King *George* the Fourth, intituled *An Act for
the more effectual Preservation and Increase of the Breed of
Salmon, and for better regulating the Fisheries in the River*
Tweed, *and the Rivers and Streams running into the same,
and also within the Mouth or Entrance of the said River;*
and another Act was passed in the Sixth Year of the Reign of
His late Majesty King *William* the Fourth, intituled *An Act to
alter, amend, and enlarge the Powers of an Act passed in the
Eleventh Year of the Reign of His late Majesty, intituled, "An
Act for the more effectual Preservation and Increase of the Breed
of Salmon, and for better regulating the Fisheries in the River*
Tweed, *and the Rivers and Streams running into the same,
and also within the Mouth or Entrance of the said River:"*
And whereas the Salmon Fisheries in the River *Tweed* of late
Years have been much less productive and have greatly decreased
in Value, and it is of public Importance that more effectual
Means should be adopted for the Preservation and Increase of
the Breed of Salmon, and for that Purpose it is necessary
and expedient that the said Acts should be consolidated and
amended, and that further Provisions should be made for the
Regulation of the said Fisheries, for the removal of Nuisances
and Obstructions, and the Prevention of illegal Fishing in the
said River; but these objects cannot be effected without the
Authority of Parliament: May it therefore please your Majesty
that it may be enacted; and be it enacted by the Queen's most

18

Excellent Majesty, by and with the Advice and Consent of the Lords Spiritual and Temporal, and Commons, in this present Parliament assembled, and by the Authority of the same, as follows:

I. This Act may be cited for all Purposes as "The *Tweed* Fisheries Act, 1857."

II. The following Words and Expressions in this Act shall have the Meanings hereby assigned to them, unless such Meanings be repugnant to or inconsistent with the Context; that is to say,

The Expression "the River" shall mean and include the River *Tweed*, and every River, Brook, or Stream which flows or runs into the said River, and also the Mouth or Entrance of the said River as described and defined in this Act:

The Word "Salmon" shall mean and include Salmon, Grilse, Sea Trout, Bull Trout, Whitling, and other fish of the Salmon kind:

The Expressions "fixed Net" and "fixed Engine" shall respectively mean and include Stake, Bag, Bob, Hang, Sole, Stell, and Cairn Nets, and all Nets, Cruives, Engines, or Devices, of whatsoever Construction or Materials the same may be or however known or termed, used or which may be used for taking, killing, leading, or turning Salmon, or for obstructing the free Passage of Salmon, and fixed to the Soil, or anchored, moored, or fixed or made stationary in any way whatever:

The Word "Fishery" shall mean a Salmon Fishery in the River:

The Word "Commissioners" shall mean the Commissioners appointed by this Act, and shall include the Representatives of Commissioners as herein-after provided:

The Words "Clerk" and "Treasurer" shall mean respectively the Clerk and Treasurer to the Commissioners for the Time being:

The Word "Sheriff" shall mean the Sheriff of the County in *Scotland* where the Matter requiring the Cognizance of such Sheriff shall arise, and shall include the Sheriff Substitute of such County:

The Words "Justice" and "Justices" shall severally mean a Justice of the Peace or Two or more Justices of the Peace acting for the County, City, Liberty, or Place in *England* or *Scotland* where the Matter requiring the Cognizance of such Justice or Justices shall arise:

The Word "Owner" shall mean any Person or Corporation

who is the Proprietor of a Fishery in the River, or who receives or is entitled to receive the Rents of such Fishery on his or their own Account, or as Trustee, Guardian, or Factor for any Person or Corporation.

III. From and after the passing of this Act the recited Acts shall be and are hereby repealed, and this Act shall commence and take effect.

IV. All Rates, Rents, Goods, Debts, Moneys, and other Property and Effects whatsoever, heritable and moveable, real and personal, belonging or owing to or held by the Commissioners and Overseers acting under the recited Acts, subject to the existing Debts, Liabilities, Engagements, Contracts, Obligations, and Incumbrances affecting the same, are hereby vested in and may be lawfully held. used, exercised, enforced, recovered, and enjoyed by the Commissioners appointed by this Act.

V. All Contracts, Agreements, and other Deeds, Instruments, and Writings made, executed, or entered into between any Person and the said Commissioners and Overseers, or by, to, in favour of, or for the said Commissioners and Overseers, shall be and continue as good, valid, and effectual to all Intents and Purposes as if the recited Acts had not been repealed; and the Commissioners shall be liable for all Debts, Obligations, and Engagements of the said Commissioners and Overseers due and owing at the Time of the passing of this Act.

VI. All Actions, Suits, and Proceedings at Law or in Equity, and all Arbitrations, to which the said Commissioners and Overseers at the Time of the passing of this Act have been or are Parties, are hereby specially saved and reserved entire, and shall not be prejudiced or affected by anything in this Act contained, and may be proceeded in by or against the Commissioners without the Necessity of intimating such Action, Suit, Proceeding, or Arbitration to the Commissioners, or making them formally Parties thereto; and all Offences against the Provisions of the recited Acts, or either of them, committed before the passing of this Act, may be prosecuted, and all Penalties and Forfeitures incurred by reason of such Offences may be sued for and recovered, by the Commissioners in the same Manner in all respects as if the recited Acts had not been repealed.

VII. Notwithstanding the Repeal of the recited Acts, and except only as is by this Act otherwise expressly provided, everything done or suffered under the recited Acts shall be as valid as if the same were not repealed, and the Repeal thereof and this Act respectively shall accordingly be subject and without Prejudice to everything so done or suffered, and to all

Rights, Liabilities, Claims, and Demands, both present and future, which, if the recited Acts were not repealed and this Act were not passed, would be incident to or consequent on any and everything so done or suffered; and with respect to all such Rights, Liabilities, Claims, or Demands which affect or should or might affect the said Commissioners and Overseers, the Commissioners shall represent the said Commissioners and Overseers, and may enforce and shall be liable in respect of such Rights, Liabilities, Claims, or Demands in the same Manner and to the same Extent as the said Commissioners and Overseers could enforce or be liable to in respect of such Rights, Liabilities, Claims, or Demands: Provided that the Generality of this Enactment shall not be restricted by any of the other Clauses or Provisions of this Act.

VIII. All Rates leviable under or by virtue of the recited Acts or any of them, and which at the Time of the passing of this Act shall be due and payable, or if this Act had not been passed would have accrued due and been payable, to the said Commissioners and Overseers, shall continue in Force and be due and payable to the Commissioners, and may be sued for, collected, and recovered by such Means and under such Restrictions and Regulations as any Rates may be sued for, collected, or recovered under or in pursuance of this Act.

IX. The Clerk, Treasurer, and other Officers of the said Commissioners and Overseers at the Time of the passing of this Act shall be Officers and Servants of the Commissioners appointed by this Act until removed, and shall be subject to the Provisions of this Act as regards both their past and future Actings and Intromissions; and all Bonds and Securities granted to the said Commissioners and Overseers for the Performance of the Duties of such Clerk, Treasurer, and other Officers, and accounting for their Intromissions, shall remain valid and effectual, and may be enforced by the Commissioners in the same Manner and to the same Extent and Effect as such Bonds and Securities might have been enforced by the said Commissioners and Overseers.

X. Every Proprietor of Salmon Fishings in the River of the annual Value of Thirty Pounds, or which extend Half a Mile in Length, where such Fishings are only on One Side of the River, or a Quarter of a Mile in Length where such Fishings comprehend both Sides of the River, the Husband of every Proprietrix or Liferentrix, One Guardian of each Minor, One Trustee of every Estate, and One Member or Trustee of each Corporation or Company respectively holding or possessing such Salmon Fishings of the annual Value or Extent aforesaid, shall be and are hereby appointed Commissioners for the Execution of this Act;

and it shall be lawful for the Commissioners of *Greenwich Hospital*, the Dean and Chapter of the Cathedral Church of *Durham*, the Mayor and Corporation of the Town of *Berwick*, and the Trustees under the Will of *Nathaniel* late Lord *Crewe*, each to nominate, by an Instrument in Writing under their Hands or Seals, from Time to Time One Person to be a Commissioner as aforesaid to represent each of them, which Person so nominated shall have the like Powers to vote and act as the Commissioners hereby appointed, and such Nomination shall be from Time to Time revocable at the Option of the Party by whom such Commissioners shall be respectively nominated.

XI. It shall be lawful for every Commissioner qualified under this Act to nominate, by any Instrument in Writing under his Hand, from Time to Time One other qualified Commissioner to be Proxy for and to represent and act in all Meetings of the Commissioners as the Representative or Proxy of the Commissioner by whom he is so nominated, which Commissioner so nominated shall be entitled, in the Absence of each such Commissioner from whom he may be so nominated, to vote at all Meetings for each Commissioner by whom he is so nominated as well as for himself.

XII. It shall be lawful for every Commissioner qualified under this Act, or the Guardians or Administrators at Law of every Person qualified to be a Commissioner who may be under Age or otherwise incapable of acting, to nominate from Time to Time his or their *bonâ fide* ordinary Chamberlain, Factor, or Attorney, holding a regular written Appointment as such, to be Proxy, and to represent and act in all Meetings of the Commissioners as the Representative or Proxy of the Person for whom he is so nominated in the Absence of such Person; but no such Chamberlain, Factor, or Attorney so nominated (unless he be himself a Commissioner qualified under this Act) shall at such Meetings vote or act on more than One Proxy, without regard to the Number of Proxies he may hold.

XIII. Every Proxy granted under the Powers of this Act, except such as are granted under the Provisions of the immediately preceding Section to a Chamberlain, Factor, or Attorney, shall be used only for the Meeting therein specified; and every such Proxy may be used for the ordinary Business to be transacted at such Meeting, and according to the Terms and Instructions therein contained as to any special Matters to be brought before such Meeting.

XIV. In case of the Absence from any Meeting of Commissioners of any Commissioner who shall not have appointed a Proxy to act for him in manner before provided, it shall be lawful for the eldest Son or other Heir apparent of such Commissioner to act and vote at such Meeting in the Stead of his Father or of the Person of whom he is such Heir.

XV. Any person not qualified as herein provided who acts as a Commissioner under this Act, or nominates any Person to act for him, shall for every such Offence be liable to a Penalty of Twenty Pounds.

XVI. Any Commissioner who accepts of any Place of Profit under this Act shall from thenceforth, and while he continues to hold such Place of Profit, be disqualified from acting or voting as a Commissioner, and from representing or voting for any other Commissioner at any Meeting of the Commissioners; and any Person so disqualified who acts or votes as aforesaid shall for every such Offence be liable to a Penalty of Twenty Pounds.

XVII. The Commissioners shall hold their First Meeting for the Purposes of this Act on the Third *Monday* after the passing of this Act at *Cornhill*, and shall hold One General Meeting on the First *Monday* of *September* in every Year thereafter at *Cornhill*, or at *Berwick*, *Coldstream*, *Kelso*, or *Melrose*, as may be fixed upon by the Commissioners at their immediately preceding Annual General Meeting; and no Matters other than the ordinary Business of the Commission shall be transacted at any such Annual General Meeting unless special Notice of such Matters has been given by Advertisement as herein-after provided in the Case of Special Meetings: Provided, that if no other Place be specially fixed upon at any such Annual General Meeting, the next Annual Meeting of the Commissioners shall be held at *Cornhill*.

XVIII. It shall be lawful for any Three Commissioners from Time to Time, by a Requisition in Writing and Signed by them, to require the Clerk to call a Special General Meeting of the Commissioners, and on the Receipt of such Requisition the Clerk shall call such Meeting by an Advertisement inserted at least twice in some One Newspaper published in the County of *Roxburgh* and in *Berwick-upon-Tweed* respectively, and if no Newspaper shall be there published, then in Two Newspapers, the one published in *Edinburgh* and the other in *Newcastle-upon-Tyne*, at least Ten days before such Meeting shall be held, and which Requisition and Advertisement shall specify the Time and Place and the Purposes of such Meeting, and it shall not be lawful at any such Meeting to enter upon any other Business than that which is specified in such Requisition and Advertisement; and all such Special General Meetings shall be held at *Cornhill*, or at such other Place as the Commissioners shall from Time to Time fix upon as the Place for holding Special General Meetings.

XIX. The Quorum of every General and Special Meeting of Commissioners shall be Five, and if less than Five shall be present at any Meeting the Commissioners or Commissioner present shall have power to adjourn the Meeting to such Time and Place as they or he shall think fit, and in that Case Notice shall be given of the Time, Place, and Purpose of such Adjourned Meeting by Advertisement inserted in any Two such Newspapers published as aforesaid at least Ten Days before such Adjourned Meeting: Provided, that it shall not be in the Power of any Adjourned or Special Meeting to alter or rescind any Act done or Resolution passed by any Annual General Meeting.

XX. The Commissioners at every Meeting shall elect a Chairman to preside for that Meeting only, and if there be an equal Division of Votes on any Question the Chairman shall, in addition to his own Vote or Votes as a Commissioner, have a second or Casting Vote.

XXI. The Commissioners assembled at their First or at any of their Annual General Meetings, or at Special General Meeting called as aforesaid, may appoint different Districts for the better conducting and managing the several Purposes of this Act, and may fix the Times and Places of Meetings of Commissioners of each District; and at such District Meetings the Commissioners appointed to act in and for such District shall have Power to name a Chairman, Clerks, and other Officers with suitable Salaries, and to take such Securities from those appointed to Offices of Trust for the due Execution of their Offices as they shall think proper; and in District Meetings of Commissioners Three shall be a Quorum, but any One or more attending shall have Power to adjourn; and a particular Report from each District, with a Copy of the Books and Minutes of the Proceedings kept within the same, shall be made to the General Annual Meeting in every Year, and in case of Failure or Neglect the Clerk to the District shall be liable to a Penalty not exceeding Twenty Pounds.

XXII. At all Meetings of the Commissioners each Commissioner having the Qualification in Extent or annual Value of Salmon Fishings defined in Section Ten shall be entitled to One Vote; and every Commissioner possessed of or representing Salmon Fishings of the annual Value of Two hundred Pounds and under Four hundred Pounds, or who shall pay towards the Funds by this Act authorized to be raised a Sum equal to the Assessment leviable for the Time on Salmon Fishings of the annual Value of Two hundred Pounds, shall be entitled to Two Votes; and every Commissioner possessed of or representing Salmon Fishings of the annual Value of Four hundred Pounds or upwards, or who shall pay towards the Funds by this Act authorized to be raised a Sum equal to the Assessment leviable for the Time on Salmon Fishings of the annual Value of Four hundred Pounds, shall be entitled to three Votes; and no Commissioner shall be entitled to more than Three Votes; and when a Proxy is given for General Meetings it shall be for all the Votes to which the Commissioner giving it is entitled, and when for District Meetings for all the Votes to which the Commissioner giving it is entitled, in respect of Fisheries within the District for which it is used.

XXIII. At all Meetings of the Commissioners they shall defray their own Expenses, except such as may be incurred for the Use of the Room in which the Meeting is held, and for Books, Stationery, and Fire.

XXIV. It shall be lawful for the Commissioners at any General Meeting to appoint a Clerk and Treasurer and Superintendent of Water Bailiffs, and such other Officers as they shall think proper, with such Salaries as they shall think fit, and from Time to Time to remove and again to replace any Clerk, Treasurer, Superintendent, or other Officer; and in case of the Clerk, Treasurer, Superintendent, or other Officer dying or being removed from or quitting the Service of the Commissioners, it shall be lawful for the Commissioners, at a Special General Meeting called for the Purpose by the Clerk or any Three of the Commissioners, of which Meeting Notice shall be given as herein-before provided, to appoint some other fit and proper Person to be Clerk, Treasurer, Superintendent, or Officer in his Place.

XXV. The Clerk shall attend the General and Special Meetings of the Commissioners, and shall, in proper Books to be provided for that purpose, enter and keep a true and perfect Account of all the Money received by virtue of this Act, and of the Application of the same, and Minutes of all the Acts and Proceedings under this Act of the Commissioners and of every Committee appointed by them; and every such Minute shall be signed by the Chairman of the Meeting at which the Proceeding took place, and such Minute so signed shall be received as Evidence in all Courts, and before all Judges, Justices, and others, without Proof of such Meeting having been duly convened or held, or of the Persons attending such Meeting having been or being Commissioners or Members of Committees respectively, or of the Signature of the Chairman, or of the fact of his having been Chairman, all which Matters shall be presumed until the contrary is proved; and every Commissioner may at all convenient Times inspect and peruse such Books and Accounts *gratis*, and may demand and have Copies of any Part thereof on Payment of Sixpence for every One Hundred Words so to be copied; and if the Clerk shall refuse to permit any Commissioner to inspect or peruse any such Books or Accounts at all convenient Times, or refuse to make any such Copies within a reasonable Time at the Rate aforesaid, he shall for every such Offence be liable to a Penalty not exceeding Five Pounds.

XXVI. The same Person shall not be appointed to the Office of Clerk and Treasurer; and if any person being the Clerk or the Partner, or in the Service of the Clerk or of his Partner, shall accept the Office of Treasurer, or if any Person being the Treasurer or the Partner, or in the Service of the Treasurer or of his Partner, shall accept the Office of Clerk, he shall for every such Offence be liable to a Penalty of One Hundred Pounds.

XXVII. Every Officer employed by the Commissioners who shall exact or accept on account of anything done by virtue of his Office any Fee or Reward whatsoever other than the Salary or Allowances fixed by the Commissioners, or who shall be in any way concerned or interested in any Bargain or Contract made by the Commissioners, shall be liable to a Penalty of Fifty Pounds, and shall be incapable of being afterwards employed by the Commissioners.

XXVIII. Before any Treasurer, Collector, or other Officer intrusted by the Commissioners with the Custody or Control of Moneys by virtue of his Office shall enter upon such Office, the Commissioners shall take sufficient Security from him for the faithful Execution thereof.

XXIX. Every Collector appointed or employed by the Commissioners by virtue of this Act to collect any Rates shall, within Seven Days after he shall have received any Moneys on account of any such Rates, pay over the same to the Treasurer to the Account of the Commissioners, and the Receipt of the Treasurer for the Moneys so paid shall be a sufficient Discharge to such Collector; and every such Collector shall, in such Time and in such Manner as the Commissioners direct, deliver to them true and perfect Accounts in Writing under his Hand of all Moneys received by him and of all Moneys paid by him to the Treasurer by virtue of this Act, and also a List of the Names of all Persons who have neglected or refused to pay any Rate or Money owing by them, with a Statement of the Moneys due by them respectively.

XXX. Every Collector and other Officer appointed or employed by the Commissioners by virtue of this Act shall from Time to Time, when required by the Commissioners, make out and deliver to them, or to any Person appointed by them for that Purpose, a true and perfect Account in Writing under his Hand of all Moneys received by him on behalf of the Commissioners, and such Account shall state how and to whom and for what Purpose such Moneys have been disposed of, and together with such Account such Officer shall deliver the Vouchers and Receipts for such Payments; and every such Officer shall pay to the Commissioners, or to any Person appointed by them to receive the same, all Moneys which shall appear to be owing by him upon the Balance of such Accounts.

XXXI. If any such Collector or other Officer fail to render such Accounts as aforesaid, or to produce and deliver up all the Vouchers and Receipts relating to the same in his Possession or Power, or to pay the Balance thereof when thereunto required, or if for Five Days after being thereunto required he fail to deliver up to the Commissioners, or to any Person appointed by them to receive the same, all Papers and Writings, Property, Effects, Matters, and Things, in his Possession or Power relating to the Execution of this Act or belonging to the Commissioners, then, on Complaint thereof being made to the Sheriff or a Justice, such Sheriff or Justice shall summon such Officer to appear before such Sheriff or before Two or more Justices, according as the Summons may have been issued by the Sheriff or a Justice, at a Time and Place to be set forth in such Summons, to answer such Charge; and upon the Appearance of such Officer, or upon Proof that such Summons was personally served upon him or left at his last known Place of Abode, such Sheriff or Justices may hear and determine the Matter in a summary Way, and may adjust and declare the Balance owing by such Officer; and if it appear, either upon Confession of such Officer or upon Evidence or upon Inspection of the Account, that any Moneys of the Commissioners are in the Hands of such Officer or owing by him to the Commissioners, such Sheriff or Justices may order such Officer to pay the same, and if he fail to pay the Amount it shall be lawful for such Sheriff or Justices to grant a Warrant to levy the same by Distress or by Poinding and Sale, or in default thereof to commit the Offender to Gaol, there to remain without Bail for a Period not exceeding Three Months, unless the same be sooner paid.

XXXII. If any such Officer summoned as aforesaid refuse to make out such Account in Writing, or to produce and deliver to the Sheriff or Justices the several Vouchers and Receipts relating thereto, or to deliver up any Books, Papers, or Writ-

ings, Property, Effects, Matters, or Things, in his Possession
or Power belonging to the Commissioners, such Sheriff or
Justices may commit such Officer to Gaol, there to remain
until he shall have delivered up all the Vouchers and Receipts
in his Possession or Power relating to such Accounts, and all
the Books, Papers, Writings, Property, Effects, Matters, and
Things in his Possession or Power belonging to the Commissioners.

XXXIII. If any Commissioner or other Person acting on
behalf of the Commissioners shall make Oath that he has good
Reason to believe, upon Grounds to be stated in his Deposi-
tion, and that he does believe, that it is the Intention of any
such Officer to abscond, the Sheriff or Justice before whom the
Complaint is made may, instead of issuing his Summons, issue
his Warrant for bringing such Officer before the Sheriff if the
Warrant be issued by him, or before any Two Justices if the
Warrant be issued by a Justice; but no Person executing such
Warrant shall keep such Officer in Custody longer than Twenty-
four Hours without bringing him before the Sheriff or some
Justice, according as he may be summoned before the one or
the other; and the Sheriff or Justice before whom such Officer
may be brought may either discharge such Officer, if he think
there is no sufficient Ground for his Detention, or order such
Officer to be detained in Custody so as to be brought before the
Sheriff or Two Justices at a Time and Place to be named in
such Order, unless such Officer give Bail to the Satisfaction of
such Sheriff or Justice for his Appearance before such Sheriff
or Justices to answer the Complaint of the Commissioners.

XXXIV. No such Proceeding against or Dealing with any
such Officer as aforesaid shall deprive the Commissioners of any
Remedy which they might otherwise have against any Surety
of such Officer.

XXXV. The Commissioners may sue and be sued for or with
respect to any Matter or Thing to be done in the Execution of
this Act, or for any Penalties recoverable under the Provisions
thereof, in the Name of their Clerk or in the Name of any
Three of the Commissioners; and no Action or Suit wherein
the Commissioners shall be concerned as Plaintiffs or Pursuers
or Defendants or Defenders in the Name of their Clerk, or in
the Name of any Three of the Commissioners by virtue of this
Act, shall abate by the Death or Removal of any such Clerk
or Commissioner; but the Clerk for the Time being, or any
Three of the Commissioners to be for that Purpose nominated,
if Plaintiff or Pursuer, or who may be sued if Defendant or
Defender, shall be deemed to be the Plaintiff or Pursuer or
Defendant or Defender (as the Case may be) in every such
Action or Suit.

XXXVI. It shall be lawful for the Commissioners assembled at any General, Special, or Adjourned Meeting to nominate and appoint such Number of Water Bailiffs for the Protection of the Fisheries and Detection of Offenders as to them shall appear expedient, or to authorise their District Meetings or any Two or more Commissioners to nominate and appoint such Water Bailiffs for such Periods and at such Salaries and on such Terms and Conditions as shall appear to be expedient; and it shall be in the Power of any General, Special, or District Meeting of Commissioners to remove such Water Bailiffs or any of them, and appoint others in their Room, and to make such Alterations in regard to their Salaries as to them shall appear proper; and it shall be lawful for any Two Commissioners to supply and fill up any Vacancy or Vacancies that may occur by the Death, Resignation, or Dismissal of any One or more Water Bailiffs till the next General, Special, or Adjourned Meeting be held; and before any Superintendent or Water Bailiff shall be entitled to act under the Authority of this Act he shall take the Oath following before any Sheriff or Justice of Peace; *(videlicet,)*

"I *A.B.* do solemnly swear, That I will duly and faithfully execute the Office of Superintendent [*or* Water Bailiff] in Terms of 'The *Tweed* Fisheries Act, 1857.' So help me GOD."

And if any Person shall act as a Superintendent or Water Bailiff under the Authority of this Act without previously taking such Oath, he shall for every such Offence be liable to a Penalty not exceeding Ten Pounds.

XXXVII. The Superintendent and Water Bailiffs appointed as aforesaid shall, after being sworn into Office, have and be entitled to exercise the Powers and Authorities of Constables in regard to all Matters connected with this Act in the same Manner as if Offences against this Act were Breaches of the Peace, and for the Purpose of preventing Offences, or of detecting and apprehending Offenders, to enter upon any Grounds adjoining the River, and at all Times with their Boats or otherwise to enter upon any Fishery in the River for the Purpose of preventing or detecting unlawful Fishings or Obstructions in the River, and to moor, anchor, or otherwise fix their Boats at such Places as they shall find convenient; provided that by such mooring, anchoring, or fixing their Boats they do not obstruct or impede any legal Mode of Fishing.

XXXVIII. It shall be lawful for every Superintendent or Water Bailiff or other Person whatsoever, without any Warrant or Authority other than this Act, *brevi manu* to seize and detain any Person who shall be found committing any Offence against the Provisions of this Act, and to convey such

Offender or cause him to be conveyed by any Constable or other Peace Officer, in case the Offence is committed in *England*, before any Justice having Jurisdiction in the Place where the Offence is committed or where the Offender resides or is found, who shall forthwith proceed against such Offender according to Law and according to the Provisions in this Act contained, and in case the Offence is committed in *Scotland* such Offender shall be conveyed by the Person apprehending him before the Sheriff or some Justice having Jurisdiction in the Place where the Offence is committed or where the Offender resides or is found, and such Sheriff or Justice shall forthwith examine and thereupon discharge or commit such Offender until Caution de Judicio sisti be found, as the Case may require.

XXXIX. Every Person who shall resist or make forcible Opposition to or assault any High or Petty Constable, Peace Officer, Sheriff Officer, Superintendent, or Water Bailiff, or any other Person employed in the Execution of this Act, shall for every such Offence be liable to a Penalty not exceeding Five Pounds.

XL. All Sheriffs, Justices of the Peace, and other Magistrates shall and may act in the Execution of this Act notwithstanding any such Sheriff, Justice, or Magistrate shall be interested in any Fishery, except in any Case where he or the Lessee or Occupier of any Fishery in which he is interested is a Party to the Prosecution or Cause to be heard and determined by him.

XLI. For the Purposes of this Act, the Limits of the Mouth or Entrance of the River *Tweed* shall be deemed to extend and shall extend from the Pier called *Queen Elizabeth's* Pier along the Sea Coast on the South Side of the said Pier Five Miles, and along the Sea Coast on the North Side of the said Pier Four Miles, and shall also extend Five Miles in front of the Mouth of the said River and of the several Lines of Boundary herein-before mentioned into the Sea, such Distance towards the Sea to be computed by Lines drawn the one from the Northern and the other from the Southern of the aforesaid Boundaries at Right Angles to a line drawn between the said Northern and Southern Extremities; and the whole Enactments and Provisions of this Act shall extend and be applicable to the Mouth or Entrance of the said River within the Limits above defined.

XLII. It shall not be lawful for any Person to fish for or take or aid or assist in fishing for or taking any Salmon in or from the River at any Time between the First Day of *October* in any Year and the first Day of *March* in the Year following, except by means of the Rod and Line, nor with the Rod and

Line at any Time between the Fourteenth Day of *October* in any Year and the First Day of *March* in the Year following, and which respective Periods above defined are in this Act termed the "Annual Close Times."

XLIII. It shall not be lawful for any Person between the First Day of *March* and the Fourteenth Day of *October* in any Year to fish for or take or aid or assist in fishing for or taking any Salmon in or from the River at any Time or in any Way whatsoever between Six of the Clock on *Saturday* Afternoon and Six of the Clock on the following *Monday* Morning, and which Period last above defined is in this Act termed the " Weekly Close Time."

XLIV. Every Person who shall during the Annual Close Times or Weekly Close Time fish for or take or aid or assist in fishing for or taking any Salmon in or from the River (excepting as aforesaid) shall for every such Offence be liable to a Penalty not exceeding Ten Pounds, and an additional Penalty of Ten Shillings for each Salmon so taken, and shall also forfeit every Salmon so taken, and every Boat, Net, Tackle, or Engine by which such Salmon has been taken or attempted to be taken.

XLV. Every Person who during the Annual Close Times fishes in the River with any Pout Net or Net of any other Kind or Description whatsoever shall for every such Offence be liable in a Penalty not exceeding Five Pounds, and every such Net shall be forfeited.

XLVI. Every Person who during the Annual Close Times has in his Possession Salmon known by such Person to have been taken or caught in the River during the Annual Close Times (except such Salmon as are taken by means of the Rod and Line between the First and the Fourteenth Days of *October*), or who sells or offers or exposes for Sale or Exchange any Salmon known by such Person to have been caught in the River during the Annual Close Times, shall for every such Offence be liable to a Penalty not exceeding Two Pounds for every Salmon so had in his Possession, or sold or offered or exposed for Sale or Exchange as aforesaid, and shall also forfeit every such Salmon, and every Boat, Cart, Basket, or Package in which the same may be found, and the Proof that such Salmon was not taken contrary to the Provisions of this Act shall lie upon the Person in whose Custody the same is found.

XLVII. On or before the Fourth Day of *October* in every Year every Occupier of a Fishery in the River shall and he is hereby required to remove from every Fishery, Fishing, Shield, and Fishing Ground and Houses and Premises occupied or used by him all Boats, Oars, Nets, Engines, and other Tackle used and employed in taking and killing Salmon (excepting Boats with their Oars and such other Implements as are used for Angling or Rod Fishing), and to carry away the same to some Place or Places to be from Time to Time appointed by the Commissioners, where the same can be securely lodged and kept until the Twenty-seventh Day of *February* in the following Year; and each Boat, with its Oars and other Implements as aforesaid, so retained for the Purpose of Angling or Rod Fishing shall be removed and carried away on or before the Seventeenth Day of *October* in every Year, and shall be lodged and kept and remain as aforesaid until the Twenty-seventh Day of *February* in the following Year; and every such Occupier who neglects or refuses to remove and carry away all and every such Boats, Oars, Nets, Engines, and other Tackle as aforesaid, and to keep the same secured from the said Fisheries and Premises during the Period aforesaid, shall for every such Offence be liable to a Penalty not exceeding Twenty Pounds, and all such Boats, Oars, Nets, Engines and other Tackle not removed or kept secured as aforesaid shall be forfeited: Provided always, that this Enactment shall not be held or construed to extend to Public Ferry Boats, or to Boats used by any Owner or Occupier of Land adjoining the River solely for the Transport of himself or his Family or Servants or any Persons in his Employment: Provided also, that all such last-mentioned Boats shall be under and subject to the Regulations herein-after prescribed with respect thereto.

XLVIII. It shall be lawful for any Superintendent or Water Bailiff or other Person employed in the Execution of this Act, without any other Authority than this Act, to seize all such Boats, Oars, Nets, Engines, and other Tackle which shall not have been so removed or kept secured as aforesaid (but excepting as aforesaid), and to convey and carry the same to some of the Places of Security to be appointed as aforesaid; and also at any Time during the Annual Close Times to enter into or upon any Fishery or Fishing Grounds, and without any Warrant to search all and every the Fishing Shields and other Premises belonging thereto for any Boats, Oars, Nets, Engines, and other Tackle that may be deposited or concealed therein; and if any such Shield is found to be locked up, and if upon being required the Occupier of such Shield shall refuse to open the Door thereof, it shall be lawful for any Superintendent or Water Bailiff or other Person employed as aforesaid to break open the Door of such Shield, and to search for such Boats, Oars, Nets, Engines, or other Tackle, and if any are found to seize and carry away the same to some of the Places of Security to be appointed as aforesaid.

XLIX. If any Net or other Engine or Tackle whatsoever adapted for taking or killing Salmon or obstructing their passage in the River shall be left or placed in the River at any Time during the Annual Close Time, or Weekly Close Time, it shall be lawful for any Superintendent or Water Bailiff, or other Person acting or employed under the Authority of this Act, to seize and carry away the same, and it shall be lawful for the Commissioners to cause the same to be cut to Pieces or otherwise destroyed, or, in their Discretion, to be restored to the Owner.

L. It shall not be lawful for any Person other than an Owner or Occupier of a Fishery in the River, or otherwise entitled to fish for Salmon therein, or having an exclusive Right of Fishing for Salmon in any Fishery beyond the River, or having a Licence under the Hand of the Clerk, to have in his Possession within Five Miles from the River any Net or Engine of the Description of those used for taking or killing Salmon, except for the Purpose of manufacturing or selling or repairing the same for the Owner or Occupier of a Fishery; and every Person who is convicted of offending against this Enactment shall for every such Offence be liable to a Penalty not exceeding Twenty Pounds; and every such Net or Engine found in the Possession of such Person shall be forfeited, and the Sheriff or Justice before whom such Person is convicted shall order and direct every such Net or Engine to be cut to Pieces or otherwise destroyed.

LI. Upon Information on Oath to any Sheriff or Justice that the Informant has probable Cause to suspect and does suspect, and stating the Grounds of such Suspicion, that any Person residing or being at the Time within the Jurisdiction of such Sheriff or Justice has, contrary to the Provisions of this Act, in his Custody or Possession, or that there is lodged, placed, or concealed in any Dwelling House, Fishing Shield, Outhouse, or Premises, or in any Boat, Vessel, Carriage, Cart, or Vehicle within the Jurisdiction of such Sheriff or Justice, or which will shortly pass through or be within the same, any Net, Leister, Spear, or similar Engine adapted for taking or killing Salmon, or any Salmon which have been illegally taken or killed in or from the River, it shall be lawful for such Sheriff or Justice to authorise and direct, by Warrant under his Hand, any Superintendent or Water Bailiff appointed and acting under the Authority of this Act, or any High or Petty Constable or other Peace Officer, to search in the Daytime every Dwelling House, and at any Time every Fishing Shield, Outhouse, or Premises, or Place, Boat, Vessel, Carriage, Cart, or other Vehicle wherein he has Information that any such Nets, Leisters, Spears, or Engines, or any Salmon, are lodged, placed, or concealed; and if upon such Search any such Nets, Leisters, Spears, or Engines adapted for the taking or killing of Salmon, or any Salmon illegally taken or killed as aforesaid, shall be there found, it shall be lawful for such Superintendent or Water Bailiff, Constable, or Peace Officer to seize and carry away or secure the same, and also the Boat, Vessel, Carriage, Cart, Vehicle, Basket, Box, or Package in which the same may be found: Provided, that every such Warrant shall be put in force within Twenty-four Hours after the same is granted, and only within the Jurisdiction of the Sheriff or Justice granting such Warrant.

LII. The Lessee, Tenant, or Occupier of every established and accustomed Ferry for the Conveyance of Passengers, Horses, and Carriages across the River shall have the Name or Names of the Owner and of the Ferry and the Number of each Boat painted upon some conspicuous Part of each and every Boat so used by him, in Letters of Two Inches in Length in White on a Black Ground or in Black on a White Ground, and shall keep such Boat locked up when not actually in use; and every such Lessee, Tenant, or Occupier who has in his Possession or uses for the Purposes of such Ferry any Boat not so marked and painted, or who does not keep such Boat locked up as aforesaid, shall for every such Offence be liable to a Penalty not exceeding Five Pounds; and every such Lessee, Tenant, or Occupier who uses or permits or allows any Boat belonging to him or to such Ferry to be used for the Purpose of Fishing in the River shall for every such Offence be liable to a Penalty not exceeding Ten Pounds, and every Boat so used may be seized and forfeited.

LIII. Every Owner and Occupier of a Fishery within or of Land adjoining the River who uses any Boat in or upon the River for the Purpose of Fishing, or for any other Purpose, shall have his Name and Surname painted upon every such Boat, with the Number thereof, in like Manner as is hereinbefore directed with respect to Ferry Boats; and no Boat which in the Fishing Season is generally and ordinarily used for fishing with Nets shall be used for Angling or Rod Fishing; and every such Owner and Occupier who uses a Boat contrary to the Provisions of this Section, or without his Name and the Number painted thereon as before provided, shall for every such Offence be liable to a Penalty not exceeding Five Pounds, and every Boat so used may be seized and forfeited.

LIV. It shall be lawful for the Commissioners at any Annual General Meeting, from Time to Time, to direct and appoint all Boats generally and ordinarily used for fishing with Nets to be painted or otherwise marked by some Colour or Mark, so that

19

the same may be known and may be easily distinguished from Ferry Boats or Boats used indiscriminately for both Net Fishing and Rod Fishing, which Direction or Appointment shall be notified to the Owner and Occupier of every Fishery using any such Boat or to his or their known Agent, and which distinguishing Colour or Mark every Owner and Occupier of every Boat generally and ordinarily used for fishing with Nets shall be bound, after such Notification, to put upon such Boat previous to the Commencement of the next Fishing Season, and also upon all such Boats as they shall afterwards use, and to keep the same thereon until such Time as some new Direction or Appointment in that Behalf shall have been made by the Commissioners; and every such Owner or Occupier who uses any such Boat without such distinguishing Colour or Mark, or with any other Colour or Mark than those specially appointed for such Boat, shall for every such Offence be liable to a Penalty not exceeding Five Pounds, and every Boat so used may be seized and forfeited.

LV. It shall not be lawful for any Person to set or place or retain in the River any fixed Net or fixed Engine, or to take or kill any Salmon by means of any such fixed Net or fixed Engine; and every Person who sets, places, or retains in the River any such fixed Net or fixed Engine, or by means thereof takes or kills any Salmon, shall for every such Offence be liable to a Penalty not exceeding Twenty Pounds, and to a daily Penalty not exceeding Ten Pounds for every Day during which such fixed Net or fixed Engine is so set, placed, or retained, and an additional Penalty of Ten Shillings for each Salmon taken by any such Means, and every fixed Net or fixed Engine so used and the Fish so taken shall be forfeited; and it shall be lawful for the Commissioners, or any Two of them, or any Person appointed or authorised by the Commissioners, or any Two of them, to remove and take away all and every such fixed Net or fixed Engine, and to dispose of the same as they shall think fit.

LVI. All Mill Dams, Dykes, Wears, Caulds, and other permanent Obstructions to the Run of Salmon in the River shall be so constructed, and if necessary shall be so altered, as to permit and allow of the free Run of Salmon over the same in the main Stream of the River in the ordinary and mean State thereof; and if the Owners or Occupiers of such Mill Dams, Dykes, Wears, Caulds, and other Obstructions, or of any Mills or Works for which they are or may be erected or used, shall refuse or neglect so to construct or alter the same within Twenty-one Days after being thereunto required in Writing by any Two of the Commissioners or the Clerk, it shall be lawful for the Sheriff in *Scotland* or any Justice in *England* within whose Jurisdiction such Mill Dams, Dykes, Wears, Caulds, and other Obstructions are wholly or partly situated, upon the Application or Information of any Commissioner, or the Clerk or any Officer or Person appointed by the Commissioners, to order and Direct such Construction or Alteration to be made in a substantial Manner under the Inspection and Direction of a proper Person to be named by such Sheriff or Justice, and at the Expense of the Commissioners in the Case of any such Mill Dam, Dyke, Wear, Cauld, or other permanent Obstruction existing at the passing of this Act, and at the Expense of the Owners or Occupiers of any such Mill Dam, Dyke, Wear, Cauld, or other permanent Obstruction that may be erected after the passing of this Act, or that shall be altered, reconstructed, or renewed in a Manner to destroy the Free Run of Salmon over the same: Provided, that the Height of no such Mill Dam, Dyke, Wear, Cauld, or other Obstruction existing at the passing of this Act shall be lowered in any part thereof by any Works or Alterations made under the Provisions of this Act for obtaining a free Run for Salmon as herein provided; and that any Mill Dam, Dyke, Wear, Cauld, or other permanent Obstruction, altered or substituted for and in the place of any existing Mill Dam, Dyke, Wear, Cauld, or other permanent Obstruction, but which shall offer the same Facilities for the free Run of Salmon over the same as before such Alteration or Substitution, shall be considered and dealt with as a Cauld existing at the passing of this Act; and in every Case all Alterations shall be made in such Manner as may sufficiently effect the Object intended with the least possible Injury to the Property and Works of such Owner and Occupier.

LVII. All Rocks, Shoals, Deposits of Stones, Gravel, Sand. Mud, or other Matter or Thing, and all natural Obstructions in the River, which prevent, obstruct, or interrupt the free Passage of Salmon therein, shall be removed or altered so as to permit and allow of the free Run of Salmon at all Times over, across, or through the same; and if the Owner of the Soil, Land, or Fishery in or upon which the Obstruction or Cause of Interruption exists or is situate shall refuse or neglect to alter or remove the same so as to allow the free Run of Salmon at all Times over, across, or through the same, within Fourteen Days after being thereunto required in Writing by any Two Commissioners or the Clerk, it shall be lawful for the Commissioners or for the Sheriff or any Justice within whose Jurisdiction the Obstruction or Cause of Interruption is wholly or partly situated, upon the Application or Information of any Commissioner or the Clerk, to order and direct that such Obstruction or Cause of Interruption shall be removed or altered by or under the Inspection and Direction of a proper Person to be appointed by the Commissioners or such Sheriff or Justice, and at the Expense of the Commissioners, in such a manner as may sufficiently effect the Object intended with the least possible Injury to the Property of such Owner: Provided that this Enactment shall not in any way extend to authorize the Alteration or Removal of any Mill Dam, Dyke, Wear, Cauld, or other permanent Obstruction now used for manufacturing Purposes, and as to which Provision is made in the immediately preceding Section.

LVIII. The Owner of every Cairn in the River, or connected with either Bank or Shore thereof, or on or connected with any Shoal or Island therein, and which in the Opinion of the Commissioners may be principally or ordinarily used or is mainly adapted for fishing with Nets, shall within Three Months after the passing of this Act remove or destroy the same; and in the event of such Owner refusing or neglecting to remove or destroy such Cairn within the Period above mentioned, the Commissioners may at any Time thereafter appoint a fit and proper person to remove and destroy the same at the Expense of the Commissioners.

LIX. Every Owner or Occupier of a Mill or Manufactory of any Description on the River shall set up and maintain in the Mill Lead in front of the Waterwheel of such Mill or Manufactory a Heck of the full Breadth and Depth of the Mill Lead thereat, and with vertical Bars having a clear Space of not more than Three and One Quarter Inches between each Bar, and that under a Penalty not exceeding Five Pounds in case of Failure; and every Person who shall wilfully injure or destroy any such Heck, or shall raise or remove the same, except for the Purpose of cleaning or repairing the same, or cleaning the Mill Lead, or any other necessary Purpose, shall for every such Offence be liable to a Penalty not exceeding Five Pounds.

LX. Every Person who beats the Water, or places, uses, or sets any White Object or any Net or other Thing whatsoever in, over, or across the River, so as to prevent or for the Purpose of preventing Salmon from entering or from going up or down the River or any Part thereof, or who in any other Way or Manner prevents or obstructs Salmon from entering or going up and down the River, shall for the First Offence be liable to a Penalty not exceeding Ten Pounds, and for every subsequent Offence to a Penalty not exceeding Twenty Pounds, and the Net or Object or Thing so placed, used, or set, may be seized and forfeited.

LXI. Nothing in this Act contained prohibiting the placing of fixed Engines or other Things whatsoever in the River shall apply to Waterwheels or other Machinery used only for manufacturing Purposes, and placed in or upon Mill Leads.

LXII. Every Person who shall shoot or work any Wear Shot Net in the River within the Distance of Thirty Yards of any other Wear Shot Net already shot or being worked in the River before such last-mentioned Net is fully drawn and landed shall for every such Offence be liable to a Penalty not exceeding Five Pounds.

LXIII. Every Person who at any Time takes or kills or attempts to take or kill Salmon in or from the River by means of any Leister or Spear or any such Engine shall for every such Offence be liable to a Penalty not exceeding Ten Pounds, and an additional Penalty of Ten Shillings for each Salmon so taken; and every such Leister, Spear, and other Engine so used or attempted to be used, and every Salmon so taken, may be seized and forfeited.

LXIV. Every Person who has in his Possession within Five Miles from the River any Leister, Spear, or similar Engine of the Description of those used for killing Salmon shall for every such Offence be liable to a Penalty not exceeding Two Pounds, and every such Leister, Spear, or similar Engine may be seized and forfeited.

LXV. Every Person who at any Time lays or places in the River, or allows to fall or run or flow into the River, any hot Lime, or Refuse of Gasworks, or Products thereof, or Prussiate of Potash, or any Water in which Green flax has been steeped, or any Matter or Thing which shall poison or kill any Salmon or Smolt, shall for every such First Offence be liable to a Penalty not exceeding Five Pounds, and for every subsequent Offence shall be liable to a Penalty not exceeding Ten Pounds, and to a daily Penalty of Two Pounds for every Day during which such Offence is continued.

LXVI. Every Person who at any Time lays or places in or allows to fall into the River at or below High-water Mark any Coal, Cinders, Coal Ashes, Dirt, or Rubbish shall for every such Offence be liable to a Penalty not exceeding Forty Shillings.

LXVII. Every Person not being an Owner or Occupier of a Fishery in the River, or otherwise entitled to fish for Salmon therein, who at any Time between the First Day of *March* and the Fourteenth day of *October* in any Year fishes for or takes or aids or assists in fishing for or taking Salmon in or from the River, shall for every such Offence be liable to a Penalty not exceeding Ten Pounds, and an additional Penalty of Ten Shillings for every Salmon so taken or killed; and every Salmon so taken, and every Boat, Net, Rod, Engine, or Tackle used in such Fishing, or by means of which any Salmon has been taken or attempted to be taken, may be seized and forfeited.

LXVIII. Every Person who enters or is found upon any Ground adjacent or near to the River or in or upon the River with Intent illegally to take or kill Salmon shall for every such Offence be liable to a Penalty not exceeding Five Pounds.

LXIX. If any Person who is found in or upon the River, or upon Ground adjacent or near to the River, has in his Possession, or if he be in Company with any Person having at the Time in his Possession, any Net or Implement wherewith Salmon are usually taken or killed during the Periods when it is unlawful to take Salmon by such Net or Implement or for such Person to have the same in his Possession (excepting in the Case of Occupiers within Half an Hour immediately after the Commencement or Half an Hour immediately before the Termination of the Weekly Close Time), or during the Periods when such Fish may be taken, unless such Person be the Occupier of a Fishery in the River or duly authorised by any such Occupier to fish in the River, the Possession of such Net or Implement shall be deemed and taken to be sufficient Evidence of the Intent of such Person to commit the Offence specified in the immediately preceding Section ; and notwithstanding of any such Net or Implement not being in the Possession of any Person who is found as aforesaid in or upon the River, or upon Ground adjacent or near to the River, it shall be lawful for the Sheriff or Justice before whom the Complaint against such Person shall be heard to infer, adjudge, and determine the Intent of such Person to commit the Offence specified in the immediately preceding Section, according to the Evidence which may be adduced on the Hearing of such Complaint, and to convict or discharge him accordingly.

LXX. Every Person who during the Periods in each Year when it is lawful to fish for Salmon knowingly takes or kills or aids or assists in taking or killing in or from the River any foul, unclean, or unseasonable salmon, or knowingly has in his Possession any such Salmon, or exposes for sale or exchanges for any Matter or Thing any such Salmon, shall for every such Offence be liable to a Penalty not exceeding Five Pounds, and every Salmon so taken, and the Net or other Engine by which the same has been taken, and the Hampers, Baskets, and Packages in which the same are found, may be seized and forfeited ; and the Proof that such Salmon were not taken in or from the River contrary to this Enactment shall lie upon the Person in whose Custody the same shall be found.

LXXI. Every Person who shall between the First Day of *March* and the First Day of *June* in fishing with a Rod and Line use any Cleek or Instrument for landing Fish other than a Landing Net shall be liable to a Penalty not exceeding Five Pounds.

LXXII. If any Person while fishing in the River for Salmon takes or captures any foul, unclean, or unseasonable Salmon, he shall immediately put back such Salmon into the River with as little injury to such Salmon as possible; and every Person convicted of offending against this Enactment shall for every such Offence be liable to a Penalty not exceeding Ten Shillings for each Salmon so taken and not put back as aforesaid.

LXXIII. If any Person while in the Act of fishing for River or Fresh-water Trout, during the Period when Salmon may be lawfully taken and killed, takes any Salmon in or from the River, he shall forthwith deliver up such Salmon to the Owner or Occupier of the Fishery where the same was taken, and every Person who fails or refuses to deliver up any Salmon so taken shall be liable to a Penalty not exceeding Two Pounds for every such Salmon.

LXXIV. Every Person who wilfully takes or kills or aids or assists in taking or killing in or from the River by any Means or by any Device (except by the Rod and Line), or wilfully sells, purchases, or has in his Possession, any Smolt, Fry, or young Brood or Spawn of Salmon, or in any Way or by any Device wilfully obstructs the Passage of such Smolts, Fry, or young Brood, or injures or disturbs any such Smolts or Fry, or any Spawn or Spawning Bed, Bank, or Shallow where the same may be, shall for every such Offence be liable to a Penalty not exceeding Ten Pounds, and to an additional Penalty of Two Shillings for each of the Smolts, Fry or young Brood of Salmon so taken, killed, or destroyed, or found in his Possession, and all Nets, Tackle, and Engines whereby the same have been taken or killed, and the Hampers, Baskets, or Packages wherein the same may be found, may be seized and forfeited.

LXXV. Every Person who wilfully kills any Smolt, Fry, or young Brood of Salmon by the Rod and Line between the First Day of *April* and the First Day of *June* in each Year, or has in his Possession any Smolt, Fry, or young Brood of Salmon taken by means of the Rod and Line during the said Period, shall for every such First Offence be liable to a Penalty of Sixpence, and shall for every Second or subsequent Offence be liable to a Penalty not exceeding Two Pounds and an additional Penalty of Two Shillings for each of the Smolts, Fry, or young

Brood of Salmon so killed or found in his Possession ; and the Rod and Line whereby the same have been killed, and the Baskets or Packages in which the same may be found, may in the Case of every such Second and subsequent Offence be seized and forfeited.

LXXVI. And whereas it is expedient that the Act passed in the Eighth and Ninth Year of the Reign of Her present Majesty, intituled *An Act to prevent fishing for Trout or other Fresh-water Fish by Nets in the Rivers and Waters in* Scotland, should apply to the whole of the River *Tweed :* Be it enacted, That the said Act shall apply and is hereby extended to the whole of the River, whether situated in *England* or in *Scotland ;* and all Offences against the Provisions of the said Act committed in or upon that Part of the River which is situated in *England* shall be heard, adjudged, and determined by or before any Justice of the Peace or Magistrate for the County, Division, Borough, or Place where such Offence is committed, or where the Offender resides or is found ; and the Penalties imposed by or under the said Act may be recovered and applied in the same Manner as is herein provided with respect to Penalties to be imposed or recovered under the Provisions of this Act.

LXXVII. In the Case of any Fishery usually fished by Nets which belongs to or is held by Two or more Owners jointly, any one of such Owners may, by Writing under his Hand, require the other Owners jointly interested therein to agree with him for the joint Fishing of such Fishery, and to fix the Number of Men, Boats, Nets, and Appurtenances necessary for such Fishing ; and on such Owner furnishing his proportionate Number of Men, Boats, Nets, and Appurtenances so fixed and agreed upon, and contributing and paying his proportionate Share of the Burdens and Working Expenses of such Fishery, such Owner shall be entitled for his own Use and Behoof to a Share of the whole Produce of such Fishery in proportion to his Interest therein ; and every joint Owner of such Fishery may lease his Interest therein to such Person and on such Terms and Conditions as he may think fit, and every such Lessee shall during his Lease have all the Rights hereby conferred on such joint Owner.

LXXVIII. If for Fourteen Days after being thereto required in Writing as aforesaid the joint Owners of such Fishery, or any One of them, shall refuse or delay to fix and agree upon the Number of Men, Boats, Nets, and Appurtenances necessary for such Fishery, any One or more of such joint Owners may, by Writing under his Hand, require that all such Matters be referred to Arbitration, and may name an

Arbitrator to act on his Behalf, and require each of the other joint Owners to name an Arbitrator to act on his Behalf; and in the event of such joint Owners or any of them refusing or delaying for Fourteen Days after being so required to name such Arbitrator or Arbitrators, any One or more of such joint Owners may apply to the Sheriff or any Justice to appoint a fit and proper Person to act as sole Arbitrator in such Matters, and to decide therein, and to fix the number of Men, Boats, Nets, and Appurtenances necessary for such Fishery, and the Shares of the several joint Owners in the Produce thereof; and on such Application the Sheriff or Justice shall and he is hereby authorised to appoint such Arbitrator; and the Arbitrators appointed by such joint Owners as aforesaid may choose an Umpire to act in case of their differing in Opinion, and the Decision or Decree Arbitral to be pronounced by such Arbitrators or Umpire, or by any Arbitrator appointed by the Sheriff or Justice, shall be final and not subject to Review in any Court or by any Process whatsoever.

LXXIX. For defraying the Expenses to be incurred in carrying this Act into effect it shall be lawful for the Commissioners at any General, Special, or Adjourned Meeting and they are hereby required to make, impose, and levy an annual Rate or Assessment of Twenty Pounds *per Centum per Annum* until the Debts and Obligations contracted by the Commissioners and Overseers acting under the recited Acts, and due and subsisting at the passing of this Act, and the Costs of obtaining and passing this Act and incidental thereto, are paid, and annually thereafter of such Amount as the Commissioners shall fix and determine, not exceeding Twenty Pounds *per Centum per Annum*, to be paid by the whole Owners of Salmon Fisheries in the River in proportion to the Rents or yearly Value of their several Fisheries as such Rents or yearly Value shall be ascertained and fixed by the Commissioners, or by the Sheriff or Justices on the Application of any Owner who may think himself aggrieved by any such Assessment, provided Notice of such Application be given to the Clerk within Ten Days after Notice of such Assessment is given to such Owner, and which Rate shall be payable either yearly or half-yearly, as the Commissioners may from Time to Time direct and appoint, by the several Tenants or Occupiers of the said several Fisheries, for and on behalf of the respective Owners of the same, and for which Payments such Tenants or Occupiers shall be entitled to Relief from the respective Owners on settling or paying their Rents; and if any such Rate shall not be paid to the Collector appointed under this Act by any Tenant or Occupier when required, the same shall on Demand be payable by the Owner of the Fishery possessed by such Tenant or Occupier.

LXXX. The Rate made at any such Meeting shall be binding upon and may be enforced against every such Owner, Tenant, and Occupier of a Fishery ; and for the Recovery of any Rates which may remain unpaid it shall be lawful for any Sheriff or Justice within whose Jurisdiction the Goods and Effects of any Owner, Tenant, or Occupier of a Fishery liable for such Rates may be found to grant Warrant for poinding or distraining such Goods and Effects, and to appraise them on the Place where found, and afterwards to sell the same by Auction for Payment of such Rates, together with the full Costs of such Poinding, Distress, and Sale, and the Surplus (if any) shall be paid, when demanded, to the Person whose Effects shall have been so distrained and sold; which Warrants shall be granted by such Sheriff or Justice upon an Application made to him by the Clerk or Treasurer or other Person authorised by the Commissioners, with an Attestation on Oath signed by the Collector appointed under this Act certifying that the Person complained of is liable for and has not paid such Rates, and specifying therein the Amount due by him ; and the Proceedings for the Recovery of such Rates may be in the Form of the Schedule (A.) hereunto annexed, or as near thereto as may be ; or the Commissioners or Clerk may bring and prosecute an Action or Actions at Law for Recovery of such Rates or Arrears thereof.

LXXXI. The Rates levied under the Authority of this Act shall be applied, first, in paying and discharging the Debts and Obligations contracted by the Commissioners and Overseers acting under the recited Acts, and due and subsisting at the Time of the passing of this Act; secondly, in paying the Costs of obtaining and passing this Act, and incidental thereto ; and, lastly, in paying and defraying Salaries and Allowances to the Clerk, Treasurer, Collectors, Superintendent, Water Bailiffs, and other Officers, and other Expenses incurred in carrying this Act into execution.

LXXXII. Every Penalty imposed by this Act may be recovered by Action of Debt in any County Court, or by summary Proceeding before the Sheriff or a Justice or Justices having Jurisdiction in the Place where the Offence is committed or where the Offender resides or is found ; and on Complaint being made at the Instance of the Procurator Fiscal or other public Prosecutor of the County, District, or Place where the Offence may have been committed, or where the Offender or Offenders shall reside or may be found, or at the Instance of any One or more of the Commissioners, or of their Clerk, to any such Sheriff or Justice or Justices, he or they shall issue a Summons or Warrant requiring the Person complained against to appear before the Sheriff or any Justice or Justices at a Time not less than Six free Days after Service, and at a Place to be named in such Summons or Warrant; and every such Summons or Warrant, with a Copy of the Complaint, shall be served on the Person complained against, either personally or by leaving the same with some Inmate at his usual Place of Abode: and upon the Appearance of the Person complained against, or in his Absence after Proof of the due Service of such Summons or Warrant, it shall be lawful for the Sheriff or Justice or Justices to proceed to the Hearing of the Complaint; and upon Proof of the Offence, either by the Confession of the Person complained against, or upon the Oath of One credible Witness or more, or in default of Appearance of such Person, it shall be lawful for such Sheriff or Justice or Justices to convict the Offender, and upon such Conviction to adjudge the Offender to pay the Penalty incurred, as well as such Costs attending the Conviction as such Sheriff or Justice or Justices shall think fit; and it shall be competent on the Hearing of every such Complaint to prove that the Person then complained against has been previously convicted of an Offence against the Provisions of this Act, and for such Sheriff or Justice or Justices to take such previous Conviction into consideration in pronouncing Sentence.

LXXXIII. If forthwith upon any such Adjudication or Conviction as aforesaid the Amount of the Penalty and of such Costs as aforesaid be not paid, the Amount of such Penalty and Costs shall be levied by Poinding or Distress and Sale, and such Sheriff or Justice or Justices shall issue their or his Warrant of Poinding or Distress and Sale accordingly.

LXXXIV. It shall be lawful for any such Sheriff or Justice to order any Offender so convicted as aforesaid to be detained and kept in safe Custody until Return can be conveniently made to the Warrant of Poinding or Distress and Sale to be issued for levying such Penalty and Costs, unless the Offender give sufficient Security by way of Recognisance, Bond of Caution, or otherwise to the Satisfaction of the Sheriff or Justice for his Appearance before him on the Day appointed for such Return, such Day not being more than Eight Days from the Time of taking such Security; but if before issuing such Warrant of Poinding or Distress and Sale it shall appear to the Sheriff or Justice, by the Admission of the Offender or otherwise, that no sufficient Poinding or Distress can be had within the Jurisdiction of such Sheriff or Justice whereon to levy such Penalty and Costs, he may, if he thinks fit, refrain from issuing such Warrant of Poinding or Distress and Sale; and in such Case, or if such Warrant shall have been issued, and upon the Return thereof such Insufficiency as aforesaid shall be made to appear to such Sheriff or Justice, then such Sheriff or Justice shall by Warrant cause such Offender to be committed to

—

Prison, there to remain without Bail for any Period not exceeding Two Months in the Case of a First Offence, for any Period not exceeding Three Months in the Case of a Second Offence, and for any Period not exceeding Four Months in the Case of a Third or subsequent Offence, unless such Penalty and Costs be sooner paid and satisfied.

LXXXV. Such Penalty and Costs shall be levied by Poinding or Distress and Sale of the Goods, Chattels, and Effects of the Party liable to pay the same; and the Overplus arising from the Sale of such Goods, Chattels, and Effects, after satisfying such Penalty and Costs and the Expenses of the Poinding or Distress and Sale, shall be returned on Demand to the Party whose Goods, Chattels, or Effects shall have been poinded or distrained.

LXXXVI. No Poinding or Distress levied by virtue of this Act shall be deemed unlawful, nor shall any Party making the same be deemed a Trespasser, on account of any Defect or Want of Form in the Summons, Conviction, Warrant of Poinding or Distress and Sale, or other Proceeding relating thereto, nor shall such Party be deemed a Trespasser *ab initio* on account of any Irregularity afterwards committed by him, but all Persons aggrieved by such Defect or Irregularity may recover by Action full Satisfaction for the special Damage.

LXXXVII. Every such Penalty, when recovered, shall be paid to the Commissioners, or to their Clerk or Treasurer, or other Person authorised by them to receive the same, to be applied for the Purposes of this Act in the same Manner as the Rates hereby authorised to be levied.

LXXXVIII. No Person shall be liable to the Payment of any Penalty imposed by virtue of this Act for any Offence made cognisable before a Sheriff or Justice, unless the Complaint respecting such Offence shall have been made before such Sheriff or Justice within Six Months next after the Commission of such Offence.

LXXXIX. If through any Act, Neglect, or Default, on account whereof any Person shall have incurred any Penalty imposed by this Act, any Damage to the Property of the Commissioners shall have been committed by such Person, he shall be liable to make good such Damage as well as to pay such Penalty; and the Amount of such Damage shall in case of Dispute be determined by the Sheriff or Justices by whom the Party incurring such Penalty shall have been convicted, and on Nonpayment of such Damage on Demand the same shall be levied by Poinding or Distress, and such Sheriff or

Justices, or one or other of such Justices, shall issue their or his Warrant accordingly.

XC. Every Summons, Warrant, Conviction, and Sentence to be issued or pronounced by any Sheriff or Justice or Justices under the Authority of this Act may be enforced against the Person or the Goods and Effects of any Party or Witness in any other County, Burgh, or Place where such Party or Witness may be found, as well as in the County, Burgh, or Place where the same is issued or pronounced, provided such Summons, Warrant, Conviction, or Sentence be endorsed by the Sheriff or Sheriff Clerk or a justice of such other County, Burgh, or Place; and such Endorsation or Warrant of Concurrence may be in the Form in the Schedule (B.) hereunto annexed, and shall be sufficient Authority to the Constables or Sheriff Officers of both Jurisdictions respectively to put such Summons, Warrant, Conviction, or Sentence into execution within such other County, Burgh, or Place.

XCI. It shall be lawful for any Sheriff or Justice to summon any Person to appear before him, or in the Case of a Justice before any One or more Justices, as a Witness in any Matter in which such Sheriff or Justice or Justices shall have Jurisdiction under the Provisions of this Act, at a Time and Place mentioned in such Summons, and to administer to him an Oath to testify the Truth in such Matter; and if any Person so summoned shall without reasonable Excuse refuse or neglect to appear at the Time and Place appointed for that Purpose, having been paid or tendered a reasonable Sum for his Expenses, or if any Person appearing shall refuse to be examined upon Oath, or to give Evidence before such Sheriff or Justice or Justices, every such Person shall for every such Offence be liable to a Penalty not exceeding Five Pounds.

XCII. In all Cases where it is provided by this Act that any Article, Matter, or Thing may be seized and forfeited, it shall be lawful for any Water Bailiff, Constable, or other Person acting in the Execution of this Act to seize and take such Article, Matter, or Thing, and to keep the same in his Custody and Possession until the Person from whom the same is taken is brought before the Sheriff or Justice; and where any such Article, Matter, or Thing shall be adjudged by the Sheriff or Justice to be forfeited under the Provisions of this Act, it shall be lawful for such Sheriff or Justice to direct such Article, Matter, or Thing to be destroyed or to be sold and disposed of as he or they may think fit, and the Proceeds of any such Sale shall be paid to the Commissioners or their Clerk or Treasurer or other Person authorised by them to receive the same, and shall be applied for the Purposes of this Act in the same Manner as the Rates hereby authorised to be levied.

XCIII. Any Information, Complaint, and Proceedings before the Sheriff or Justice or Justices before whom any Person shall be complained of or proceeded against for any Offence under the Provisions of this Act, and the Warrants, Sentence, or Conviction thereon, may be in the Form of the Schedule (B.) hereunto annexed, or as near thereto as may be, and may be printed or written or partly printed and partly written, and no written Record of Evidence shall be necessary unless either Party before such Complaint shall be heard requires the Sheriff or Justice or Justices to take Notes of the Evidence to be adduced, which such Sheriff or Justice or Justices shall do or cause to be done, and the Notes so taken shall be deemed and held in any subsequent Proceedings as a sufficient Record of the Evidence under such Complaint.

XCIV. No Proceeding in pursuance of this Act shall be quashed or vacated for Want of Form, nor shall the same be removed by Certiorari or otherwise into any of the Superior Courts in *England*, or be subject to Appeal or Review by any of the Supreme Courts in *Scotland*, except as herein-after provided.

XCV. It shall not be necessary in any Proceeding against any Person under the Provisions of this Act to negative by Evidence any Licence, Consent, Authority, or other Matter of Exception or Defence, but the Person seeking to avail himself of such Licence, Consent, Authority, or other Matter of Exception or Defence shall be bound to prove the same.

XCVI. It shall be lawful for the Complainer or for any Party charged to appeal against any Adjudication or Conviction pronounced by any Sheriff or Justice or Justices in *Scotland*, with respect to any Complaint or Penalty or Forfeiture under the Provisions of this Act, by which he thinks himself aggrieved; and in case such Adjudication or Conviction shall be pronounced by any Sheriff, the Appeal therefrom shall be made to the next Circuit Court of Justiciary in the Manner and by and under the Rules, Limitations, Conditions, and Restrictions contained in the Act passed in the Twentieth Year of the Reign of His Majesty King *George* the Second for taking away and abolishing Heritable Jurisdictions in *Scotland;* and in case such Abjudication or Conviction shall be pronounced by any Justice or Justices, the Appeal therefrom shall be made to the next General, Stated, or Adjourned Meeting of the Justices of the County, Burgh, or Place for which such Justice or Justices shall act, in Quarter Sessions assembled, but no such Appeal to the Quarter Sessions shall be entertained unless it be made within Four Months next after the pronouncing of such Adjudication or Conviction, nor unless Ten Days Notice in Writing of such Appeal, stating the Nature and Grounds thereof, be given to the Party against whom the Appeal shall be brought: Provided, that with every such Appeal against the Adjudication or Conviction pronounced by any Sheriff or Justice or Justices a Bond of Caution for the Payment of any Penalty or Costs which may have been awarded against the Appellant by the Adjudication or Conviction appealed from, together with the Costs of the Appeal, shall be lodged with the Sheriff Clerk or Clerk of the Peace, and the Sufficiency of the Cautioner in such Bond shall be judged of and determined by the Sheriff Clerk or Clerk of the Peace, as the Case may be; and it shall not be competent to appeal from or bring any Adjudication or Conviction pronounced by any Sheriff or Justice or Justices acting under this Act under Review in any other Way than as herein provided; and the Decisions of the Circuit Court of Justiciary and of the Justices in Quarter Sessions assembled in any of the Matters aforesaid shall be final, and not subject to Review by Advocation, Suspension, Reduction, or any other Process whatsoever.

XCVII. If any Party shall feel aggrieved by any Adjudication or Conviction pronounced by any Justice or Justices in *England* with respect to Penalty or Forfeiture under the Provisions of this Act, such Party may appeal to the General Quarter Sessions for the County or Place in which the Cause of Appeal shall have arisen, but no such Appeal shall be entertained unless it be made within Four Months next after the making of such Determination or Adjudication, nor unless Ten Days Notice in Writing of such Appeal, stating the Nature and Grounds thereof, be given to the Party against whom the Appeal shall be brought, nor unless the Appellant forthwith after such Notice enter into Recognisances, with Two sufficient Sureties, before a Justice conditioned duly to prosecute such Appeal, and to abide the Order of the Court thereon.

XCVIII. At the Quarter Sessions in *England* or *Scotland* for which such Notice shall be given the Court shall proceed to hear and determine the Appeal in a summary Way, or they may, if they think fit, adjourn it to the following Sessions; and upon the Hearing of such Appeal the Court may, if they think fit, mitigate any Penalty or Forfeiture, or confirm or quash the Adjudication, and order any Money paid by any Party or levied by Poinding or Distress of his Goods to be returned to him, and they may make such Order concerning the Costs, both of the Adjudication and of the Appeal, as they may think reasonable.

XCIX. Every Person who upon any Examination on Oath under the Provisions of this Act shall wilfully and corruptly give false Evidence shall be liable to the Penalties of wilful and corrupt Perjury.

C. Nothing in this Act contained shall diminish, prejudice, take away, alter, suspend, or affect any Right, Power, Authority, Privilege, or Jurisdiction of the Lord High Admiral of the United Kingdom of *Great Britain* and *Ireland*, or of the Commissioners for executing the Office of Lord High Admiral.

THE 1859 ACT.

WHEREAS an Act was passed in the Twentieth and Twenty-first Year of the Reign of Her present Majesty, intituled *An Act to consolidate and amend the Acts for the more effectual Preservation and Increase of Salmon and the Regulation of the Fisheries in the River* Tweed: And whereas it is expedient and would be for the Advantage of the Salmon Fisheries in the said River that the Annual Close Times defined by the said Act should be altered, and that the Limits of the Mouth or Entrance of the said River should be extended, and that further Provision should be made for the Regulation of the Fisheries in the said River and within the said extended Limits; but these Objects cannot be effected without the Authority of Parliament: May it therefore please your Majesty that it may be enacted; and be it enacted by the Queen's most Excellent Majesty, by and with the Advice and Consent of the Lords Spiritual and Temporal, and Commons, in this present Parliament assembled, and by the Authority of the same, as follows:

I. This Act may be cited for all Purposes as "The *Tweed* Fisheries Amendment Act, 1859."

II. The Expression "the River" in the recited Act and this Act shall mean and include the River *Tweed*, and every River, Brook, or Stream which flows or runs into the said River, and also the Mouth or Entrance of the said River, as described and defined in this Act; and the several other Words and Expressions interpreted in the Second Section of the recited Act shall, when used in this Act, have the same Meanings as are by the recited Act assigned to them respectively.

III. From and after the Fifth Day of *October* One thousand eight hundred and fifty-nine, the Forty-first, Forty-second,

Forty-third, Forty-fourth, Forty-sixth, Forty-seventh, Sixty-seventh, and Seventy-first Sections of the recited Act shall be and are hereby repealed, and this Act shall commence and take effect: Provided always, that the recited Act, except in so far as expressly repealed by this Act, shall be and remain in full Force and as valid and effectual as if this Act had not been passed; provided also, that, notwithstanding such Repeal, all Penalties in respect of Acts done before the Commencement of this Act may be enforced, and all Proceedings instituted before and pending at the Commencement of this Act may be continued and prosecuted, and all Resolutions duly made and Acts duly done under the Authority of the said repealed Enactments shall be and remain valid and effectual, to all Intents and Purposes as if this Act had not been passed; provided further, that the Forty-first Section of the recited Act shall, notwithstanding such Repeal, be read and continued as an operative Definition for the Purpose of distinguishing the Limits of the Mouth or Entrance of the River *Tweed* as defined by the recited Act and the extended Limits defined by this Act, and for such Purpose only.

IV. For the Purposes of the recited Act and this Act, and subject as herein-after provided, the Limits of the Mouth or Entrance of the River *Tweed* shall be deemed to extend and shall extend from the Pier called *Queen Elizabeth's* Pier, along the Sea Coast on the South Side of the said Pier to a Point at High-water Mark on the said Sea Coast on the South Side distant Seven Miles measured in a straight Line from the Lighthouse on the said Pier, and along the Sea Coast on the North Side of the said Pier to the Point of Boundary at High-water Mark between the Borough of *Berwick-on-Tweed* and the Kingdom of *Scotland*, and shall also extend Five Miles in front of the Mouth of the said River and of the whole Line of Sea Coast within the Points of Boundary herein-before mentioned into the Sea, such distance towards the Sea to be computed by Lines drawn at Right Angles to a Line drawn between the said Northern and Southern Extremities; and the said Limits on the South shall be deemed to include and shall include the Fishery now known as the *Holy Island* Station of the *Goswick* Fisheries.

V. The Rates or Assessments by the recited Act authorised to be levied shall be leviable on and in respect of all Salmon Fisheries within the Limits of the Mouth or Entrance of the River *Tweed* as above defined, and shall be payable by and recoverable from the Owners, Tenants, or Occupiers of such Fisheries in manner provided by the recited Act; and the whole Enactments and Provisions of the recited Act (so far as not hereby repealed) and of this Act, except as herein-after

20

provided, shall extend and be applicable to the Mouth or Entrance of the said River within the Limits above defined: Provided always, that the Provisions of the Fifty-fifth and Sixtieth Sections of the recited Act shall not be applicable to any Stake Net or Bag Net which may be set or placed beyond the Limits of the Mouth or Entrance of the said River, as defined by the Forty-first Section of the recited Act, and within the extended Limits defined by this Act; provided also, that the Rates or Assessments to be levied on and in respect of the Fisheries situated beyond the Limits as defined in the recited Act, and within the said extended Limits, shall not be applied in or towards the Payment or Discharge of any Debts or Obligations contracted by the Commissioners previous to the passing of this Act.

VI. It shall not be lawful for any Person to fish for or take or aid or assist in fishing for or taking any Salmon in or from the River at any Time between the Fourteenth day of *September* in any Year and the Fifteenth day of *February* in the Year following, except by means of the Rod and Line with the artificial Fly only, nor with the Rod and Line at any time between the Thirtieth Day of *November* in any year and the First Day of *February* in the Year following, and which respective Periods above defined shall be and be held to be the "Annual Close Times," within the Meaning of the recited Act and this Act; provided that the Commissioners or any Five of their Number may, by Writing under their Hands or under the Hand of their Clerk, authorise any Persons appointed by them to fish for and take Salmon in or from the River, with the Consent of the Owner of the Fishery from which such Salmon are taken, during the Annual Close Times, for the Purpose of artificial Propagation.

VII. It shall not be lawful for any Person, between the Fifteenth day of *February* and the Fourteenth Day of *September* in any Year, to fish for or take or aid or assist in fishing for or taking any Salmon in or from the River at any Time or in any Way whatsoever, except by means of the Rod and Line, or by means of Stake Nets and Bag Nets, as herein-after provided, between Six of the Clock on *Saturday* Afternoon and Six of the Clock on the following *Monday* Morning; and it shall not be lawful to fish for or take or aid or assist in fishing for or taking any Salmon in or by means of any Stake Net or Bag Net set or placed as provided for by the Twelfth Section of this Act at any Time between the Low Water next in point of Time before Six of the Clock on *Saturday* Afternoon and the Low Water next in point of Time before Six of the Clock on the following *Monday* Morning; and which respective Periods above defined shall be and be held to be the "Weekly Close Times," within the Meaning of the recited Act and this Act.

VIII. Every Person who during the Annual Close Times or Weekly Close Times fishes for or takes or aids or assists in fishing for or taking any Salmon in or from the River, excepting as aforesaid, shall for every such Offence be liable to a Penalty not exceeding Ten Pounds, and an additional Penalty of Ten Shillings for each Salmon so taken; and every Salmon so taken, and every Boat, Net, Tackle, or Engine by which such Salmon has been taken or attempted to be taken, may be seized and forfeited.

IX. The whole Enactments and Provisions of the recited Act with respect to the Annual Close Times and Weekly Close Time therein defined (so far as not hereby repealed) shall be and are hereby made applicable to the Annual Close Times and Weekly Close Times respectively defined by this Act.

X. Every Person who during the Annual Close Times has in his Possession Salmon known by such Person to have been taken or caught in the River during the Annual Close Times (except Salmon which have been taken by means of the Rod and Line between the Fifteenth Day of *September* and the Thirtieth Day of *November*, both Days inclusive, or between the First and Fourteenth Days of *February*, both Days inclusive, or which have been taken for the Purpose of artificial Propagation, under the Authority of the Commissioners, as herein-before provided), or who sells or offers or exposes for Sale or Exchange any Salmon known by such Person to have been caught in the River between the Fifteenth Day of *September* in any Year and the Fourteenth Day of *February* in the Year following, both Days inclusive, shall for every such Offence be liable to a Penalty of not less than Ten Shillings and not exceeding Two Pounds for each Salmon so had in his Possession, or sold or offered or exposed for Sale or Exchange as aforesaid, and every such Salmon, and every Boat, Cart, Basket, or Package in which the same may be found, may be seized and forfeited; and the Proof that such Salmon was not taken contrary to the Provisions of this Act shall lie upon the Person in whose Custody the same is found.

XI. On or before the Seventeenth Day of *September* in every Year, every Occupier of a Fishery in the River shall and he is hereby required to remove from every Fishery, Fishing Shield, and Fishing Ground, and Houses and Premises occupied or used by him, all Boats, Oars, Nets, Engines, and other Tackle used and employed in taking and killing Salmon (excepting Boats with their Oars and such other Implements as are used for Angling or Rod-fishing) and to carry away the same to some Place or Places to be from Time to Time appointed by the Commissioners, where the same can be securely lodged and kept until the Thirteenth Day of *February* in the following Year; and each Boat with its Oars and other Implements as aforesaid so retained for the Purpose of Angling or Rod-fishing shall be removed or carried away on or before the Third Day of *December* in every Year; and shall be lodged and kept and remain as aforesaid until the Thirtieth Day of *January* in the following Year; and every such Occupier who neglects or refuses to remove and carry away all and every such Boats, Oars, Nets, Engines, and other Tackle as aforesaid, and to keep the same secured from the said Fisheries and Premises during the Period aforesaid, shall for every such Offence be liable to a Penalty not exceeding Twenty Pounds, and all such Boats, Oars, Nets, Engines, and other Tackle not removed or kept secured as aforesaid shall be forfeited: Provided always, that this Enactment shall not be held or construed to extend to public Ferry Boats, or to Boats used by any Owner or Occupier of Land adjoining the River solely for the Transport of himself, or his Family or Servants, or any Persons in his Employment; provided also, that all such last-mentioned Boats shall be under and subject to the Regulations prescribed in the recited Act with respect thereto; provided further, that this Enactment, so far as it requires Nets to be carried away to some Place or Places to be appointed by the Commissioners, shall not apply to the Stake Nets or Bag Nets to be set or placed as provided for by the Twelfth Section of this Act, but that all such Nets shall, on or before the Seventeenth Day of *September* in every Year, be removed and carried away from the said Fisheries and from the Strand or Shore, and kept in such Places as may be provided by the Owners of such Nets.

XII. All Stake Nets and Bag Nets set or placed beyond the Limits of the Mouth or Entrance of the said River, as defined by the Forty-first Section of the recited Act and within the extended Limits defined by this Act, shall be subject to the following Provisions and Regulations:

The Nets used in the Formation and Construction of such Stake Nets and of the Leaders of such Bag Nets shall be extended evenly in such Manner that the Meshes of such Nets shall be stretched to their full Opening:

Every such Stake Net shall be so placed and constructed as that clear Openings for the free Passage of Salmon, as herein-after provided, can be made in the Traps or Chambers thereof:

In every such Stake Net there shall be made, and kept free from Obstruction during the whole Period of the Weekly Close Time, a clear Opening of at least Three Feet in Width in the Traps or Chambers of such Stake Net from the Bottom to the Top thereof, so as effectually to allow of the free Passage of Salmon through such Traps or

Chambers during the whole Period of the Weekly Close Time:

Every such Bag Net shall be so placed and constructed as that the Netting of the Leaders thereof can be raised and kept out of the Water:

The Netting of the Leader of every such Bag Net shall during the whole Period of the Weekly Close Time be raised and kept out of the Water:

And every Person committing any Breach or Contravention of the said Provisions and Regulations shall for every such Offence be liable to a Penalty not exceeding Ten Pounds, and an additional Penalty of Ten Shillings for each Salmon taken in or by means of any Bag or Stake Nets set, placed, or used contrary to the said Provisions and Regulations, and shall also forfeit any Salmon so taken, and every Bag or Stake Net so set, placed, or used; provided that nothing herein contained shall be construed to render liable to any Penalty or Forfeiture any Person who shall be prevented by Storm or Stress of Weather from making such Openings in Stake Nets, or removing such Leaders of Bag Nets as aforesaid, or from removing such Stake Nets or Bag Nets at the Commencement of the Annual Close Time, in respect of any such Act or Omission while he shall be so prevented.

XIII. From and after the Fifteenth Day of *February*, One thousand eight hundred and sixty it shall not be lawful to shoot, draw, or use in the River any Net of which the Meshes shall be less than One Inch and Three Quarters of an Inch from Knot to Knot, or Seven Inches round (except Nets which shall be used solely for the taking of Herrings or Shrimps, and Nets which shall be used solely for the Purpose of landing Fish taken with the Rod and Line); and every Person who shoots, draws, or uses in the River, or has in his Possession within Five Miles of the River, any Net adapted for taking or killing Fish with Meshes of smaller Dimensions than those above specified (except as aforesaid), or shoots, draws, or uses any double Net, shall for every such Offence be liable to a Penalty not exceeding Ten Pounds, and an additional Penalty of Ten Shillings for each Salmon taken by means of such illegal Net or double Net, and every such illegal Net and every Salmon so taken may be seized and forfeited.

XIV. Every Person who at any Time takes or kills or attempts to take or kill Salmon in or from the River by means of any Pout Net, Rake Hook, or similar Engine of the Description of those used for killing Salmon, or who has in his Possession within Five Miles from the River any such Pout Net, Rake Hook, or similar Engine, shall for every such Offence be liable to a Penalty not exceeding Two Pounds, and an additional Penalty of Ten Shillings for each Salmon so taken; and every such Pout Net, Rake Hook, or similar Engine, and every Salmon so taken, may be seized and forfeited; provided that nothing in this Section contained shall apply to any Scoop Net or other similar Implement used solely for the Purpose of taking Fish out of the Chambers of the Stake Nets or Bag Nets within the extended Limits of this Act.

XV. Every Person, not being an Owner or Occupier of a Fishery in the River, or otherwise entitled to fish for Salmon therein, who, at any Time between the First Day of *February* and the Thirtieth Day of *November* in any Year, fishes for or takes or aids or assists in fishing for or taking Salmon in or from the River, shall for every such Offence be liable to a Penalty not exceeding Ten Pounds, and an additional Penalty of Ten Shillings for each Salmon so taken or killed, and every Salmon so taken, and every Boat, Net, Rod, Engine, or Tackle used in such Fishing, or by means of which any Salmon has been taken or attempted to be taken, may be seized and forfeited.

XVI. Every Person who shall between the Fifteenth Day of *September* in any Year and the First Day of *May* in the Year following, in fishing with a Rod and Line, use any Cleek or Instrument for landing Fish other than a Landing Net, shall be liable to a Penalty not exceeding Five Pounds.

XVII. Nothing contained in the Seventy-second Section of the recited Act shall require the putting back into the River of any foul, unclean, or unseasonable Sea Trout, Bull Trout, or Whitling taken or captured by means of the Rod and Line, or render liable to any Penalty any Person who shall not put back into the River any such Sea Trout, Bull Trout, or Whitling so taken or captured; provided that the Proof that any such Sea Trout, Bull Trout, or Whitling was taken or captured by means of the Rod and Line shall lie upon the Person in whose Possession the same shall be found.

XVIII. Complaints and Proceedings for Offences against or Penalties or Forfeitures incurred under the Provisions of the recited Act and this Act may be made, prosecuted, and taken at the Instance of the Superintendent of Water Bailiffs for the Time being appointed and acting under the recited Act and this Act; and such Superintendent shall be entitled and is hereby Authorized to make and prosecute such Complaints and to take such Proceedings in his own Name in the same Manner and to the same Effect as Complaints may be made and prosecuted and Proceedings may be taken by the Procurator Fiscal or other Public Prosecutor, or the Commissioners or their Clerk, under the Provisions of the recited Act and this Act.

XIX. The whole Enactments and Provisions of the recited Act with respect to the Apprehension and Punishment of Offenders, and the Recovery, Application, and Disposal of Penalties and Forfeitures, are hereby incorporated with and made applicable to this Act, and to Offences committed against and Penalties and Forfeitures to be imposed and recovered under the Provisions of this Act; and all offences committed against the Provisions of this Act shall be prosecuted, and all Penalties and Forfeitures imposed under the Provisions of this Act shall be sued for, recovered, applied, and disposed of, in the Form and Manner (as nearly as may be) prescribed by the recited Act and this Act.

XX. Any Sheriff or Justice before whom any Offender is convicted of any Offence under the Provisions of the recited Act or this Act, on the Failure in Payment by such Offender of the Penalty and Costs which he has been adjudged to pay, may, without issuing any Warrant of Poinding or Distress and Sale for the Recovery of such Penalty and Costs, at once issue his Warrant for the Commitment to Prison of such Offender for the Periods specified in the Eighty-fourth Section of the recited Act, unless such Penalty and Costs be sooner paid and satisfied.

XXI. Every Proxy granted under the Provisions and for the Purposes of the recited Act or this Act shall be chargeable only with the Stamp Duty imposed on Proxies by the Act of the Nineteenth and Twentieth Years of Her Majesty's Reign, Chapter Eighty-one.

XXII. Nothing in this Act contained shall diminish, prejudice, take away, alter, suspend, or affect any Right, Power, Authority, Privilege, or Jurisdiction of the Lord High Admiral of the United Kingdom of *Great Britain and Ireland*, or of the Commissioners for executing the Office of Lord High Admiral.

XXIII. Nothing in the recited Act or this Act contained shall be deemed to exempt the River from the Provisions of any General Act relating to Salmon Fisheries which shall be passed in the present or any future Session of Parliament.

ROYAL SOCIETY OF EDINBURGH.

January 9th, 1843.—The following communications were read:—

1. "On the Growth of the Salmon," by Mr. John Young, Sutherlandshire.

Mr. Young has here taken up the subject of the salmon's growth where it was necessarily left off by Mr. Shaw. So far as the earliest or fresh-water state of the fish is concerned, he entirely agrees with the observer just named. He then states the various opinions which prevail regarding the more or less rapid growth of smolts and grilse, and shows, by tabular lists (the result of frequently repeated experiments), that the increase in their dimensions is extraordinary, so soon as they descend into the salt water. So far back as the months of April and May, 1837, he marked a number of descending smolts, by making a peculiar perforation in the caudal fin by means of small nipping-irons constructed for the purpose. He recaptured a considerable number of them ascending the rivers as grilse, in the course of the ensuing months of June and July, weighing several pounds each, more or less, according to the difference in the length of their sojourn in the sea. Again in April and May, 1842, he marked a number of descending smolts, by clipping off the little adipose fin upon the back. In June and July he caught several of them returning up the river, and bearing his peculiar mark, the adipose fin being absent. Two or three specimens were exhibited to the Society. One marked in April, and re-captured on the 30th of July, weighed three and a half pounds.

As the season advances grilse increase in size, those being the largest which abide the longest in the sea; they spawn in the rivers after their first ascent, and before they have become adult salmon.

Mr. Young also described various experiments instituted with the view of showing the transition of grilse into salmon. He marked many small grilse after they had spawned in winter and were about to re-descend into the sea. He had re-captured them in the course of the ensuing summer as finely formed salmon, ranging in weight from nine to fourteen pounds, the difference still depending on the length of their sojourn in the sea. He has tried these experiments for many seasons, but never twice with the same mark. A specimen marked as a grilse of four pounds in January, 1842, and re-captured as a salmon of nine pounds in July, was exhibited to the Society; it bore a peculiarly twisted piece of *copper* wire in the upper lobe of the caudal fin. Those marked and retaken in 1841 were marked with brass wire in the dorsal fin. With these and other precautions, Mr. Young debarred the possibility of any mistake as to the lapse of time. Both grilse and salmon return uniformly to their native streams; at least it very rarely happens that a fish bearing a particular mark is found except in a river where it was so marked. Salmon in the perfect state, as to form and aspect, also increase rapidly in their dimensions on again reaching the sea. A spawned salmon weighing twelve pounds was marked on the 4th of March, and was recaptured on its return from the sea on the 10th of July, weighing eighteen pounds.

Mr. Young is of opinion that salmon rather diminish than increase during their sojourn in rivers, and he illustrates this and other points of his subject by numerous experiments and observations.

THE END.

GLASGOW: PRINTED BY HAY NISBET AND CO.